Dresden

Dresden

A City Reborn

Edited by

Anthony Clayton and Alan Russell

With a foreword by

HRH The Duke of Kent

Oxford • New York

First published in 1999 by
Berg
Editorial offices:
150 Cowley Road, Oxford, OX4 1JJ, UK
838 Broadway, Third Floor, New York, NY10003-4812, USA

Berg is an imprint of Oxford International Publishers Ltd.

Library of Congress Cataloging-in-Publication Data
A catalog record for this book is available from the Library of Congress.

British Library Cataloguing-in-Publication Data
A catalogue record for this book is available from the British Library.

ISBN   1 85973 229 1 (Cloth)
         1 85973 441 3 (Paper)

Typeset by JS Typesetting, Wellingborough, Northants.
Printed in the United Kingdom by Biddles Ltd, Guildford and King's Lynn.

**Published with the support of Historical Collections Group Plc.
All royalties from the sale of this book are being donated to the
Dresden Trust.**

dedicated
to all those seeking to convert
the evils of the past into the
achievements of the future

Contents

Contents

List of Colour Plates

List of Black and White Pictures

Acknowledgements

This book is the fruit of many people's work and interest, in Germany and in the United Kingdom. Its main chapters, which can be read either randomly or in sequence, were all written by British authors, but to give the work authentic local flavour we have included some shorter contributions made, inter alia, by influential Dresdeners.

We should first record our thanks to His Royal Highness the Duke of Kent for his kindness in contributing a Foreword, which accurately explains the inspiration behind this book. We would like to express our gratitude to our authors and to our graphic artist, Stephen Conlin, all of whom have given their time unstintingly and without remuneration (all royalties go to the Trust). And we are grateful to the members of the Board of the Dresden Trust for their continuous support and especially to John Beale for his personal commitment.

It gives us particular satisfaction that Baumeister Burger (who has overall responsibility for the rebuilding of the Frauenkirche), Pfarrer Karl-Ludwig Hoch (who has witnessed everything that has happened in his native city from the 1930s to the present day), Deputy Mayor Gunter Just (who is master-minding the replanning of Dresden), and Professor Hans Nadler (who for decades fought tooth and nail to save as much as possible of old Dresden), should have found time – along with Lord Menuhin and Canon Paul Oestreicher nearer home – to contribute to the book.

For more general but nevertheless valuable assistance we would like to express our thanks to Dr. Jäger and the Gesellschaft zur Förderung des Wieder-aufbaus der Frauenkirche, to the librarian and staff of the Royal Military Academy at Sandhurst and to staff members of the Conflict Studies Research Centre there, and to the German Historical Institute in Bloomsbury. The Gemäldegalerie, the Sächsische Landes – und Universitätsbibliothek, the Planning Department of Dresden City Council and Manfred Lauffer, have been important sources of information and of illustrations. We are indebted to Germany's Grand Lodge of Ancient, Free and Accepted Masons for the award to the Trust of its 1999 Humanitarian Prize which, inter alia, made an expanded colour section possible.

The list of the many others who have helped is too long to present in full but we would like in particular to mention the following: Dr. Peter Barker, Mr. Michael Barnes, Pastorin Ulrike Birkener-Kettenacker, Dietrich Graf Brühl, Dr. Friedrich Georgi, Professor Jürgen Paul, Major-General Graf von Stauffenberg, Dr. Trevor Waters, Mr. Martin Williams and Mrs. Erika Woollams. We should also record that the secretarial skills of Carolyn Jordan, Monica Alexander, and Select Office Services Chichester, have been invaluable throughout. To the many others involved, we would also offer our sincere thanks for all their help and advice.

Anthony Clayton and Alan Russell

NB   The names of the Wettin House are usually given in their German form (with the exception only of Augustus the Strong and his son): for the convenience of readers both forms are set out in Appendix 1. Italics are used for short quotations in German and other foreign languages and for the titles of works – save those in English translation.

Foreword

Every so often the name of a city comes to stand for something more than just its own achievements, however great these may have been, like the Hague for peace, Hiroshima for atomic warfare and Dresden for the horrors of conventional carpet bombing. Where the symbolism is just and humane, understanding and creative, we all gain.

For many decades, Dresden lay sequestered in ideological quarantine and political isolation. Whatever the tyrannies imposed upon it, however, its great cultural heart never stopped beating. Just as in the 1930s Fritz Busch went on conducting until the Nazis drove him from the rostrum and Hanns Ander-Donath kept his celebrated organ concerts going in the Frauenkirche during the war years, so, on 4 August 1945, the Kreuzkirche choirboys sang, amid the ruins of the devastated city, the haunting Requiem that is still performed there annually. In the 1950s and the 1960s, the Opera and the Staatskapelle flourished once again and the city's museums once more displayed the great art treasures for which they were renowned and which the Russians had returned. Many baroque buildings, and indeed streets, fell victim to financial constraint and to ideological prejudice, but the Dresdeners' profound faith in their heritage, and in the future of their city, never failed.

They also kept alive the flame of freedom by placing candles every year on the massive pile of rubble that had been their beloved Frauenkirche. And since the Berlin Wall came down, the outpouring of creativity has been truly astonishing. The civil and cultural renaissance that has been taking place since that time has to be seen to be believed.

As patron of the British German Association and of the Dresden Trust, and as a member of the British Royal Family, I salute all those involved. I was deeply moved to be able to take part in the ceremonies that took place in Dresden in February 1995 to commemorate the fiftieth anniversary of the destruction of the city. It was a great privilege for me to be able to present the Bishop of Saxony with a picture of the Orb and Cross that the British people are contributing to the rebuilt Frauenkirche. To be able to share in the pain of others and – in a small way – to work with them in building reconciliation into friendship and cooperation is at once healing and fulfilling.

It is in this spirit that I am delighted to contribute this Foreword to a book written to recall the greatness of Dresden's past, to remember its devastation and to inform and inspire, as the work of recreating its physical, social and cultural fabric forges ahead. It tells a story that should be better known in the English-speaking world: of artistic achievement, of human courage and dedication, and of patient work towards the re-emergence of Dresden as an important centre of European culture. I hope you will visit it. I congratulate the Dresden Trust on its work and, on behalf of everyone in the United Kingdom, I extend warm greetings to the city and its people.

HRH The Duke of Kent
Patron of the British-German Association
and of the Dresden Trust

Dresden and the Dresden Trust

Alan Russell

The City of Dresden was and is unique – in its beauty, in its achievements, in its tragic fate, and in the national and international support it is receiving – from 15–20 support groups in Germany and from at least three overseas (see Appendix 2).

In its own way the Dresden Trust is unique too. No other British charity focuses so specifically on one foreign city in the pursuit of a universal aim, in this case of reconciliation after one of the twentieth century's saddest tragedies.

As the Duke of Kent says in his Foreword to this volume, behind Dresden – and therefore behind the Trust – there is a deep underlying symbolism. Dresden represents some of the best as well as some of the most terrible elements in British–German history and, although the Trust's message of reconciliation has a particular resonance in the city itself, it is not just for Dresden alone. It is – and it is seen, in Germany, in Britain and elsewhere – to be a far broader and very special act of international friendship and goodwill.

This book, the first comprehensive English-language work on the Saxon capital in the twentieth century, tries to reflect this combination of the universal and of the particular. It begins by taking a brief look at the origins and inspiration of the Trust, and then proceeds to examine Dresden's history, its replanning and its architecture, its fine art collections, its music and its theatrical and literary traditions. It is the story not so much of destruction in war as of a courageous people's determination to rebuild its heritage and to mould a tragically decimated but nevertheless culturally rich city for the twenty-first century. It is also a cautionary tale about British–German relations, appropriately told as one millennium gives way to another.

Germany's and Dresden's links with Britain

There can be no better starting point, perhaps, than the recollection that, despite its Celtic origins, Britain has always had strong Germanic elements in it. A recurrent theme is that we have more in common than many of us often think.

Britain's Beaker Folk came from the Rhineland. Many Romanized Germans served in Britain in the Imperial Armies. The Jutes, Angles and Saxons, who constituted this country's first big wave of immigration in modern times (up to 10 per cent of the population) put their mark on the early English kingdoms; and smaller but influential waves of traders, investors, religious refugees and other immigrants – including royal immigrants – continued to arrive across the succeeding centuries.

Neither Dresden nor Saxony (in its modern geographical form) played a *leading* part in these movements. The establishment of the Leipzig Trade Fair in the fourteenth century stimulated early commercial exchanges, but the merchants who negotiated special privileges with Henry II, Henry III, Richard III and Edward III, and who developed the Hansa trade up and down the east coasts of England and Scotland, came rather from Cologne and Lübeck and the other northern German towns. In the same way, the English merchant adventurers knew Flanders, Frisia and the Baltic far better than they did Middle Europe. Shakespeare's plays were produced in Danzig well before Dresden, which, significantly, receives no mention whatsoever in the recently published study of *Germans in Britain since 1500*.

Was it, therefore, only the horrors of twentieth-century aerial warfare that brought Dresden into the consciousness of the British people? The answer must be emphatically 'no', although this has certainly been an important recent factor.

The fine 'china' or porcelain, whose manufacture Augustus the Strong so strongly encouraged, became a fashionable adjunct to many a British household in the middle to late eighteenth century. Around the same time, the British Royal House of Hanover began to open Britain up much more than hitherto to German music and musicians, often from Saxony and from Dresden. Dresden's famous Kapellmeister, Johann Adolf Hasse, was intensely disappointed when he was unable to make the journey to London to visit England's most famous resident Saxon, Handel, whose music he had so much influenced. When the Seven Years War ended opportunities in Dresden, Johann Christian Bach, brother of Wilhelm Friedemann Bach of Dresden's Sophienkirche, did, however, make the journey to become Master of the Queen's Music. Zumpe and other Saxon makers of musical instruments followed in his footsteps and founded Britain's first piano-manufacturing businesses. Later in the century, Mozart and Haydn also reached Britain, where London's musical reputation was growing rapidly. In the late eighteenth century and the early nineteenth century, literary and artistic romanticism flowered famously in both England and Saxony.

Figure 1. Dresden's Old City seen from the Marienbrücke in 1935. Courtesy of the Sächsische Landesbibliothek, Deutsche Fotothek.

The economic and political world that emerged from the Napoleonic wars complemented these culturally convergent trends. Many of the five million nineteenth-century German emigrants to America, Canada, and the colonies passed through Britain and some of them stayed on, mainly in London and Liverpool, Manchester, Hull and Bradford. Industrial development stimulated trade, investment and risk, and Ludwig Mond prospered as surely in Manchester as did the Schröders in London. The reputation for excellence built up by the German Hochschulen made them natural partners for Britain's new municipal universities and Thomas Carlyle, George Eliot and others (much helped by the Prince Regent) were able to make German philosophy, art, manufactures and music fashionable, something that would have been unthinkable two hundred years earlier.

It was against this sense of culture and commercial – and sometimes racial – affinity that, in the nineteenth century, Dresden became one of the major overseas destinations favoured by the British for settlement and leisure. An *Englisches Viertel* (English Quarter) was built up, with its own churches (Scottish as well as Anglican), which survived intact until 1945, and across the city, very much under the influence of Ebenezer Howard's Garden City movement, Germany's first garden suburb came into being at Hellerau. Between the city and the British who knew it, something like a love affair developed. A. F. Chorley, whose book *Modern German Music* was published in 1854 wrote, in a typically lyrical way, of his stroll through the Zwinger Gardens:

> along a solemn avenue of chestnut trees . . . through a courtyard . . . into a meadow stretching down to the placid Elbe, garnished with pollarded trees such as Paul Potter loved to paint . . . and divided by a brook . . . with stepping stones

and looking back at the city as he left it in a carriage, he

> beheld it with the mist of early day wreathing round the beehive – like the dome of Our Lady's Church and the spires round it . . ., [with] the Elbe below and behind the bridge . . ., under a mantle of deep empurpled shadow, mak[ing] as fair a town picture as one of those splendid clusters of Italian architecture which Caspar Poussin loved to build into his landscapes.

In a quiet but continuous way, until the First World War blew it all apart (and incidentally reduced Britain's German community from close on 80,000 to less than 5,000), a web of professional and personal links with the city grew up, many of which have only come to light again in the hundreds of letters that have poured into the Trust.

One striking example is the Welshman who cherishes his descent from the Maréchal de Saxe who, despite his title, was a German. Another concerns the Hampshire lady whose ancestor, John Osborne, had been Ambassador to the Court in Dresden between 1771 and 1775. Two more examples come from the academic world: the Fellow of Jesus College Cambridge who married his German bride in the Frauenkirche in 1919 and the Emeritus Professor of Classics from Exeter who taught in Dresden in the 1930s, met his wife there and wrote a novel, *The Cloven Pine*, about his experiences there, under the pseudonym of Frank Clare. Trade and industry have produced a similar crop of stories. The donor of a stone for the Frauenkirche wrote from the Isle of Wight to explain that her grandfather came to work for the Dresdner Bank in the City of London in Edwardian times and ended up staying on. Conversely, a ninety-year-old English businessman living just outside Oxford has retold the story of his life in Dresden with his wife and two sons. Artistic links were of course many and varied. Stephen Conlin, the graphic artist who has done so much for the Trust, acquired his love of Dresden and of German architecture from his British soldier father who had been horrified by the city's destruction. Lord Menuhin one of the Trust's earliest patrons, frequently recalled, with great depth of feeling, his first visit to Dresden in 1929, when, as a boy of 13, he gave his first concert in the Opera House. More recently Joan Woolley has recorded the history of her Dresden-born mother's 'survival' in her book of that name.

Towards the end of the 1920s, links were established against a more sombre background as political and racial refugees arrived – for example, the biologist Dr Fritz van Emden, the painter Kokoschka and the one time staff member of the Gemäldegalerie, Nikolaus Pevsner.

The near total destruction of Dresden in February 1945 and the vast movements of people that came as the war ended, gave the situation a savage twist as families were scattered all over Europe and indeed the world. Instead, however, of the bitterness that so characterized the end of the First World War, there was a sense of simple relief, well expressed by Katrin FitzHerbert in her book *True to Both My Selves*, that normal life could begin again.

No-one connected with the Dresden Trust allows any moral equivalence (as one writer put it), between 'an act of war . . . however misguided . . . and systematic and sadistic cruelty and extermination'. But in the many letters that the Trust has received, the feeling comes through that, as Harold Nicholson wrote in the *Observer* in 1963, 'in Dresden something not quite worthy of Britain had taken place'. The *Daily Telegraph* wrote seven years later in its editorial on the 25th commemoration of the raid that 'no nation is diminished by acknowledgement of a desolating and dreadful act.'

The Dresden Trust

This said, the Trust has always sought to look forward, not back, and to seek out the path of reconciliation so courageously indicated in earlier years by Victor Gollancz, by Yehudi Menuhin and by the young people of Coventry, Cambridge, and elsewhere, who went out to Dresden to help rebuild the Deaconess Hospital with their own hands. When, therefore, in 1992, Bomber Command Association understandably decided to honour the heroism and sacrifices of its aircrews, the founders of the Dresden Trust decided to seek out ways of honouring the victims of aerial bombing as well (whether in Dresden, Hamburg, London, Coventry, Clydeside or elsewhere) through a contribution to Dresden's rebuilt Frauenkirche. Formally established on 16 August 1993, it began its fundraising six months later.

The Trust has always stressed the non-political, non-confessional and non-judgemental nature of its appeal and, right from the start, consulted many political, religious and other leaders of opinion, including the military. In the course of the service held in Chichester Cathedral in July 1994 to commemorate the Bell-Bonhoeffer tradition, His Grace the Archbishop of Canterbury paid tribute to the work of the Trust, and in November of the same year the then Chief Rabbi in Britain expressed his 'interest in the project and his hope that it (might) indeed come to fruition'. Contacts with the Catholic Church,

Figure 2. The pre-war Frauenkirche seen through the Münzgasse. Courtesy of the Sächsische Landesbibliothek, Deutsche Fotothek.

with the United Reformed Church, with the Church of Scotland and with the Society of Friends have all been very positive and representatives of all political parties, of educational and professional bodies, of business and of the broadsheets have been supportive. Expressions of understanding, relief and support have reached the Trust from people in all walks of life, including ex-fliers, and their widows – who have written of the anguish suffered over many years. Many links with families and friends have been re-established.

In September 1994, five members of the Trust's Board of Trustees visited Dresden to meet representatives of the Stiftung Frauenkirche Dresden and of the Gesellschaft zür Förderung des Wiederaufbaus der Frauenkirche (the Foundation and the Society – in effect the management and fund-raising arms of the local organization). It was on this occasion, in the earliest days of the Trust's work, that it was – informally – invited to make the financing and manufacturing of the eight-metre-high baroque Orb and Cross, which are to complete the dome of the rebuilt church, the centrepiece of its appeal. Five months later, at a dinner that he gave in St James Palace in honour of

Saxon Minister President Kurt Biedenkopf, the Duke of Kent formally communicated the Trust's grateful acceptance of this signal honour, stating that 'nothing could better symbolize the message which the British people want to give to Dresden . . . of gratitude and pleasure at the links of friendship that we now enjoy.'

Just four weeks later, in the course of the very moving ceremonies held on 13 February, 1995 to mark the fiftieth anniversary of Dresden's *Untergang*, both sides did everything possible to set old historical animosities aside. In a city decorated everywhere with posters of the destroyed baroque centre carrying the bold heading *Dank Hitler* (meaning 'you can thank Hitler for this'), Mayor Herbert Wagner, Minister-President Kurt Biedenkopf, and Federal President Roman Herzog all stressed in unambiguous terms that the war that had destroyed Dresden had originated in Germany itself.

In Dresden's Heidefriedhof (the cemetery in the heathland just outside Dresden) the Duke of Kent walked with his wreath (recorded the *Guardian* in its report)

> . . . 'down a long avenue to the memorial marked by concrete plinths which left no doubts about Germany's wartime atrocities. With the names of Auschwitz, Theresienstadt, Buchenwald and four other notorious death camps . . . on one side . . . and on the opposite side, (those of) places where Germans had killed hundreds of other innocents – Coventry . . . marked [by] three red tulips and a single candle . . . Leningrad, Lidice, Oradour, Rotterdam, Warsaw . . . [On] the main memorial stone, . . . [were however] etched words for Dresden itself. '*How many died. Who knows the number? Your wounds betray the torment of the nameless ones, burnt here in a hell fire, lit by human hands.*'

Here, in dignified and solemn silence, the Duke laid his wreath on behalf of the government and people of the United Kingdom.

Later in the same day, in the Kreuzkirche, he gave expression, in the language of his hosts, to the anguish that he shared with them. His words translate as follows:

> On behalf of Her Majesty The Queen and the people of the United Kingdom I offer you a drawing of the Cross that will stand on the top of the dome of the Frauenkirche when it is rebuilt. We want this Cross to be a symbol of the reconciliation between Britain and Germany. We give it in remembrance of those who died in Dresden in February 1945, and in the conviction that there will forever be peace between our two peoples. We deeply regret the suffering on all sides in the War. Today we remember especially that of the people of Dresden.

And in the raw, still-scarred chancel he presented the Bishop of Saxony with the Trust's specially commissioned drawing of the Orb and Cross. There could not, commented *The Times* (14 February 1995) have been any more fitting gesture. 'Some Germans may interpret it as a discreet apology. All can agree that it is a sincere act of reconciliation.'

President Herzog who, in December 1994, had cited the Dresden raid as an example of inhumanity in war, accepted the drawing in just that spirit. In the Palace of Culture, in the afternoon of 13 February 1995, he recalled that when the Frauenkirche stood again – proudly – as the symbol of Dresden reborn, the Dresdeners would have their British friends to thank for the Orb and Cross standing at its peak. That evening, as the bells of around 100 churches rang out above the milling crowds, the city began, both physically and spiritually, to live anew, and real forgiveness and friendship took root.

The Rebuilding of the Frauenkirche and the Making of the Cross

Since that time, the rebuilding of the Frauenkirche has gone ahead rapidly: the Engineer in Charge gives a summary on pp 141–143. The beautiful new Crypt was opened in August 1996 and as the walls of the Church above rose up to the level of the main Cornices, the many galleries and prayer rooms have taken shape inside. A new organ, to include a Silbermann replica, will be installed and Johann Baptist Grone's beautiful ceiling frescoes re-created.

In Britain meanwhile, the new Orb and Cross, precise replicas of the 18th century originals, were manufactured and were placed on display in Windsor during the German President's State Visit in December 1998 and thereafter in Coventry, Liverpool, Edinburgh and London – prior to their handover in Dresden by the Duke of Kent, on 13 February 2000 (see Plates 1 and 2). The Trust has, in addition, financed one of the ground-floor Windows and hopes to make further contributions not only to the fabric of the church, but also – through lectures, scholarships, artwork, books and visits – to the religious vocation and cultural life of the reborn church and city.

All of these things mark the culmination of a dream born 61 years earlier. On 13–14 February 1945, as the Silesian poet Gerhart Hauptmann helplessly watched his adopted city go up in flames, he asked, through his tears, whether the British (and Americans) had lost sight of the cultural riches that had flowed out to them from Dresden. In September 1994, the Chairman of the Trust assured Hauptmann's successors that they had not; and when Dresden celebrates the eight-hundredth anniversary of its incorporation, in 2006, the symbol of reconciliation and of renewed understanding and interchange will be there, at the very pinnacle of the Frauenkirche, for all to see.

Dresden, 1206–1918

Anthony Clayton

What made a minor German city, of no particular fame until the end of the seventeenth century, suddenly develop into one of Europe's richest cultural and artistic centres? The story is intriguing and important.

Medieval and Renaissance Dresden

Dresden was not one of the great medieval German cities such as Nuremberg or Cologne. Its origins were humble; it was a trade settlement founded by a minor local prince, Margrave Dietrich of Meissen, as a German colony on the south bank of the River Elbe, at a natural crossing point on the east-west trading routes.

This settlement became a town in the early thirteenth century, as was noted in a charter of 1206. Later in the same century, another minor German prince, Margrave Heinrich, known as Henry the Illustrious, built a castle there, which became a centre of local culture, medieval poetry and song. In 1220 the first bridge across the Elbe was built, at the same crossing point as the present Augustusbrücke (Augustus Bridge). Unusually for the period, the bridge was built of stone; it served to link the town with its Slav Sorb forest-dwellers' village suburb of 'Drezdane' and, later, after German penetration across the river, with the plains of the north-east. After the death of Heinrich, Dresden passed through various hands until it once again came under the Margraves of Meissen.

Both townships were composed of narrow, evil-smelling streets of small one-or-two-storeyed houses, mean in appearance, mostly timber with a few stone-built reed-thatched roofs. Goats and pigs wandered through the streets, and the gutters of those streets formed the only municipal drainage. In the centre, and on the present-day site, was the Altmarkt, or Old Market, adjacent to the town hall and the tall spire of the first Kreuzkirche, the Church of the Cross (so named as Constance, the first wife of Margrave Heinrich, had brought what was believed to be part of Christ's Cross with her in her dowry). The town's layout followed a grid-like pattern, with streets at right angles to each other and named after the trade or occupation of the residents – Weber-gasse (Weavers Street), Schössergasse (Tax Collectors Street), Fressgasse (Grocers Street). In Schulgasse (School Street), was the original Kreuzschule, a grammar school whose continuing existence and fame owe much to its world-renowned boys' choir. In Badergasse (Bath Street) there was a town bathhouse.

The medieval life of the town was typical of minor German town principali-ties; in good times there was trade and prosperity from the work of craftsmen, tailors and merchants; there was drink, there were games, festivities, religious processions and street plays based on events in the Bible including Christ's passion and crucifixion, with thousands of visitors to the Kreuzkirche and its relic. In bad times there was pestilence, superstition, fire, violent crime, disease and warfare. The Jews were often held to blame for such disasters and, in 1349, they were accused of poisoning the city's wells and members of the Jewish community were burnt at the stake. The Jews were expelled in 1411 and again in 1430. The town, for most of the Middle Ages, boasted only one doctor – the court physician. Ordinary people had recourse to bloodletting barbers, charlatans or hopes of a miracle. One fire in 1491 destroyed the Kreuzkirche and most of the surrounding streets and houses.

The Holy Roman Empire of the German Nation, the loose community of over 1,800 political units, principalities, imperial cities, imperial villages and lands held by imperial knights, included Saxony. The ruler of Saxony, styled the Elector, was one of the seven hereditary leading princes with the right to elect one of their number as Emperor. The electoral processes involved bargaining, bribery and, on occasion, conflict. Electors could use the elections to their advantage. In 1485 the two ducal brothers of the Saxon House of Wettin, who were ruling several Saxon lands, agreed to divide their patrimony. The elder, Ernst, retained the title of Elector and the Ernestine House's lands to the west and north, and the younger, Albrecht, took the Meissen-Dresden areas for his branch of the family (see Appendix 1). Dresden now became the capital of a small state. Although not yet the capital of the Saxon Electorate, the new status was a first step towards the city's great future, its development assured through the silver-mining industry and the skill of the Saxon craftsmen who wrought the metals.

In the late Middle Ages there appeared the early signs of the second great division to set German against German – religion. Dissenting Hussite preachers from Prague taught briefly in the first decade of the fifteenth century, at Dresden's Kreuzschule, until they were expelled. A century later the notorious Dominican monk Tetzel openly sold his 'indulgences', forgiveness of sins by payment, in the streets of Dresden; these were to be the final provocation for Martin Luther, who had also preached in Dresden at this time. The open corruption led Luther to publish his attack on the authority of Rome in Wittenberg in October 1517. Luther's arguments were essentially religious, taking as their main theme the notion that the evil in human nature was only redeemable by the grace of God and that mortals only experience this grace by living by simple faith, without the intervention of a priest. The arguments, however, presented a challenge to the political and religious establishment, Papal theocracy and clerical privileges. The disaffected, notably princes in need of monies for their states and jealous of Church wealth, and townspeople, all increasingly chose Lutheranism. The population of Dresden followed the teaching of their fellow Saxon, Luther; on the occasion of the publication of the Papal Bull excommunicating Luther, they burned down the house of a noted opponent of the Reformation.

A little later, in 1524, the Saxon Elector was converted to the Lutheran church, despite his status within the supposedly Catholic Holy Roman Empire. Saxon Lutheranism, however, was to include certain specific features that were all to prove significant for Dresden. The Protestant church in Saxony supported the ruler and the state structure and was opposed to the more extreme Calvinist Protestantism that questioned the authority of rulers; the Saxon church also maintained ritual and pageantry in its services – it was 'High Church' in English terms. The Holy Roman Emperor, Charles V, attempted to reassert his authority and discipline over the Ernestine Saxon Elector using the jealousy and the aims of Duke Moritz, the Albertine prince ruling in Dresden. Despite initial military advantage and the capture of the Ernestine Elector, defection by Moritz robbed him of success. The wily, if unscrupulous, Moritz emerged victorious and won the Electoral title for his Albertine line of the Wettin House (see Appendix 1).

Dresden was now the capital of an Electorate and an important city, but a prize for whose wealth and allegiance other competitors in this arena of inter-German politics and warfare were to strive. Saxony was also, unfortunately, placed in this arena, between north and south German interests, and was to suffer accordingly. Duke – later Elector – Moritz who ruled from 1541 to 1553 and his successors Electors Augustus (1553–86) and Christian I (1586–91), transformed Dresden into a fine Renaissance city of houses, mostly stone-built with elaborate gables, stone sculpture and painted designs on the exterior walls. Some of this work still survives. Moritz rebuilt and extended the Royal Palace, which had originated as a fort guarding the Elbe Bridge, into a splendid four-winged multi-gabled building with a central courtyard and a main entrance facing the Elbe Bridge. Later centuries were to bring additions, destruction and reconstruction. Augustus added the Arsenal, now the

Albertinum with its famous Grünes Gewölbe (Green Vault), the treasure house of the Saxon kings. Christian I rebuilt the town's rampart fortifications, one section of which is now the Brühl Terrasse, and added the Stallhof (Stable Court) with its long colonnade, decorated with the Wettin coats of arms, open on the courtyard side so as to serve as a tilting yard spectators' gallery, and equipped with a horse pond and two bronze pillars used for 'tilting at the ring', a form of jousting.

The Kreuzkirche was rebuilt with a magnificent Renaissance façade. This was later destroyed but it was recorded for posterity in the painting of Bernardo Bellotto. The foundations of Dresden's later fame as a centre of music were laid with rich early baroque Protestant church music in the Court Chapel, and the Saxon Staatskapelle, the first orchestra in Dresden, was founded in 1548.

This first Renaissance age of splendour was, however, followed by the first catastrophe, the trauma of the Thirty Years War. The war represented the last military effort of the Habsburg Holy Roman Emperors to restore Catholicism and their authority in Germany, beginning with the suppression of the Calvinists under their chosen ruler, the Elector Palatine, in Bohemia. Saxon Protestantism, in the form of the ultra-conservative Lutheran Elector Johann Georg I, a man of integrity but limited intellectual ability, was totally opposed to Calvinism. Saxony therefore sided with the Habsburg Imperial cause. This cause at first gained spectacular military victories, only to suffer an even more spectacular defeat at the hands of the Swedes, who came to the help of the northern Protestants for a mixture of religious reasons and their own strategic interests, and the French who were anxious to acquire Alsace and Lorraine. In the final balance, the Habsburg cause was lost and the position of the Empire's great princes was strengthened, thereby setting back the cause of German unity for over 200 years with far-reaching and disastrous results. The Lutheran princely states were, however, saved from the Catholic Counter-Reformation.

The war was a terrible experience for Saxony, which found itself on the losing side between the powers to the north and south. For the rural areas the passage of armies brought devastation, the extermination of villages and decimation of the population of towns, rapine, disease, starvation, beggary and wholesale misery. Literature and art virtually ceased to exist, music survived with difficulty thanks to Dresden's first great composer and conductor, Heinrich Schütz. The city itself was marginally more fortunate than the rural areas, being secured against sacking and pillages by its rebuilt fortifications, but it was not spared the wider economic and social consequences including inflation, taxation, hunger and disease.

Augustus the Strong and his Successors

The void created by this catastrophe was nevertheless an important reason for the great flowering of culture that followed, after a brief period. One positive general result of the war was further erosion of medieval superstitions – an erosion that contributed to the eighteenth century Age of Enlightenment and, in architecture, to the baroque. Other factors peculiar to Saxony were also to contribute to this cultural flowering in Dresden. One of these, undoubtedly, was the gentle rolling hill-country of the Elbe Valley. As one moves along road or river the patterns of hills and smaller valleys ceaselessly change. This sense of movement influences the baroque in Dresden in the same way as the Danube Valley contributed to that of Vienna, where the Habsburgs believed splendid architecture would contribute to the restoration of their authority. The return to Roman Catholicism of the Saxon Court was to bring some of the style of the baroque of Vienna and Munich to Dresden, where religious toleration and the preference of the local Lutheran Church for splendour and ritual could all fuse. Saxony gained in self-confidence from its contribution to the army led by King Jan (John) Sobieski of Poland, which defeated the Turks outside Vienna in 1683; this self-confidence was commemorated with the Türkenbrunnen, the Turkish Fountain. This fountain, originally erected in 1649 to mark the end of the Thirty Years War, was given statues of a goddess of victory and a Turk's head entwined with snakes spouting water. The Georgentor, the George Tower and Gateway, into the Royal Palace, built in 1693, also marked this event.

All of this, however, was influenced by the towering personality and ambition of the most remarkable ruler in the history of Saxony, Elector Friedrich August II, August der Starke, known in English as Augustus the Strong. Augustus was not a pleasant man either in appearance or in behaviour. He was ruthless, self-indulgent, corrupt and an uncontrolled womanizer. Physically he was endowed with enormous strength, hence his additional name; he could bend and break pokers and horseshoes with ease. He had, however, a vision for his land and dynasty that was to transform his Saxon capital. As a second son he had not been destined for the Electorate and as a prince he had been allowed to visit Catholic countries, namely France – where he had met Louis XIV at Versailles – Italy and Spain, and also Catholic Vienna; these clearly impressed him. In 1694 he became Elector of Saxony following the death of an elder brother, and then shortly afterwards following a necessary preliminary – and unpopular – conversion to the Roman Catholic Church, King of Poland. Augustus saw the linkage of Saxony and Poland as profitable for the two countries for both economic and cultural reasons. He was, however, only elected king after some bribery within the Polish Diet, meeting under very heavy pressure, from the Tsar of Russia, Peter the Great. The kingship was to bring its problems in the Great Northern War, which started in 1700. Augustus unwisely tried to occupy Livonia, (now part of Lithuania and Latvia), which was held by Sweden. Charles XII of Sweden, a remarkable warrior king, fought back, drove Augustus out of Poland in 1702, and forced his deposition in 1704. Charles XII's power was, however, to be destroyed by Peter the Great in 1709, after which Augustus regained the throne of Poland, which remained linked to that of Saxony until 1763.

Augustus followed the Habsburg belief that building prestige would strengthen both the legitimacy of the state and his own personal authority. He was fortunate that Saxony, with its mineral and agricultural resources and a hard-working population, could support his designs, despite wars and the need to maintain a standing army, either by borrowing or through taxation, by using the wealth of the silver mines, and through the exploitation of Poland.

A newly formed Privy Council extended his authority over Saxon cities and improved greatly the efficiency of government. However, there were incidents of industrial unrest, which are interesting in view of Dresden's subsequent associations with socialism. Dresden's craft and small-trader tradition had, from the late Middle Ages, been fashioned on independence and self-confidence of spirit, characteristics that can be seen repeatedly throughout the city's history, and in 1712 builders on one royal project came out on strike over the non-payment of arrears of wages.

Augustus's first major project was the Grosser Garten, the Great Garden. Gardens with fountains and running water were an essential component of baroque design and living. People could sit in them and stroll or debate in peace and quiet. The site, a little outside the city at the time, had been acquired by Elector Johann Georg II as a private pheasant enclosure in 1674, and work on the palace had begun two years later. Augustus directed that the park and palace should become a great public garden, to be his Versailles. It was designed for the public to admire, while at the same time breaking through the confines of the old walled city.

The whole area was now planned in the French style, in a rectangular form with a central *parterre*, dominated in the middle by the palace. The gardens were laid out in a complex pattern of hedges and flower borders on either side of the main axis through the park. There were two lesser avenues running parallel to this avenue, and it was crossed by another running north to south. Eight elegant small houses for royal guests were placed symmetrically around the inner garden. To the side of the palace, facing away from the city, was a large rectangular pond, the scene of the pageants and festivals. The H-shaped palace itself was of three storeys. The exterior reflected the transition from Renaissance to baroque, the overall design being essentially

Figure 3. The Zwinger, looking towards the Kronentor entrance to the south-west wing. Courtesy of the Sächsische Landesbibliothek, Deutsche Fotothek.

Renaissance but with baroque decoration and double flights of steps up from the garden. Italian, Dutch, and French influences are all present. The most important feature of the interior was the central banqueting hall, rising to two storeys in height. Order and symmetry were made to predominate in the close linkage of house, gardens and early baroque statuary and sculpture.

Augustus left two additional world-famous baroque legacies in the city: the Zwinger and the Frauenkirche.

The Zwinger was an exuberant piece of architecture that was as elaborate as any of the most flamboyant in Vienna. It was the work of Matthäus Pöppelmann, an architect who had just arrived in Dresden from Westphalia but who was then sent by Augustus to study the architecture of Vienna and Prague. The name 'Zwinger' meant an outer bailey, an open space surrounded by fortified walls, and the original concept was relatively simple: an orangery with low, curved galleries adjoining the royal palace. The concept was developed to provide for a stage set, and arena, for the great Court pageants, tournaments and displays, with the elaborate Long Galleries, and sinuous staircases, the superb Wall Pavilion and Rampart Pavilion, and the elegant onion-domed Crown Gate at the entrance. All were decorated with rich baroque sculpture, the finest being the work of Balthasar Permoser. His themes were those of nature in the form of fountains, satyrs, nymphs, putti and figures from classical antiquity, together with dynastic coats of arms to emphasize Augustus's authority. The concept was further developed between 1723 and 1728 to provide for the use of the pavilions and galleries to house the royal art collections. Like the Grosser Garten, the Zwinger was open to the general public to admire. The Zwinger, although developed further in the nineteenth century and much restored after many vicissitudes, remains one of the most magnificent examples of baroque architecture in Europe with its rocking curves and sense of movement and creativity.

Although he was by now a Catholic, Augustus's second major work in the city was the great Protestant Frauenkirche, the Church of Our Lady, the jewel in the crown. The church was designed with remarkable boldness for the confined area of its Neumarkt (New Market Place) site, the cramped space being turned to advantage, the church's four towers presenting the same image from any direction. It took seventeen years to complete, from 1726 to 1743. The architect was George Bähr and the design of the Frauen-kirche reflected contemporary Protestant theology: there was a large central space where services would centre around preaching to galleries crowded with worshippers. Great importance was attached to a High Altar for Eucharist, and a great organ for music. But the church also represented a spiritual unity in the city, its dedication to Our Lady being unusual in a Protestant church. Its size, its brilliant and daring handling of interior space, and its huge 352-foot-high stone dome, which formed the physical and spatial centre point of the pre-1945 Dresden skyline, all made the Frauenkirche arguably the world's most important pure baroque Protestant building. The church's interior with its richly sculptured high altar, pulpit and painted galleries and dome left an unforgettable impression.

Another notable building owing its existence to Augustus is the Taschenberg Palace, a reflection of the less conventional side of Augustus's character. The Palace, connected by a covered passage to the Royal Palace, was built for Constantia von Cosel, a favourite among Augustus's numerous mistresses (the baroque age was tolerant of such matters). The elegant baroque facade has been restored following its destruction in 1945.

Augustus re-planned and largely rebuilt the city itself as well as the major public buildings, his instrument for control being a Board of Public Works established in 1718. Wide streets, planned to open upon a vista, replaced narrow lanes, and houses were all built of stone, with stone staircases and with French style mansard roofs replacing span-roofs and gables. Around the Neumarkt a number of fine baroque palaces and houses were built; none of these have survived. A number of Italian architects were employed. Augustus wanted to make the Elbe into a waterway comparable with the Grand Canal in Venice and Pöpplemann was commissioned to build an elegant bridge, later replaced for navigation reasons.

Following a disastrous fire in 1685, Augustus directed the rebuilding of Altendresden (Old Dresden) by his state architect von Klengel. It became known as the Neue Königstadt (New Royal Town), soon shortened to Neustadt. His plans for it provided for a road leading across the now-renamed Augustus Bridge to a central point from which a number of roads radiated out in different directions. Traffic was so heavy that within twenty years a one-way system had to be introduced on the bridge. Only a few features of the original plan have survived the alterations of later centuries and the destruction of the Second World War. The splendour of the past is, however, evidenced by the statue of the *Goldener Reiter* (Golden Horseman), an idealized representation of Augustus himself, erected three years after his death, and a number of baroque houses in the Königstrasse (King Street), leading to the Japanisches Palais (Japanese Palace) built for the housing of porcelain, Japanese, Far Eastern and local. The Japanese Palace is another work by Pöppelman, aided by two assistants – Zacharias Longuelune and Jean de Bodt.

Augustus carried his fascination with the Orient further at a large riverside summer palace, Pillnitz, some six miles from Dresden. The palace, like the Japanese Palace, was the work of a team headed by Pöppelman, its curved 'pagoda' roofs, lantern-shaped chimneys and Chinese scenes on the stucco of the river facade are highly unusual (see Plate 12). Augustus also treated himself to an elegant country lodge for large hunting parties – Moritzburg castle, fifteen miles north-west of Dresden. Built of a yellow stone and surrounded by water, the castle features four large round towers, each topped by a dome. A striking chapel with a well-proportioned spire completes the composition. The Saxon princes staged mock sea battles on the water surrounding the castle. Finally Augustus founded, in the old cathedral city of Meissen, the world-renowned porcelain craft industry whose products are often referred to as Dresden china. The first director, Johann Böttger had been ordered to make gold to pay for Augustus's court and projects; he failed in this but his alternative, hand-reared porcelain, which he invented in Dresden in 1709, was to prove profitable.

Under Augustus Dresden had become a city of over 40,000 people, a major European capital with a court renowned for its splendour. Dressed in rich clothes adorned with jewels, Augustus would himself participate in the lavish and Bacchanalian court festivals dedicated to Mars, Diana, Venus, Neptune, Saturn and Jupiter, the last held in celebration of the wedding of his son. Opera, ballet, comedy were all performed. In all music, Italian composers and performers were in the lead. Augustus acquired his magnificent collection of gold and silver work, porcelain and painting for the greater glory of his court and his rule. The rich cultural life of the city in which architecture, art, music and drama were all inter-related both complemented and developed

Figure 4. The Hofkirche, Dresden's Catholic Court Church, photographed before World War II with, on the left of the picture, the Georgentor. Courtesy of the Sächsische Landesbibliothek, Deutsche Fotothek.

the special characteristics of the Saxon people, who liked to live in harmony, avoid war, and enjoy life.

Augustus was succeeded by his son, Frederick Augustus II of Saxony (Augustus III of Poland) in 1733 (see Appendix I). The son continued his father's work, his contribution to the city being the lovely late Italian baroque style Hofkirche (Court Church), the work of an Italian architect, Gaetano Chiaveri, and built between 1739 and 1755. The design is unusual, the front aligned towards Warsaw, a raised roof over the nave, a graceful tower and, around the two balustrade roof lines, rows of sculptured figures of saints that provide a superb silhouette effect. These figures were the work of another Italian, Lorenzo Mattielli. The Hofkirche's interior contained a glittering ceiling fresco and a famous 3,000-pipe organ. Augustus, like his father, had converted to Rome to ensure his succession in Poland, but Roman Catholicism was still unpopular in Dresden. The foundations of the Hofkirche had to be laid in secrecy, with Catholic priests entering and leaving in disguise.

The Hofkirche's beautiful spire, the Frauenkirche's well-proportioned dome, and the palace towers all completed the unique Dresden skyline; even today the impact of the Hofkirche, when crossing into the city over the Augustus-brücke, is unforgettable. The original state of these buildings, and other aspects of the life of mid-eighteenth century Dresden, have been recorded for us in superb paintings by Bernardo Bellotto Canaletto, the nephew of the great Venetian, who was invited to Dresden by Augustus, (see Plates 16 and 18), and also in literature by James Boswell who visited the city after the Seven Years War. Bellotto's works show not only Dresden's buildings, including the Kreuzkirche, in their Renaissance form the Altmarkt town houses, Pöppelmann's bridge and the baroque buildings of the 500-metre-long Brühl Terrace, but also much fascinating detail of the life of the city's inhabitants, their dress, transport and occupations.

Gracious and elegant though Dresden was, the social and political developments of the eighteenth century were the reverse. Court life sank into a measure of corruption, Count Brühl, Augustus's Chief Minister, amassing a vast wardrobe, coach and jewellery collections for his luxurious lifestyle. Boswell was present at a sale of upwards of 700 gold snuffboxes, many of them 'very rich in diamonds' after Brühl's fall from office. Brühl's personal extravagances were legendary; he kept twelve tailors permanently employed and wore a new suit every day. In his defence, however, Brühl fully supported his king in furthering Dresden's artistic and cultural life. In policy he sought stability for Central Europe and feared Prussian ambitions. His fears were justified as, in the Seven Years' War (1756–63) the Prussian king, Frederick the Great, invaded Saxony and occupied Dresden. His artillery damaged the Zwinger and destroyed the Kreuzkirche and he ruthlessly exploited Saxony's wealth to fund his war against the Emperor. The Kreuzkirche was later rebuilt with its present late baroque tower. At this time, in the years 1770 to 1776, the *Landhaus* (State Government and Legislature Building, now the Dresden City Museum) was built. With its large hall and splendid wide curving stairs the *Landhaus* reflects the move away from pure baroque to a more severely classical style (see Plate 15).

More warfare was, however, to follow. The upheavals in Europe, inspired by the French Revolution, led to a minor Saxon peasants' rebellion in 1790 and a rebellion of apprentices led by journeymen tailors in Dresden itself in 1794. Both were put down severely by the Elector's troops and were followed by censorship and the control of journals and books. At the death of Augustus, the Saxon Electors lost the title of King of Poland. After the French Revolution Saxony joined the successive groupings of German states that in intermittent warfare attempted to contain French efforts to control German affairs, but in 1806 Napoleon's defeat of Austria led to the end of these attempts and

Figure 5. The Kreuzkirche as rebuilt after the Seven Years War, seen across the Altmarkt as it was before 1945. Courtesy of the Sächsische Landesbibliothek, Deutsche Fotothek.

the final demise of the Holy Roman Empire. A loose Confederation of the Rhine was created under Napoleon's protection. Saxony, which had continued in its opposition to France and Napoleon, then joined the Confederation, which served to reduce the number of sovereign political entities to forty.

Nineteenth-Century Dresden

The Elector took the title of King of Saxony and then became a loyal supporter of Napoleon. His support gave Napoleon the opportunity for his last but short-lived military success at the battle of Dresden in October 1813. The battle was fought in and around the city following a series of street skirmishes over the preceding five months, but the outcome left Saxony once again on the losing side. Prussia, which had deserted Napoleon's cause following his disastrous invasion of Russia, accordingly sought to add Saxony to her territories, and only the diplomatic vigour of the French statesman, Talley-rand, and the British Foreign Secretary, Castlereagh, secured the survival of a very greatly reduced Saxony at the Congress of Vienna peace-making in 1814–15. For Germany as a whole this settlement provided a 'German Confederation' of thirty-nine states, with the Habsburg Emperor at Vienna as president.

The city's cultural life continued despite the political and military turmoil. Goethe and Schiller both found inspiration for their writing in Dresden; Weber was director of the opera, and the young Richard Wagner was amongst the *Kreuzschule's* schoolboys. The beauty of the city and the Elbe valley inspired numbers of Romantic writers and artists, such as the Dresden-born poet Theodor Körner, the writer Ludwig Tieck and the landscape painter Caspar David Friedrich.

As with all Europe, the nineteenth century was to be one of dramatic change for Saxony and its capital. The Napoleonic Wars – in particular the arrival in the city of Lützow's *Freikorps* of partisans – had aroused a new German consciousness and spread ideas of political liberation, but the conservative rulers of both the major powers in rivalry for leadership, Austria and Prussia, were opposed to any reduction of their authority, as were most of the other German princely rulers. Dominated initially by Austria, an era of repression opened, although this was light in Saxony and Dresden compared with other states. Until the great popular explosion of 1848 the only significant developments for Saxony were a measure of constitutional government granted by King Friedrich August II in 1831 and Saxony's entry into the Prussian-sponsored *Zollverein*, Customs Union, which by 1834 covered most of the German Confederation but not Austria.

The revolutions that swept Europe in 1848 momentarily shook the foundations of the German princely states. At first frightened rulers, including the King of Saxony, conceded liberal constitutional concessions; Austria and Prussia allowed a national constituent assembly for all Germany to meet at Frankfurt. The rulers, finding that the land-owning, business and wage-earning classes did not generally support the Frankfurt assembly, then recovered their nerve and began to withdraw the concessions. The idealistic and not-very-practical delegates to the Frankfurt assembly drafted an imperial constitution, deciding to exclude Austria because of the vast non-German Habsburg territories, and to offer an imperial crown to the King of Prussia. The King preferred a conservative Prussian kingdom to a possibly dangerous liberal German empire and refused the offer. His refusal and the failure of the Frankfurt assembly marked perhaps the last opportunity for German unification by democratic means. In Saxony itself political liberals had made gains in the state parliamentary elections; these gains were unacceptable to the King, Friedrich August II, who dissolved the legislature. An uprising in Dresden followed in May 1849, in which some Saxon rebel troops, allied with students, democrats, miners and a number of the city's workforce all took to the streets singing the *Marseillaise* and proclaiming a provisional government in the Town Hall. The first Opera house was burned down in the street fighting and eventually Prussian troops, hurriedly brought in, together with Saxon troops loyal to the King, restored order, killing over 150 people in the city's streets and filling the prisons. Richard Wagner, who had fought at the barricades, was forced to flee the country.

If a liberal German unification was now impossible, economic and infrastructure developments ceaselessly involving Saxony in wider German interests were under way, all of which later served Bismarck's forceful unification. The year 1839 saw Dresden's first railway, linking the city to Leipzig; in 1837 steamboats began carrying cargoes on the Elbe.

The second half of the century saw a vast expansion of light and medium industry, breweries, chocolate, furniture, precision instruments, paper, textiles and the woollen industry, a sugar refinery, warehouses, road and rail networks, with large railway stations, banks and hotels all appearing in the city. In 1872 the Dresden Bank was founded, to this day one of Germany's most important banking houses. The bank developed interests in Middle Eastern railway construction, and mining trading interests in Russia, China, South America and German colonies in West Africa. The population of the city grew at great speed from some 50,000 in 1848 to over 400,000 by 1914.

Saxony's formal political inclusion into a Greater Germany followed successive moves, carefully planned and based essentially on military power, by the Prussian Minister President from 1862, Bismarck. He first picked a quarrel with Austria, with whom Saxony was allied, and then defeated her in a brief military campaign in 1866. He next created a North German Confederation, which included a reluctant Saxony, supposedly federal but in practice dominated by Prussia and in particular by Bismarck himself as Chancellor. Finally he picked a quarrel with France and defeated her in the 1870–1 Franco–Prussian War. On the basis of these stunning military successes, and together with massive economic development especially in heavy industry, Prussia's domination of Germany became unchallengeable. In 1871, in the Hall of Mirrors in the Palace of Versailles and in the presence of other leading German princes and rulers, the German Empire was proclaimed, with the King of Prussia its Emperor. In the imperial constitution the larger states, including Saxony, kept State military contingents, but Berlin assumed full overall control of the new nation's foreign and defence policy. Germany had been unified, but within a political culture that was to lead, with a tragic inevitability, to more wars and disaster.

The architectural development of the city reflected the major social change; the dominant social group was no longer the old Saxon aristocracy but the

Figure 6. The Semper Opera House before 1945 (since, faithfully rebuilt). Courtesy of the Sächsische Landesbibliothek, Deutsche Fotothek.

new thrusting energetic bourgeoisie, creating and created by economic expansion. Building reflected their needs and tastes. In the early years of the century, the city's old fortifications were pulled down and the moat was filled in. They were replaced with a broad ring of roads and gardens. In 1830–32 the famous Berlin architect, Schinkel, built the Altstädterwache (Guard House) near the Royal Palace, intended for the Palace guard troops but now used as a coffee house and for the sale of theatre tickets. In 1838 Gottfried Semper began work on a new Opera House, which became a victim of fire in 1869. Two years later he also began work on an impressive synagogue.

In 1847 Semper turned to the Zwinger, building what is now called the Semper Gallery thus enclosing the Elbe side of the complex. The work, in an Italian Renaissance style, was finished in 1855. In 1871 Semper began his most famous work, the Semper Opera House, to replace that destroyed in the fire of 1869. The Opera House is a remarkable combination, with a functional interior and an exterior that contributes to the centre of the city with its Court Church, Zwinger and Royal Palace. The facade of the Opera House is a structure of segmental arches in two stories with a raised central roof over the auditorium and stage, and an elaborate central portal surmounted by ebullient sculpture. The whole forms a splendid centre for Dresden's rich music life.

The Royal Palace was extensively rebuilt in the years 1883–1901 in a Renaissance style. The most striking addition to the Palace complex, however, originally dated from twenty years earlier when the sixteenth-century Stallhof (Stable Court) was refurbished as a museum. The building's exterior wall was decorated by a long frieze of figures of the Saxon Wettin princes, originally in s'graffito but replaced in 1907 by 24,000 Meissen tiles. Each of the princes is portrayed on horseback and at the end of the procession there are representatives of the professions, scholars and arts.

Other works included the enlargement of the Great Garden, the building of today's Albertinum housing the Galerie Neue Meister, the New Masters Gallery, and four new bridges across the Elbe. More practically, the city was provided with electric lighting and modern drainage systems. A tramway system was built within the city and suburbs. The new bourgeoisie had large pleasant houses and villas, stretching out into the suburbs. Dresden's bourgeois suburbs of villas and houses, of which many were destroyed in the raid, were unique in their overall size and in the variety of designs they used.

Amongst Dresden's bourgeoisie there was an English community that found Dresden to be an agreeable and civilized city in which to live. For the working-class population of the city, however, tenement buildings, somewhat drab and ugly, were erected.

The working day was long, nine-and-a-half to eleven hours. Although, except for a few skilled workers, the wage levels were not generous, they were adequate if prudently managed; these and the social security system of Bismarck's Germany ensured there was none of the squalor of St Petersburg or Moscow – despite much subsequent political rhetoric. The political atmosphere was, however, far from liberal: socialist politicians and trade unions were repressed by stringent legislation. Moreover, an international anti-semitic congress met in Dresden in 1882. Despite all this, the liberal tradition and radical socialism, the latter to prove such an important feature of Dresden's post-1918 life, remained alive. In 1866 August Bebel, the founder of German socialism, had addressed a mass meeting in Dresden warning against the threat of Prussian domination. In the mid-1890s, Rosa Luxemburg, the future Communist leader, was editor of a radical Dresden newspaper, and in 1903 Bebel returned to Dresden for a Social Democrat rally in which he declared war on the 'bourgeois social order'. Bebel, although a Rhinelander, won his first seat in the German parliament in Dresden, deliberately choosing the city. Socialism was studied by working men in legal and underground meetings, and there were occasional demonstrations and strikes.

Figure 7. Hellerau, the Festspielhaus (theatre) before 1945. Courtesy of the Sächsische Landesbibliothek, Deutsche Fotothek.

Dresden, 1900–18

The last years of the nineteenth century and the first years of the twentieth saw further building on both banks of the Elbe – mostly of large government offices. Notable amongst them was the *Landtagsgebäude*, the Saxon State Parliament building, designed by Wallot (the architect of the Berlin Reichstag) and completed in 1903, and Roth and Bräters impressive new *Rathaus*, Town Hall, (1910) now rebuilt around its surviving tower – the tallest in the City, with a gilded figure stretching an arm out over the city's roofs, which has survived.

The buildings of these years generally reflected the bureaucratic, hierarchical nature of both the German Empire and the Saxon State. One remarkable exception to this structured social order was the garden suburb city of Hellerau, built in 1910 by an enlightened factory owner for his workers. Modelled on English garden city concepts, Hellerau consists of neat, well-designed houses, open public spaces, and educational and recreational facilities. Its centrepiece was a Festspielhaus (theatre) that could hold 600 people; this was revolutionary in design, having no barrier between audience and stage. Greek-patterned eurhythmic dance performances were staged in this theatre. The interior was lit by thousands of lights installed behind translucent linen. The lights were controlled centrally so that the walls and the ceiling would radiate light in harmony with the emotional nuances of the music and the gestures and movements of the dancers. All was intended to create an atmosphere of social harmony in which the minds, emotions and bodies of the workers would be reunited. Hellerau achieved world fame and leading theatre artists of the time, including Shaw, Diaghilev and Nijinsky visited the Festspielhaus before its closure in 1914.

The First World War from 1914 to 1918, while leaving Dresden as a city unscathed, saw not only the defeat of the German state but also the end of an age. Many young Saxon men perished in the fighting on the various fronts. The iron grip of the British Royal Navy's blockade of Germany imposed increasing hardship on the populace – a hardship compounded by inflation, the fall in the value of money beginning a process of ruin for the middle classes that continued after the war. By 1918 the German nation was reduced to weekly rations of four pounds of bread, seven-and-a-half pounds of potatoes, half a pound of meat (if it was available), with small portions of fish, butter, fats and jam (less than 10 per cent of pre-war consumption). The German Empire's government collapsed amid demonstrations of war-weary and hungry crowds in Berlin and elsewhere. Twenty thousand people had demonstrated in Dresden in September, and even larger demonstrations followed in the city on 8 and 9 November. The Kaiser fled into exile and the other German rulers, including the King Friedrich August III of Saxony, were forced to abdicate. None were physically molested, the German revolutions at this point not carrying the regicidal passions and hatreds that had character- ized the events in Russia. The end of the monarchy, however, terminated the court-based culture that had been the centre of Dresden's life in the seventeenth, eighteenth and nineteenth centuries. The twentieth century was now to usher in misfortune worse even than the Thirty Years War, and catastrophe in which Dresden, with all its beauty, culture and history was to be reduced, in apocalyptic horror, to a ruin.

Dresden, 1919—45

Anthony Clayton

The Weimar Republic, the name given to the German state system that existed between the collapse of Imperial Germany and the accession to power of Adolf Hitler, was born in conditions of military defeat and the Versailles peace settlement, which most Germans saw as humiliating. The post-armistice months and years were marked by unemployment, particularly severe in Saxony, limbless ex-soldiers begging in the streets, and a sour climate of opinion in which all the respected authorities of the past – state, church, army, parents, teachers – seemed discredited and were ignored. Crime, venereal disease, promiscuity, divorce were all claimed to be spiralling. Many saw in these conditions a moral decline. Taking flight into the unreal, people believed that the degeneracy could be arrested only by a revived authority, for some Communist, for others National Socialist. Division was to be the *leitmotiv* of Germany from 1918 onwards. Weimar Germany, however well meaning its liberal founders were, was to be the overture to the Nazis.

The City under Weimar and under the Nazis

Soldiers and workers' councils overthrew the Saxon monarchy and hoisted the red flag on the Royal Palace. The more moderate socialist national government in Berlin, supported by the Army and extreme right-wing armed groups, and with dubious legitimacy, restored a fragile and illiberal order. This order was challenged unsuccessfully, first by an attempted communist coup, the 'Spartacus Rebellion', in January 1919, in which the Army assassinated the communist leaders; and then in March 1920 by a coup attempt mounted by right-wing militants, the Kapp Putsch, which the Army decided – after some wavering – not to support. The national government tried to take refuge in Dresden, but was refused permission to do so by the military commander. A general strike was called in protest at the coup attempt; this, in turn, led to the most vicious of the ongoing 1920s Dresden street battles between the political right and left, fifty-nine people being killed. In the next two years there followed spiralling inflation of the German currency, with covert government support in order to invalidate the reparations payment clauses of the Versailles Treaty. This meant ruin for even more of the middle classes and for the small traders, with workers' wages always rising below the level of inflation. At the start of the inflation the German mark stood at twenty to the pound, by the end of 1923 it had reached 23,000,000,000 to the pound. A man's life savings were perhaps enough to buy a postage stamp. All this added to a sense of disillusionment with the new regime and widened the divisions in German society.

In practice the constitution of Weimar Germany greatly strengthened the authority of the central national government, the Army in particular retaining strong emergency powers and requiring only presidential authority. In 1923 the political parties of the moderate left that had been elected to the Saxon State Assembly and Dresden City Council rashly permitted the Communists first to form a 'Red Militia' and then to enter the state government. The government then made demands on Berlin for the recognition of the militia – demands backed by sabotage and rioting. The Berlin government, in response, deployed the Army that, using its emergency powers, removed the Dresden government by decree, disbanded the militia, and imprisoned leading members of the administration, Socialist and Communist alike, and including the State Premier, Dr Zeigner.

Thereafter, on the surface, conditions seemed to improve, the currency was stabilized and the nation appeared to accept the democratic system. At the end of the decade, however, the Great Depression, the recession in world trade, threw scores of thousands out of work in a renewed atmosphere of hopelessness; the street battles between left and right, the latter now the Nazi brownshirt storm troopers, broke out again.

In a series of brilliantly managed electoral campaigns – the work of Göbbels – the Nazis under Hitler steadily increased their vote in the years 1929 to mid-1932. The appeal to the ballot box was accompanied in the streets by the bullying of the stormtroopers, whose ranks were filled by the unemployed; in the case of Dresden, for example, 61,000 people, one man in four, was out of work. In a final election, in November 1932, the Nazi vote dropped, leading Hitler to his January 1933 decision to take office as Chancellor in case of any further fall. The same month saw an anti-Nazi demonstration of some 45,000 people and a bitter street battle in Dresden in which non-Nazis, mostly Communists, suffered severely.

In power as Chancellor, Hitler successfully marginalized other non-Nazi ministers, took total power, and finally, on the death of President Hindenburg, proclaimed himself *Führer* (leader), both ceremonial and executive head of state. The other features of the Nazi system soon followed: huge rallies and

Figure 8. Hitler's accession to power acclaimed in Dresden, 1933. Courtesy of the Sächsische Landesbibliothek, Deutsche Fotothek.

parades, propaganda on the theme of national regeneration, suppression of the free press, the development of Nazi youth organizations, secret police and concentration camps and the distortion of education. The Churches were expected to align their worship and teaching with Nazism; critics such as a senior pastor at the Frauenkirche, Hugo Hahn, a leading member of Pastor Martin Niemöller's anti-Nazi groups within the Lutheran church, were discharged from their posts. Hahn was expelled from Saxony. In the words of Victor Klemperer, the renowned Dresden philologist, all this represented the 'destruction of speech and thought' in what he called LTI, *Lingua Tertii Imperii*, the title of his 1947 book.

The Nazi era, from its early days, began systematic persecution of Jews and all others opposed to Nazism. Dresden's Jews in the professions were first deprived of their work and status, then their civic rights and finally, in most cases and after much prior cruelty, their lives at Auschwitz. Works by Jews were removed from the Dresden State Art Collections; music scores and books by Jews – even acknowledged musical and literary masterpieces – were burned publicly. Jewish children and students were expelled from schools and the Technical High School. In the November 1938 *Kristallnacht*, Crystal Night, pogrom destruction or 'general aryanization' of Jewish property,

Semper's synagogue was burnt down and Jews were banned from entering the centre of the city and later made to wear a yellow star badge. Victor Klemperer's diary provides a moving personal account. Although a decorated veteran of the First World War, a patriot and married to a non-Jew, he received the full treatment of terror and degradation. He first lost his university appointment and found himself shunned by colleagues and former students. He was then made to assume 'Israel' as his first name and wear a yellow star. He was ordered out of public transport and amenities. Only his marriage to a non-Jew saved his life. Finally he was imprisoned and forced into slave labour before fleeing into the countryside in the confusion following the air attack on Dresden, to live under an assumed name during the last months of the war. His diaries, however, also record many acts of kindness from Germans and his continuing steadfast faith in Germany, which he saw betrayed by the Nazis, who were, in his view, 'un-German'. Dresden's main achievement in the Weimar period, the city's lead in the field of health education and the German Hygiene Museum, was used to further Nazi ideological study of superior and inferior races. The only notable addition in the Nazi era was the 1935 motorway bridge. The Theaterplatz (Theatre Square), between the Opera and the Zwinger, was renamed the Adolf Hitler

Figure 9. Boycott of a Jewish shop in Dresden 1936. Courtesy of the Dresden City Museum.

Figure 10. Hitler visits Dresden, May 1934. Courtesy of the Dresden City Museum.

Platz and other streets received names reflecting the Nazi version of history. The garden city of Hellerau was given to the SS for use as a recreation camp. As German historians have subsequently commented, the evil that was to destroy this superbly beautiful 700-year-old city had some of its roots within the city walls.

The nature of the Nazi state, with its all-pervading secret police system, was such that resistance in Germany could only be limited. Fear dominated the non-fanatical section of the population, with a fatalistic acceptance of events as a by-product. The general populace was not sympathetic to resisters; many would willingly inform against them. Nevertheless, in Saxony as elsewhere in Germany, a few brave figures were prepared to protest; an even smaller number was prepared to act. The protesters included churchmen and students; those who acted were mainly individuals or very small groups of workers, socialists or communists, engaged in secret political discussion meetings or industrial sabotage. The names and occupations of some of the Dresden activists well illustrate the style and nature of their activities: pre-war Communist Party members such as Wilhelm Firl, a journalist, Otto Galle, a cobbler, Albert Hensel, Franz Hoffman, Kurt Schlosser and Herbert Blochwitz, all carpenters, Arno Lade, a tram conductor, Franz Latzel, a metal worker, Hans Rothbarth, a textile worker, and Hans Daukner, a Jewish gardener; all were arrested and later killed in concentration camps. Others also killed in camps included Alfred Schmieder, a Social Democrat Party member and a bookkeeper by trade, and Bernhard Wensch, a Roman Catholic priest whose opposition to Nazi youth education brought about his death in Dachau. In general most of the opposition was caught apart from a few fortunates who escaped into Czechoslovakia; those caught and convicted were executed by decapitation in the yard of Dresden's Supreme Court. One report claims 1,069 headless corpses were removed from the yard in the war years.

There were a number of Saxons present in the Free Germany organization sponsored by Moscow in 1943.

Only the military possessed the physical means to eliminate the Nazi regime. In the honourable if ultimately unsuccessful tradition of resistance to Hitler within the German Army, two Saxon officers from Dresden were conspicuous. Both were devout Christians, free of personal ambition, their beliefs leading them to oppose Nazism. The first was General Friedrich Olbricht who had moved among groups of officers critical of Hitler since 1938 and who became an active conspirator in February 1943. He agreed to co-operate with the second, Major-General Hans Oster, chief of staff of the Abwehr (Armed Services Counter-Intelligence) in the creation of a network of reliable military contacts across Germany to prepare to seize power should Hitler be assassinated, a contingency referred to as 'Operation Flash' and planned for March 1943. In the event Hitler escaped death because bombs planted in an aircraft in which he was travelling failed to explode. Olbricht, nevertheless, remained an active conspirator, assisted by an officer who joined his staff, Colonel Count von Stauffenberg. Stauffenberg was himself a south German but, curiously, his grandmother came from Dresden's small nineteenth-century English community. Both Olbricht and Stauffenberg were leading members of the group of conspirators in the 20 July 1944 attempt on Hitler's life, Operation Valkyrie. As chief of staff to the Commander of the Home Army, Olbricht's role was to move troops into Berlin on the pretext of suppressing an uprising of foreign workers, so as to secure the capital for the conspirators after Hitler had been killed. The bomb planted by von Stauffenberg, however, failed to kill Hitler yet again, and the plot fell apart. The conspirators felt deeply that the world must know that there were Germans who were totally opposed to the Nazi regime, to the point of losing their lives. General Olbricht made no attempt to flee and after a brief struggle was overpowered. On the orders of his commander he was executed, with von Stauffenberg and others, in the courtyard of the War Ministry. Dresden's Olbricht Platz, the site of the military History Museum, commemorates his name. Other less senior Saxon officers figured in the Moscow-sponsored League of German Officers, led by Field Marshal Paulus after his defeat at Stalingrad.

General Oster was a more complex character. His hatred of Nazism dated from the years before Hitler's accession to power and included involvement in a conspiracy to remove Hitler at the time of the 1938 Sudetenland crisis, if the *Führer* had involved Germany in war. After the collapse of this project Oster used the Abwehr as a channel of communication for officers opposed to Hitler and warned the British government in March 1939 of Hitler's plan for Poland through a British journalist, Ian Colvin.

Following the outbreak of war, Oster and Admiral Canaris specifically recruited a number of known opponents of Nazism. In despair at his failure to motivate senior commanders to act against Hitler, in November 1939, Oster deliberately passed guarded warnings of a planned German invasion to the Belgian and Netherlands governments; the invasion was, however, deferred at the last minute. Other warnings of planned invasions of Norway and Denmark in 1940 and Yugoslavia in 1941 were almost certainly the work of Oster. An honourable soldier who believed the role of an army was the defence of its country, his Christian principles led him to increasing hatred of aggression; his counter-intelligence work revealed Nazi methods of warfare to him, daily reinforcing his loathing of the regime. Until early 1943 Oster continued to provide a variety of undercover arrangements and help for conspirators, but in April of that year the Abwehr was investigated. Several

Figure 11. General Friedrich Olbricht, executed for complicity in the 20 July 1944 bomb plot. Courtesy of Dr F. Georgi.

of Oster's contacts were arrested and he himself retired. In July 1944 Oster's name was found on lists of appointments that would have been made had the bomb plot against Hitler succeeded. He was arrested and, after a hurriedly convened SS court martial, he was executed in Flossenburg concentration camp just before the camp was liberated by the Americans in April 1945.

The Second World War, 1939–44

The outbreak of the Second World War had briefly seen Dresden as the centre of much military activity, preparing, supplying and moving units of the

German Army's Army Group South for their part in the invasion of Poland. Thereafter, until October 1944, the city remained of very secondary importance in military terms, only its barracks being used for training and staging of troops. A few factories around the city were engaged in a small way with direct military production, precision instruments, shell fuses, aircraft components and gas masks. Other factories were at work on goods needed by any population at any time, cigarettes, breweries, soap, radio receivers, and baby powder. No factories lay in the city centre, although the city centre was important for posts and telegraph communications, particularly after the opening of the Russian campaign. Numbers of British prisoners of war were directed to work in the postal sheds. Despite the compulsion, they were well treated.

The revival of industry with, in the case of Dresden, its very limited rearmament component had resolved the problem of unemployment and as the war progressed older men and women and slave labour were all directed into factories. Rearmament specifically enhanced Dresden's importance as the centre of one of the military districts into which Germany was subdivided by creating a parallel air district. This new administration was responsible for the city's anti-aircraft artillery defence. Until the autumn of 1944 this defence had been based upon nine heavy anti-aircraft gun batteries distributed in and around the city, the guns being either the extremely efficient German 88 mm gun, or captured Russian 85 mm guns rebored to 88 mm. As the war situation worsened, Dresden's batteries were moved away, either to defend other cities that were already under air attack or for use as anti-tank batteries in ground fighting. Dummy guns of wood and papiermaché were positioned to replace them. The re-development left Dresden with only a small number of light 20 mm cannon and no searchlights for anti-aircraft defence. This reduction in turn created a widely held illusion that the city would never be bombed – even that some understanding to this effect had been reached with the Allies. The movement of the guns had a further tragic consequence as the gun crews of one of the batteries included a number of young boys, Hitler Youth members from the Kreuzschule, several of whom were later killed fighting the Americans far from their native city.

Until the winter of 1944–45, then, the effects of the war upon Dresden had been only those general to all of Germany: the drafting of more and more men to the armed services, the grief following news of men killed, wounded or missing, food rationing, and shortages of fuel and consumer goods. Half-starved Red Army prisoners of war provided street labour. German school children who, in compassion, gave them a crust of bread were severely reprimanded. There had been only a few small-scale air attacks upon targets in the Dresden area; these had been directed against industrial targets in the suburbs, and had hardly affected the city's life at all. Earlier in the war some dispersal of the city's art treasures had been undertaken but as the Red Army advanced towards northern Germany, some works of art were actually brought back into the city. From the late summer of 1944 the city also began to fill with refugees fleeing from East Prussia and Silesia as the Red Army advanced, its soldiers raping, slaughtering and looting as revenge for their own country's suffering under German occupation. By late January 1945, trainloads of miserable refugees were arriving in the city under an official evacuation programme for Silesia, their whole world collapsing around them; others arrived on foot, the 'Frostbite March'. The city's major schools were converted into hospitals or reception centres, their pupils were turned out to assist with welfare work, and numbers of refugees were billeted in the spacious late-nineteenth-century houses and villas. Earlier in the month, on 18 January, the United States Air Force's 2nd Air Division, using some 400 Liberator bombers in a high altitude day attack, had bombed the railway installations and yards in the city's outer and inner suburbs, causing some damage and casualties. The military, however, made virtually no preparations for any ground fighting defence of the city, although Dresden was formally proclaimed to be a fortress zone.

The Allied Air Attack

Grim though these events were, they provided no real warning for the horror to follow in the next month, one of the most traumatic events to befall any city in human history. For its origins it is necessary to look back into some of the strategic thinking of the inter-war years as well as to examine the decision-making process in minds of Allied commanders, whose judgements had become eroded by the attrition of war.

The trench warfare stalemates of the First World War had led some commanders to argue that the developing possibilities of air warfare could win wars. They could bring successes that neither ground troops nor naval blockades could continue to deliver. The first theorist was an Italian general, Douhet. In Britain the leading exponent was Marshal of the Royal Air Force Lord Trenchard. Both Douhet and Trenchard saw strategic bombing as capable of delivering these successes following attacks on enemy economic targets, particularly industrial targets. Civilian populations, it was assumed, would be safe in air-raid shelters. The RAF's Bomber Command was built up on the basis of this strategic concept taught at the Service's Cadet and Staff Colleges. But the Bomber Command Chiefs never fully foresaw the technical difficulties in achieving the necessary precision, or the gut-reaction emotions that could be aroused by initial enemy bombing of their home country and a long, exhausting war.

Following the collapse of France and the consequent German domination of Europe, only the Bomber Command of the Royal Air Force had any capacity to strike at Germany itself. This was of enormous importance to a Britain, suffering as she was from nightly German aerial bombardment. The German air attacks on Rotterdam, Coventry, London and other British cities, although not always fully understood, called for retribution as far as British opinion was concerned. The slow pre-war bombers could not be used by day so the rapidly expanding Bomber Command mounted night air attacks on Germany in the years 1940–3. These were proclaimed to be against economic targets but, by accident at first and then increasingly by design, they came to be targeted against whole cities. As the number and range of British bombing aircraft increased, to be joined from 1942 by United States Air Force squadrons operating from Britain, it became increasingly tempting and increasingly possible to carry out area bombing raids on major German cities. The attraction of this became stronger among the decision makers as it became clearer that, despite much propaganda rhetoric, allied attempts to bomb purely industrial and economic targets were not proving successful. The vast reserve capacities of German industry had been badly under-estimated. Only a few, amid the anxieties and hardships of wartime Britain, sought to question the propriety of these developments; these doubters were led by George Bell, the Bishop of Chichester and Richard Stokes, the MP for Ipswich. In the RAF itself there was a division between those who believed, on either moral or practical grounds, that bombing should be strictly confined to purely economic or military industrial targets, and others who believed Germany could most quickly be brought to her knees by area bombing, the devastation of her cities. Such bombing, it was argued, would have a general effect on the morale of the civilian population, and the military value of destroying a city's water, electricity and gas systems would deny the public utilities essential for production in surrounding industrial suburbs and towns. The speed of such a success and the saving of Allied – and in the end German – lives would justify civilian casualties. More powerful four-engine bombers and path-finding aircraft were accordingly put into production, together with navigation devices, aiming equipment and bombs, incendiary and high-capacity high explosive (the first to start fires and the second to expand the devastation).

The first major air attacks using these developed technologies and seeking to destroy city centres took place in 1943, on Wuppertal in May and June, four raids on Hamburg creating an intense fire-storm two months later, and on Kassel in October. Over 700 bombers flew on the first Wuppertal raid,

2,450 people being killed with industrial production retarded for seven weeks. In Hamburg, the most thorough air-raid precautions could not withstand the 7,931 tons of bombs dropped. Ascertained casualties totalled 31,647, including over 7,000 women and 1,735 children; the actual total may well have been several thousand more. Reports of the raids and devastation led to further expressions of concern from Members of Parliament and church leaders in Britain. They were, however, speaking against the strong tide of public opinion, inflamed from the summer of 1944 onwards by the destruction and casualties caused by German VI flying bombs and V2 rocket attacks on Britain. These attacks, the heavy losses Germany was inflicting on Bomber Command, and American preferences for concentration on precision targets of economic importance, led to Bomber Command temporarily being given new priorities. Mass firestorm attacks were only resumed in the late summer and autumn of 1944 after successes of American day bombing raids and German loss of the fighter airfields in France. The first attack was on Stuttgart, others followed on Darmstadt, on Brunswick and on Heilbronn, all with devastating effects.

By early 1945 other factors were present. The Allied armies had liberated France but had not brought the end of the European war that all had hoped for. The German Army, clearly not yet defeated, had mounted the Ardennes offensive; Germany was still introducing the most technically advanced rockets, aircraft and submarine equipment, and the Japanese war was demanding more and more resources. It was not, at the time, clear that Germany was tottering. There were fears of a post-occupation guerrilla campaign and that Germany might still turn the fortunes of war with an atomic weapon. Inevitably, war-weary minds turned to a strategic air knockout blow that might end the war in Europe. Initial thinking for this blow, Operation Thunderclap, had centred on Berlin as the target.

There was also a belief that help should be given to the advancing Red Army. The motives for this belief were mixed. It was partly inspired by a wish to provide assistance to a brave ally, but it was also seen as a demonstration to that ally of Anglo-American power. At the early February 1945 Yalta conference a senior Red Army officer, General Antonov, had suggested that Allied strategic bombing could greatly assist the Red Army's advance, but no mention was made of any specific target city or axis of advance.

Finally there was the fact that aircraft flight over eastern Germany was now less dangerous – German air defence being overstretched – and it was also considered that this area of the Reich should also be chastised for its own future political good in the same way as other areas.

These conditions and mind-sets, rather than the orders or personalities of any one individual or individuals, lay behind the chain of events and decisions that led, remorselessly as in some classical tragedy, to the destruction of Dresden, the scale of which none of the remote and war-weary decision makers fully foresaw.

The final specific decision to target the city was a product of the long-standing preference, amounting to insistence, of the Air Officer Commanding-in-Chief, Bomber Command, Air Chief Marshal Sir Arthur Harris, for a return to area bombing. It was also the strongly expressed wish of the Prime Minister, Winston Churchill, to strike at the Germany Army, in its retreat eastwards, while he was attending the Yalta Conference.

Dresden appeared on a list of priority targets produced by a special Anglo-American target-selecting committee. The inclusion of Dresden on the list was unexpected, and was queried by Bomber Command's deputy head, Air Marshal Sir Robert Saundby. The decision was confirmed, an attack almost certainly being seen as in accord with the wishes of the Prime Minister, even if no clear record of his, or any other single individual's directive specifically to destroy Dresden, existed or was even prepared. Adverse weather then delayed the launching of the attack for several days.

The original plan for the assault had provided for an opening daylight raid on 13 February by American Flying Fortress Boeing B17 bombers. The actual first strike was originally planned to be the second phase, a massive night attack by RAF Bomber Command on the night of the 13–14 February. This attack was to be preceded, as a diversion, by an earlier attack on a synthetic oil plant at Böhlen, near Leipzig, by 320 Halifax heavy bombers. The night attack was to be followed, as part of the Anglo-US 'around the clock' bombing concept, by a daylight raid by Flying Fortress bombers escorted by Mustang fighters on the following day, 14 February. Again diversionary attacks were to be mounted simultaneously on other cities.

The initial RAF night attack was a double blow, the theory being that the first blow would paralyse the city's defence and communications, give the first fires time to take hold, and leave any night interceptor fighters on the ground refuelling and rearming at the time of the arrival, three hours later, of the second blow. The first blow force was to be guided in by two squadrons of Lancaster heavy bombers carrying target illuminating parachute flares and delayed action target indicator bombs, together with eight Pathfinder fast light-bomber Mosquito aircraft for lower level precision target indication. These Lancasters and the Mosquitoes were equipped with new American-made long-range electronic navigation equipment, *Loran*, which was needed to guide the force over the long distance. The first blow was timed for 10.15 p.m., the Pathfinders and 244 Lancaster heavy bombers all being airborne by 6 p.m. The aircraft flew out in a formation two miles wide and 1,000 feet deep. The second blow was to be led in by sixty-one Pathfinder Lancasters, some tasked for diversionary raids, and was to be mounted by 350 British and sixty-seven Canadian Lancasters, escorted for part of the way by night fighter aircraft.

The weather conditions for the night flight, nearly ten hours flying outward and return, were initially thought to be hazardous. In the event, however, the clouds had largely cleared by the time of the bombers' arrival. North German radar warning systems had been confused. The Luftwaffe could only put one night fighter squadron in the air, and one of this squadron's aircraft was shot down in error by the airfield's anti-aircraft defence guns. The absence of any opposition, aircraft or heavy gun, enabled the Lancasters to bomb from a lower altitude. The overall plan, with all its complex timing, worked with almost complete efficiency. Cold was the main enemy for the crews of the aircraft, with icicles growing on oxygen masks and their electrically heated flying suits and automatic pilot systems occasionally failing, and with static electricity, 'St Elmo's fire', flashing from bombers' wings.

Crew members of the first wave aircraft could see the brilliant red and green lights of the first markers and the orange sparkle of the early fires started by the incendiaries (see Plates 5 and 6). By the time aircraft of the second wave were arriving, the first firestorm, spreading to the city's inner suburbs, had become an inferno, already visible when the aircraft were 200 miles away (see Plate 7). Over the city the sky was scarlet and white; crew members could write their log reports in the eerie light and physically feel the heat from the burning city. At least one aircraft's crew was so horrified that they dropped their bomb load away from the city in open country.

The US Air Force daylight attack on the following days appears to have struck Dresden Neustadt rather than the still-burning city (see Plate 8). The majority of the aircraft were tasked to bomb Magdeburg and Chemnitz. Some of the escorting fighters, however, machine-gunned columns of lorries on their way into Dresden for relief work, and also columns of refugees leaving the city.

The City after the Bombing

Even the most graphic medieval metaphors of hell are inadequate to describe the scenes in Dresden's streets during and after the raids. The city's old buildings, once hit, blazed and quickly linked together in an all consuming inferno that in some areas of the city reached a temperature of over 1,000 °C. The inferno created fire tornadoes of hurricane force that flung burning property, furniture and people with their clothes on fire into the air and over considerable distances. Many areas of the central city burned for three days, a few for up to a week. A pall of smoke three-and-a-half miles high containing paper, wood and other items hung over the city for three days. People, after cowering terrified in cellars and basements, died either by incineration trying to escape amid huge curtains or jets of flame, or by asphyxiation from smoke and fumes where they hid. The noise, especially during the RAF's second blow, was indescribable, combining the explosion of the bombs, the roar of the flames, which one eyewitness described as like a thundering waterfall, and the crashing of collapsing buildings. The city's streets became littered with burned-out lorries and tramcars, and scores of corpses mostly maimed, burned or showing final agony all too clearly; some had been shrivelled to a stature of just three feet by the heat. A few of the corpses were dressed for the opera. Others, including a number of children, were in carnival dress and wearing face masks, as 13 February was Shrove Tuesday, the height of the pre-Lent carnival season. The aged and infirm, unable to move quickly, and the thousands of newly arrived refugees, strangers to the city, suffered above all. In one of the city's park squares, hundreds of naked corpses were scattered. Elsewhere scores of people had attempted to take refuge in the city's very large static water tanks, only to meet death by asphyxiation as the water evaporated in the heat. In another basement ninety young girls were all found sitting as if alive. Animals from the city's zoo, crazed with fear, were loose on the streets.

The city's neglected air raid protection and control systems collapsed at the outset with the early destruction of the telephone system. The fire brigades, although reinforced by detachments from outside the city, were totally overwhelmed, scores of firemen dying in fruitless attempts to contain the spreading inferno. The tunnel escape systems became smoke or carbon monoxide-filled death traps, killing hundreds, sometimes quickly but more often painfully. For hours after the raids were over, streets were full of the screams of the injured and those looking for relatives and the bereaved.

Eight square miles of the city centre, including its finest streets and squares, were totally devastated (see Plate 3). The royal palace and opera house were burned out, and the Zwinger and Hofkirche very badly damaged. On the day after the raid, the dome of the Frauenkirche, badly damaged by fire, collapsed, reducing the great church to a pile of rubble. For forty-eight hours it remained impossible to enter some areas of the city centre at all, what had been streets being filled with the masonry of collapsed buildings many still dangerously scorching. In a few areas weeks passed before the heat subsided. None of the major monuments survived unscathed, even the Palace in the Great Garden, some distance from the city centre, was burnt out. Over 25,000 homes were destroyed.

The total number of people killed will never be known, on account of the influx of refugees prior to the raid, and the fact that many bodies were never recovered. At least 22,000 identified people are known to have died; the probable overall total is more likely to be between 35,000 and 40,000. Much higher figures have been put forward but some of these appear exaggerated, as a proportion of the refugees were billeted outside the city centre in less severely damaged suburbs. At the time of the raids the city's normal population of 600,000 had been swollen, probably to about a million, by the refugees. There was no military profit from the attacks. The barracks surrounding Dresden and Dresden's Luftwaffe air base at Dresden-Klotzsche were all untouched. Trains were carrying supplies to the German Army fighting the Russians two days after the raid. The Red Army was in any case not particularly concerned with Dresden, Berlin being the aim of its commanders.

Industrial plant, except for the Zeiss-Ikon optics factory that was destroyed, was generally undamaged, lying outside the city centre. There were, nevertheless, delays in resuming production following the breakdown of electricity and gas supplies and the city's public transport system, together with the heavy casualties amongst the work forces.

Relief columns, the first two named after two Nazi leaders, Göring and Göbbels, and comprising food supplies, field kitchens and medical equipment, together with groups of able-bodied men volunteering to help with rescue work, were all rushed to the city from Germany and Austria. Nazi Party women's organizations were also mobilized. Specialist technical military engineer units were immediately sent in to restore communications. Troops from the Dresden-Neustadt barracks arrived for relief work on 14 February, after the American daylight attack; further general military assistance was, however, delayed until 16 February. Russian and Ukrainian forced labourers were committed to rescue work. The British and American prisoners in the area worked with a will and compassion from the day after the raid onwards, though on a number of occasions they were attacked by Dresden civilians and had to be rescued by their guards. Looting by anyone, prisoner, forced labourer or German relief worker, was met by summary execution.

The immediate work involved clearing the streets of wounded and dead, opening up cellars, occasionally finding a few survivors clinging to life, but more often incinerating corpses with army flame-throwers. As time passed, troops had to wear gloves and boots, together with respirators, or be issued with alcohol-soaked facemasks for the handling of corpses.

The hospital services were, of course, totally overwhelmed. Although prior to the raid a number of temporary hospitals had been opened in schools and other buildings, these were already full of wounded and convalescing soldiers. Most of these, together with the city's permanent hospitals, were destroyed

Figure 12. Funeral pyre in the Altmarkt, February 1945. Courtesy of the Sächsische Landesbibliothek, Deutsche Fotothek.

or severely damaged in the raids. The inevitable consequence was that hundreds of injured died before they could receive medical attention. People gave clothes, curtains and bed linen to make bandages for the injured; the linen curtains of the Hellerau Festspielhaus were pulled down for the same purpose. The elderly and mothers and children were ordered to make their own way, on foot, to Marienberg in the Erzgebirge hills.

An information service for missing persons was opened with branches in each of the large suburbs. This was followed by an office charged with compiling lists of identified dead. Filing systems based on samples of clothing, personal effects, personal papers and wedding rings, in Germany often inscribed with names and worn by both men and women, were built up for identification purposes.

Bodies were lined up on the pavements for the identification procedures; thereafter they were stacked with pitchforks high on horse-drawn farm carts for removal. Near the main railway station the corpses, including a number of children from a children's refugee train, were piled in 10-foot-high mounds, 20 yards square. Distraught men and women would come to try to find corpses of relatives, sometimes taking the corpses away in old bags or wrapped in newspaper for burial. Mass graves were dug or excavated by road repair machinery in the country areas immediately surrounding the city. The sheer numbers buried soon made any attempt to record who was buried where impossible, even if the bodies had been identified. Finally, with the approach of warmer weather, some 9,000 remaining corpses, most in a state of decay, were taken in secrecy to the Altmarkt and then placed in groups sandwiched between wood and straw. These then were trampled down by Ukrainian soldiers of the anti-Soviet General Vlasov and the pyres were set on fire by flame-throwers. The ashes were later taken in a grim lorry and small cart convoy for burial in the heathland outside the city. Heavy rain followed a few days later and the city became a morass of mud, rubble and corpses.

The population of Dresden remained in collective shock for a long time. At the outset, shock seemed to have had for many the effect of numbing even the capacity for grief; the daily struggle for survival in the ruins was inevitably uppermost in people's minds. There followed, with sensitivities still dulled, tears, uncertainty, a sense of helplessness, despair. In turn, 'why' became the question, with introspective analysis of human behaviour, to be followed a little later with a mixture of views – tolerance, scepticism, a search for sincerity, a bitter distrust of all ideologies, and a belief that each individual should do his duty, should work to destroy evil and should make his own contribution, however small, to recovery.

Church services, where pastors had survived, had initially to be held in the open air for their dazed and shivering flocks on account of fumes and gases, or unsafe buildings. The mood was neither words nor tears but profound shock. For Christians there was the particular difficulty in reconciling the events with their faith.

Accordingly, a little later, in May, a newly reconstructed Lutheran hierarchy, purged of its Nazi fellow travellers, came to offer more specific counsel, to this day profoundly moving to read. Its encyclical urged priests to preserve Church communities, and to teach parishioners that by carrying each other's burdens they were following Christ's laws. It continued to say that Divine mercy was evident from the continuity of Church work, but this was not the time for any grand designs for the future. Parishioners were urged to 'think over, review and record their lives and experiences, to work industriously, and to go forth as fishers of men and seek out people in need of the Word of God.' It was pointed out that Churches would have to live very simply, remembering that grace and mercy would follow as the reward of poverty and hardship. The encyclical urged congregations to think of 'the God of Patience and Comfort', always with them in this time of need, and to be linked together in his praise. Parishioners were reminded in a second letter that Jesus would comfort and strengthen believers and that the alien voices that had so distorted Church teachings in the past were now no more. In this new setting the Church remained, as in the past and in the future, men's true spiritual home; kingdoms could come and go, people could be oppressed, but the eternal truths and enduring comfort of the Church would always remain. Believers were warned that the world was watching them. 'What would they do, what would they say, in this predicament?' The answer, in the view of the new Church hierarchy, was to serve God, witness God, comfort and be comforted, offer penance for sins, for neglect and for the blind following of instincts, for which all were guilty but all could nevertheless receive grace. Families should attend divine service, prepare their children for confirmation and return to traditional family and community piety and Bible reading. Whatever the unforeseeable future might bring, the most important point was to remain true to belief and to witness that belief.

The conductor of the Kreuzkirche choir, Rudolf Mauersberger, who had narrowly escaped death, conducted the choir in the battered shell of the church for the first time after the raid on the 4 August, and also composed a lament for the city and several boys of the choir who had lost their lives in the raid.

Predictably the Nazi government sought to make political capital from the raid, developing the theme that the raid was clear evidence of the barbaric determination of the Allies to exterminate the German nation; all would be avenged by Hitler, it was said. Rumours exaggerating the casualties were allowed to leak, a technique designed for maximum effect, but the war was drawing to its end and the propaganda made little impact in Germany. Reports of the devastation published in Sweden and Switzerland, however, led to a renewal of criticism of area bombing both within the British and American military and in Parliament. On 28 March Churchill directed that the policy be reviewed. No more area bombing of Germany took place, although other raids continued. Dresden suffered small scale US Air Force day raids on railway marshalling yards and other economic industrial targets until 17 April, on which day Dresden-Neustadt was again severely damaged.

Troops of Marshal Koniev's 1st Ukrainian Front armies began their dreaded entry into Dresden on the 8 May, the day of Germany's surrender. The Nazi Gauleiter, Mutschmann, had fled to an area occupied by American troops, but was recognized there and arrested. The first Red Army troops were Russian and tank units; these behaved well. The infantry that followed was mainly from Soviet Asia and there were a number of incidents of rape, looting and drunken behaviour. The entry, however, accompanied as it was by white sheets hung from undamaged house windows, had none of the inflamed passions of battle that had marked the rape of Breslau or East Prussia.

The Army commander immediately ordered a curfew and imposed a military administration. A garrison was installed at Hellerau. Overall the Red Army took measures, as best it could, to help the population of the stricken city and there were numerous acts of kindness by individual personnel to the civil population when it was clear the war was finally over. The Red Army sponsored a group of 'Activists of the First Hour' drawn from known Communists and Social Democrats, refugees and freed political prisoners, to work with the military administration of the city. One of these, Rudolf Friedrichs, a veteran Social Democrat, was provisionally appointed mayor.

The new political order was clear. The city was to be included in an area of Germany controlled by the Soviet Union. For the next forty-four years Dresden was to be a part of the Communist world.

Out of the Fire – the Enduring Friendship of Coventry and Dresden

Canon Paul Oestreicher, Director of International Ministry at Coventry Cathedral, 1986–97

After the raid that destroyed the centre of Coventry, Luftwaffe Chief Hermann Göring, threatened to 'coventrate' the cities of England one by one. In so doing he invented a word to describe the process of city annihilation that had begun. And Coventry itself became a symbol, a powerful weapon, in the war propaganda of both sides – of Nazi prowess on the one hand and of Nazi brutality on the other.

Understandably, the immediate instinct of the people of Coventry was for revenge – which was, indeed, to come. Having sown the wind, Hitler's Germany reaped the whirlwind as cities, one by one, but in Germany, not in Britain, were indeed 'coventrated', many in the dying days of the war. Dying days indeed: in Coventry there had been almost 1,000 dead; in Dresden, which was symbolically to become the German Coventry, there were at least 35,000 – probably many more.

Richard Howard, the wartime Provost of Coventry's ruined cathedral, had, however, always repudiated the instinct to retaliate. In his 1940 Christmas sermon he broadcast his conviction that ways of building a kinder, simpler and more Christlike world had at all costs to be found. This was not an easy message to put over as the war progressed and news of the atrocities perpetrated at Belsen, Auschwitz and elsewhere leaked out. Is it ever? Yet Coventry, church and city, where the Cross of Nails had early set the tone, set its feet firmly on the path of reconcili-ation. Its early 1947 partnership with Kiel was an important beginning and when the Cold War began to create a new division in Europe, its decision to twin with Dresden (1959) – the eastern city with all the symbolism of Coventry and more – was an apt response.

Just as the Kiel link was initially far from universally popular, so this new partnership was also controversial, although for very different reasons. It meant having dealings with the Communist authorities of an unpopular regime. Like all such arrangements, however, it was concerned with people rather than with political systems, and it underlined the need to be able to live at peace with difference. It pioneered the approach that was eventually known, and approved, as *Ostpolitik*. Whilst each fragment of recognition was welcomed by the East German government, it also served to undermine the isolation it imposed on its people, which was so brutally symbolized after 1961 by the Berlin Wall.

In Coventry itself, the Dresden link became a cornerstone of the cathedral's Ministry of Reconciliation. In the late 1950s, sixteen young West Germans were sent by *Aktion Sühnezeichen* (Action for Reconciliation/ Reparation/Expiation) to live and work in the city, where they sought to make something good come out of the destruction wrought by their parents' generation by transforming part of the cathedral ruins into an International Centre. As soon as this centre had been opened by Bishop Dibelius of Berlin, and shortly before the consecration of Basil Spence's new cathedral, Provost Williams embarked on the complex negotiations that proved necessary with the East German Government to allow an equivalent group of young Britons to go to Dresden. Agreement was finally obtained and they helped to rebuild the Lutheran Church's Deaconess Hospital. Each ward carries an inscription explaining the inspiration of the project and the meaning of Coventry's Cross of Nails, and the friendships then established have amply stood the test of time.

Music, so central to all that Dresden means to the world, has always been prominent in the Dresden–Coventry link. One of the first live television broadcasts transmitted from East Germany to the United Kingdom was a performance of Britten's *War Requiem* (composed in 1961 for the consecration of Coventry Cathedral). It was followed by a visit to Coventry of Dresden's famous Kreuzchor, by the simultaneous broadcasting from the two cities of the BBC's Songs of Praise, by a joint performance (in New York on the occasion of the fiftieth anniversary of the founding of the United Nations) of the choirs of Dresden's Hofkirche and of Coventry Cathedral, and by consecutive performances (in Coventry and Dresden to mark the fiftieth commemoration of the destruction of Dresden, in February 1995) of Mozart's Requiem Mass, conducted in both cities by Yehudi Menuhin.

The spiritual dimension was always powerfully present. It was on this last occasion in February 1995, that Coventry's Lord Mayor Nolan defined the partnership ideal as the healing of wounds and the opening

Figure 13. Coventry, the blessing of British volunteers, 1963. Photograph by
Michael Barnes, Courtesy of the Provost and Chapter of Coventry
Cathedral.

of hearts, and that the Bishop of Coventry reminded a hushed congregation in the Kreuzkirche that only through repentance and forgiveness
can the ruins of greed, hatred and racism that persist in our own hearts
be cleared away. In both cities, indeed, the ruins of war became poignant
symbols of what it means to remember and yet to forgive, and some,
certainly, in Dresden would have preferred the rubble pile that had
once been the mighty Frauenkirche to have remained, like the fragments
of the old cathedral walls in Coventry, as a permanent reminder of
this. Illuminated on significant occasions by a sea of guttering candles,
it had the added historical depth of a shrine to lost freedom.

When, however, the church, the people and the public authorities in
Dresden together decided to rebuild the Frauenkirche in all its architectural glory, the church in Coventry immediately decided to offer what
help it could. The Bishop readily accepted the invitation of his opposite
number to become a Trustee of Dresden's Frauenkirche Foundation

and, as Director of International Ministry in Coventry, I was similarly glad to help set up and promote Britain's own Dresden Trust (which is promoting a contribution from the British people as a whole). I have, in addition, been proud and privileged to place our experience with our world-wide peace mission in Coventry at the disposal of Bishop Kress and of all those working with him to breathe life into the emerging new Frauenkirche as an international centre in its own right, worthy of its distinguished past.

The dramatic peace vigils held by thousands of people in the last years and days of communist rule must always be remembered and the Frauenkirche developed as a place of pilgrimage, of prayer and of culture, which, like Coventry, speaks to all of the essential unity of the human race. It is gratifying, therefore, that the great project of restoration is already being supported by so many people – in Germany, in the United Kingdom, in the United States and elsewhere. Something is afoot that looks back to the past but augurs well for the future, which is bringing peoples together, which is arousing wonder and admiration, and which is helping Dresden to reformulate an important piece of its historic identity.

Dresden's twin cities – first and foremost Coventry – have of course developed ongoing cooperative activities that transcend the importance of any one building, however famous and splendid this may be, for example youth, educational and cultural exchanges. As the new century and millennium approach, these cities will need to redefine what partnership and friendship, at their many levels, ought now to mean to Europe and to the world – and what fun they can be!

Dresden and East Germany, 1945–90

Anthony Clayton

Any account of Dresden in the years that followed the end of the Second World War needs to be set in broad political context. Until 1990 the context was that of inclusion in the communist world, first as part of the Soviet zone of occupation of Germany and, from October 1949, as a city in the German Democratic Republic (GDR). After 1990 the context changed dramatically following German reunification, but until that time ideology dominated all aspects of life.

The Soviet Army occupied an area devastated by the fighting that followed its own entry into Eastern Germany and in the case of Dresden by the destruction of the February 1945 air attacks. The area was perceived by Stalin and his successors as one of special strategic significance for the security of the Soviet Union, itself laid waste by war. The Soviet leadership was determined that a future war with the West, which was believed to be probable, if not inevitable, must be fought outside its own borders. Eastern Germany therefore required a massive Soviet Army garrison, twenty divisions in five armies with the most modern equipment for most of the period. It was also a country to be ruled by a regime of unswerving loyalty to Moscow.

The earliest step to ensure a subservient regime was taken in April 1946 with the forced marriage, within the Soviet sector as it then was, of the region's Socialist and Communist parties to form the Socialist Unity Party, *Sozialistische Einheitspartei Deutschlands* (SED), a party that was in practice controlled by the Communists under Walter Ulbricht, the General Secretary. A little later the SED was officially proclaimed to be a Marxist-Leninist party, with an institutionalized leading role as the vanguard of the proletariat.

The next step, in 1949, was the formation of the GDR, a gain that offset the overall failure of the Soviet Union's attempt to blockade the Western allies out of Berlin. Later, the GDR became a member of the Warsaw Pact, and was permitted a six-division army integrated into the operational plans of the Group of Soviet Forces in Germany. Dresden became once again an important military centre, the headquarters of an armoured division.

The GDR, 1949–89

The GDR's government was organized on Soviet lines, effective power lying in the hands of an SED politburo, and the execution of its policies directed by the Party Secretariat with the General Secretary being the regime's most powerful figure. A single-chamber legislature existed, its role being to rubber stamp executive decisions. Centralization of power was completed in 1952 when the regime abolished the five regional governments that had been formed in 1945, among them that of Saxony. At local level, city councils such as that of Dresden had to conform with the directives laid down in Berlin.

Eastern Germany, particularly Saxony, had always possessed a strong left-wing political tradition and, at first, the accession to power of an eastward-looking left-wing local administration following the collapse of the Nazi regime seemed to many to be correct. Eastern Germany also had a Protestant culture different from that of Adenauer's Catholic West. With the emergence of the much larger Federal Republic of Germany and its astonishing economic recovery in the 1950s, however, the flaws in the GDR, the state's legitimacy in a divided country, and political oppression, began to show. By the time Erich Honecker had replaced Ulbricht and Stoph in 1976 a popular nightclub joke ran:

'On Honecker's desk, which is the telephone to Moscow?'
'The one without a mouthpiece.'

The joke was nearer the reality than Honecker's claim that the GDR had attained 'actually existing socialism'.

Official rhetoric met the legitimacy issue by the presentation of a divided Germany as merely a stage in the world class war. This rhetoric was necessary to justify, at day-to-day level, the increasing restrictions on travel and to prepare the population for a situation where, should it be necessary, German soldier could be sent to fight against German soldier. 'Who is my friend, who is my foe can only be seen in class terms' declared the GDR's Army commander, General Heinz Hoffmann.

The GDR, then, was to be legitimized as the showpiece of the new communist Europe, its citizens to be educated and trained to be the *neuer Sozialistischer Menschentyp*, the new socialist human being. German history was also rewritten to try to legitimize the regime by research into the past. The leaders of the 1525 Thuringia Peasants Revolt, Bebel and other socialists of the nineteenth century, the mutinous High Seas Fleet sailors of 1916 and 1918, the Communist leaders of the 1920s and 1930s, Germans who fought for the republican cause in Spain, Communist resistance figures, and occasional Cold War heroes, such as a young soldier (unfortunately named Göring) killed in a brush with the Americans in Berlin, were the new historical heroes. Streets, schools, barracks and regiments were given their names. Any figures in German history who had collaborated with Russia against the West were also considered to be politically correct; the East German Army on parade, for example, marched to Beethoven's Yorck march, a march dedicated by Beethoven to General Yorck von Wartenburg who, in 1813, led the Prussian Army out of Napoleon's camp to join that of Russia. The march was a Prussian Guards march in the *Kaiserzeit* but its inclusion in the GDR's repertoire was meant to highlight a praiseworthy feature from the past, and so demonstrate continuity and legitimacy as the true, anti-fascist, Germany.

The GDR, unlike the Soviet Union, was never a one-party state. Four non-communist parties were permitted on sufferance as a transition concession. Elections for the single chamber were held in which a National Front of Democratic Germany, dominated by the SED but including token representation from the other parties, presented a pre-arranged list of candidates; the list also included candidates from SED-sponsored organizations. As in the Soviet Union electoral success was measured by the percentage, generally over 90 per cent, of the Front coalition. At official levels the Soviet system of *nomenklatura* – only those of proven political conformity need apply – was set up in 1951.

The regime could justly claim a measure of success in post-1945 economic recovery – an achievement that was all the more remarkable in view of the ruthless Soviet plundering of economic assets in the immediate post-war months, and the absence of any Marshall Aid. Nationalization of industry and a policy of equal pay for women were both popular measures. The success was continued briefly after the building of the Berlin Wall in 1961, obliging East Germans to abandon hope of escape to the West, and therefore concentrating their minds and energies on the domestic scene. Precision instruments, chemical technology and heavy industry were all near world class. In the 1970s and 1980s, however, the GDR's industries, not responsive to market needs and tied firmly to the Soviet Union and East European markets, fell behind, the State's economic plans becoming less and less real.

The quality of consumer goods fell. A particularly dismal product was to be the Trabant car. Industry came to need more labour and men were brought in from Bulgaria, Mozambique, Vietnam and elsewhere. These generally lived in special areas of towns and contact with the East German population was severely limited. The regime, dominated by politicians from industrial backgrounds, also never really understood the problems of the agriculture. A system of agricultural collectives was introduced after a successful and popular breaking-up of the estates of the former land-owning classes. Joining these was at first voluntary. Coercion, including arrests, followed and eventually the policy was abandoned. However, unnecessarily rigid production plans and targets continued to be set and inflexible harvesting programmes, taking little or no account of changes in the weather, were laid down.

Nevertheless for ordinary people, after the difficulties of the 1950s, life improved, offering the best general standards of living in the communist world. Social and medical services were of a good standard, with free childcare provisions and liberal abortion laws. Food rationing was eventually ended and, although food may not have been very varied, there were no important shortages. Job security was protected and assured. Individuals in most areas could still retain possession of their own houses. At the same time, the regime embarked on the construction of vast urban complexes of large slab-sided blocks of flats, the individual flats being very small, to house – and regiment – the city populations.

It was, in fact, the regimented, coercive aspect of the regime, a product of its own ideology and questionable legitimacy, that was to be a major factor in its eventual collapse. The regime sought to control the population from cradle to grave, in the frame of its ideology and rhetoric. The doctrine of 'socialist military upbringing' governed education. Books for the very young would depict flaxen-haired small children being shown over a Soviet tank by a beaming Russian soldier, school textbooks were full of military mathematics, physics and geography instruction. Schoolchildren were expected to join the Pioneers movement and teenagers were expected to join the Society for Sport and Technology, both heavily loaded with ideological teaching and emphasizing visits to suitable sites and memorials. A *Jugendweihe* ceremony, a form of Marxist confirmation, marked entry into adolescence. The Soviet-patterned Society for Sport and Technology provided physical training – one reason for the GDR's athletics achievements - and pre-military map reading, grenade throwing and shooting. Acceptable performance in this training was required for university entry. National service in the GDR's armed forces was obligatory. Construction work was permitted as an alternative for conscientious objectors but anyone who refused any form of National Service was guilty of a crime. In National Service political education was taken further by regimental political officers and cells of party members. After National Service, a whole range of SED-directed youth, women's, cultural and trade union organizations existed to continue the process. A British visitor to a well-run and comfortable old people's home was told by a group of old ladies 'we are members of the Knitting Brigade'. Initially – and particularly after the Nazi era – people welcomed the feeling of belonging to an organization of a new society, but the feeling soon turned to a resentment at their coercive nature. The press and media invariably reflected SED ideology and politics. When protest or dissent was expressed, as happened from church pulpits from time to time, it was simply not reported. The GDR public became increasingly sceptical and able to read between the lines of what became nicknamed *Parteichinesisch* – Party gobbledegook. School and university teachers were expected to conform politically. Those who did not do so found themselves marginalized or sacked. All cultural life, very rich in the immediate post-war years following the return of anti-Nazi writers and intellectuals, fell progressively under the control of the SED to ensure political rectitude.

Within these constraints Dresden fought to revive its traditions as a centre of culture. The shattered Zwinger was restored, the Semper Opera House rebuilt, and the Kreuzkirche choir re-established. But a number of the surviving old buildings, among them the medieval Sophienkirche, were pulled down unnecessarily, and no attempt was made to restore the former Royal Palace. Those buildings were seen as part of an evil past.

A British visitor to Dresden, Alexander McKee, in 1958 described his impressions very vividly in his book *Dresden 1945: The Devil's Tinderbox*:

> The train drove over the Elbe bridge with the river curving away in what used to be the famous view of the city . . . gardens and meadows going to the river on the left bank, the cluster of spires, towers and turrets rising on the right bank. What came into view now made one gasp. It was all shabby and stained, and the corner of a large building was still collapsed, the flat roof hanging down like the corner of a blanket draped over a fence. It was as though a woman reputedly the most beautiful in Europe turned out to be an old hag, wrapped in rags, with a cigarette dangling from her lips.
>
> The train sped on, to show the historic buildings of the Old Town from a different view point – as an oasis of darkened stone in a desert of wild green. Between the train and the spires was a distance of perhaps one and a half miles. It was all green covered with grass and bushes growing in what had been houses: the cellars filled in.

One problem faced by the GDR more than other communist countries was its transparency. Much of the GDR was within range of West German television, although this was not the case in the Dresden area until late in the GDR era (as a consequence the Elbe valley was known as the *Tal der Ahnungslosen* – the valley of the people without a clue). There was also, as there had to be, an ever-increasing number of family visitors, relatives and

Figure 14. The destroyed city seen from the tower of the Town Hall, 1946.
Courtesy of the Sächsische Landesbibliothek, Deutsche Fotothek.

Figure 15. The post-war challenge: ruins in every direction, 1949. Courtesy of the Sächsische Landesbibliothek, Deutsche Fotothek.

others, from West Germany. To counter any malign influence from these and also the wider consequences of *détente* and *Ostpolitik*, the regime introduced the concept of *Abgrenzung* (delimitation) – in day-to-day terms 'your cousin from Hanover may seem a friendly, good person, but keep your distance. Remember he is from capitalist NATO land.'

Coercion was enforced when necessary. Any major criticism of the regime rendered an individual liable to severe punishments, although the death penalty was not imposed after 1968. A prison for political offenders existed in Magdeburg. As late as 1968, a Dresden schoolgirl was expelled from school for refusing to send a packet of sweets to a soldier in the Soviet Army occupying force in Czechoslovakia. The major instruments of coercion are, of course, well known: the border system with its complex structures of electrified wire, minefields and watchtowers with military personnel tasked to shoot would-be escapees along the inner German border, and the infamous Secret Police (Stasi) of the Ministry of State Security, a ministry created in 1950.

The GDR could perhaps lay claim to being the world's most closely spied-upon society. For a population, in the 1960s, of some seventeen million, the Stasi was already employing 20,000 full-time personnel, a figure that had increased to over 95,000 by the mid-1980s. At least 170,000 unofficial collaborators and regular informers backed these full-time officials. In the early 1950s some were motivated by genuine patriotic ideological beliefs. Later, people became informers for money, for benefits such as a chance to travel, or simply because it was necessary for their own career development – a Stasi reflection of the change in the nature of the GDR's rulers from party faithful to technocrats. By the late 1980s it was unclear whether the state was directing the Stasi or whether – in increasing alarm following events in Poland – the Stasi was directing the state.

Opposition to the regime came first, and very surprisingly, from the working class, with mass demonstrations on 17 June 1953. The immediate cause was an increase in working norms to meet production targets, but there were also calls for free elections. The weight of the Soviet Army's tanks in the streets of Berlin and elsewhere quickly suppressed the protest but the event served to further raise the question of the state's legitimacy. Opposition then took to 'voting with their feet'. Anyone who possibly could escaped through Berlin, the numbers increasing dramatically in 1961 and resulting in the building of the Berlin Wall in August of that year, simply to stop the haemorrhage.

In the 1970s, particularly after the signing of the Helsinki agreements, free political debate centred more and more around and in the churches, especially the Lutheran Church. The Church had drawn the correct lesson from its experience in the Nazi era, that its own safety and preservation were not its main concern but that it must accept being an outsider, taking risks, speaking out when necessary. Accordingly the Church had steadfastly refused to become an additional voice of the state, a 'Socialist Church', instead defining its role as uncommitted, 'the Church in Socialism'. In churches people could talk and debate freely, and they facilitated the 'swords to ploughshares' demonstrations. The Church continuously expressed its opposition to the continuing militarization of GDR society and in 1988 sought to express the repentance of Dresdeners for their persecution of the Jews by affixing a Memorial Tablet, composed by Siegfried Reimann the Pastor at the Annen-kirche, to the exterior of the Kreuzkirche which in English reads as follows:

"In shame and sorrow we Christians remember the Jewish citizens of this city. In 1933, 4,675 Jews lived in Dresden. In 1945, there were but 70. We were silent when their houses of prayer were set aflame, when Jews were deprived of their rights, were driven out, were murdered, we did not acknowledge them as our brothers and sisters. We beg for forgiveness and *shalom*".

(Ten years later, on 16 November 1998, the State and City joined the Church and the city's remaining Jews in inaugurating the building of a new synagogue to replace Semper's).

Dresden and the End of the GDR

The causes of the collapse of the GDR will have been evident from earlier paragraphs in this chapter – the absence of legitimacy, the staleness and boring irrelevance of the SED's annual *Losungen* (slogans), the stagnation of the economy, and the stiflingly oppressive curtailment of freedom of speech and thought. A dissident, rather sad, political joke of the time says all in respect of the failure of the GDR. A Polish dog and German dog met on the Oder. The German dog said to the Pole 'Why do you want to come to GDR?' The Pole replied 'I want to eat, but why could you possibly want to come to Poland?' The German dog replied 'I just want to bark'.

There can be little doubt that the absence of violence in the regime's collapse, when it came, was in large part due to the work of the Lutheran Church. The Democratic Awakening movement, linked to the Church, had provided a safety valve and the evident strength of the Church's following provided the regime with an indication of the weight of feeling mounting against it.

In January 1988, opposition groups in Berlin infiltrated the regime's official commemoration of the death in 1918 of the two communist leaders, Karl Liebknecht and Rosa Luxemburg, the ceremony being interrupted by shouting, leaflet distribution and placards. A number of demonstrators were arrested, two later being deported to Britain.

The year 1989 was tumultuous, beginning with small demonstrations to remind people of the events of the previous January. In the May 1989 municipal elections, opposition groups exercised their rights to monitor the elections by being present at the counting of votes. The figures that they produced of people voting against the official candidates differed widely from the official results; this falsification was shown on West German television, greatly adding to the unrest.

Two leading Dresden political figures, both on the reformist wing of the SED, Hans Modrow, the first secretary of the SED in the Bezirk Dresden (Dresden district) and Wolfgang Berghofer, the *Oberbürgermeister*, attempted to enter into dialogue with opposition groups. Their first attempts became the model for regional round-table groups that subsequently appeared in many GDR towns.

In the summer, hundreds of tourists from the GDR took refuge in West German embassies in Prague and Budapest; others escaped via Hungary and Austria. Mass protest meetings, many centred on churches, took place in cities and towns in September. In Saxony the crowd in Leipzig totalled 70,000. Implosion followed in the next month. On 4 and 5 October, trains carrying thousands of GDR citizens who had occupied the West German Embassy in Prague and who were being allowed to emigrate to West Germany were

Figure 16. Central Dresden 1955: sheep grazing in the Neumarkt. Courtesy of the
Sächsische Landesbibliothek.

routed through Dresden. At the main railway station, hundreds tried to storm
the station to jump on the trains and so escape to the West. The police, under
orders from Berlin, broke up the crowds. Faced with petrol bombs the police
used considerable violence. Further demonstrations followed on 8 October.
On this occasion the demonstrators avoided violence while the police did
not. A group of church leaders set up a local committee which, on the evening
of 9 October, secured agreement with Oberburgermeister Berghofer to avoid
further violence. On 5 October, at the military parade in Berlin for the fortieth
anniversary of the GDR, the drill and marching of the troops had been notice-
ably slovenly; more important, Gorbachev, the Soviet leader, visiting Berlin
for the occasion, told Honecker that he must reform the SED and that Soviet
troops would not be made available to secure the regime. On 9 November,
following revised and ambiguous instructions, the Berlin Wall border guards
made no effort to prevent mass crowds bursting through the Berlin Wall.

From that moment the GDR was dead. The country moved quickly to a
free multi-party system that led, with surprising speed thanks to the personal
political involvement of the West German Chancellor, Kohl, to reunification
in 1990 and to the final withdrawal of Russian troops in 1994.

In the build-up to these dramatic events the ruins of Dresden's Frauenkirche,
two fifty-foot high stumps surmounting a pile of rubble, served as a spiritual
and spatial centre point. The GDR had sought by propaganda to present the
ruins as the work of the West, but they had remained a place of open worship
and hope for thousands, especially on the anniversary of the raids and at
Christmas time.

Always in Dresden – A Personal Memoir

Dr Karl-Ludwig Hoch, retired Dresden Pastor and one of the founders of the Society for the Promotion of the Rebuilding of the Frauenkirche

For more than two hundred years our ancestors have lived in Dresden, always on the slopes above the Elbe at Loschwitz. The family home affords a lovely panoramic view over our city. It was returned to us after the end of the GDR regime and I am writing this memoir of six decades of life in Dresden there.

Once during my childhood, in November 1938, it transpired that, along with some guests, my mother was watching the burning of the Synagogue on *Kristallnacht*. Mother was appalled. One of the guests said something about 'deserved punishment'. Everyone was shouting at everyone else. Mother, who had been a widow for years, said to me and to my brother 'This is aimed at Jesus as a Jew; I expect they'll soon be setting fire to our churches as well.' So it was, seven years later, when almost all the churches of Dresden were in flames, except that the fires were not started as my mother had expected by the Nazis, and they were not aimed at the Church as such.

During my childhood we always had an au pair girl in the summer months, often from England, where we had close relations. In those days Dresden was the most popular German city with both English and American tourists. There was an 'English Quarter'; complete with an Anglican church (All Saints, built in 1868), an 'American Quarter', with its St John's church (built in 1883) and there was even a Scottish Presbyterian church. Dresden's magic lay in its combination of high art and beautiful natural surroundings, and our au pair girls, like everyone else, were fascinated by it. It was not only the musical quality of the State Opera and the choir of the Kreuzkirche that inspired them to go into raptures. They stood in amazement before Raphael's Sistine Madonna, Giorgione's Venus, the magical Zwinger courtyard, the mighty stone cupola of the Frauenkirche, and the Hofkirche with its organ by Silbermann. And they were almost more enthusiastic about the Sächsische Schweiz, bounded by its rocky cliffs, and about the royal castles of Pillnitz and Moritzburg.

I have a memory of one of these English girls urging on the rowing eights as they rounded the glorious sweep of the Elbe below our property to where the finishing posts stood and I can still hear her voice shouting 'Go on, go on.' The majestic dome of the Frauenkirche, which rode

Figure 17. Dr Hoch's drawing (above) of the Frauenkirche, as a young boy, showing the view of it from Loschwitz in 1941 and Figure 18 (below) the remains of it in 1945. Courtesy of Dr Karl-Ludwig Hoch.

above the scene, may well have evoked in her memories of the dome of St Paul's Cathedral in London.

All through the war we kept in touch with our relatives in England through the Red Cross and we regularly listened to the BBC's broadcasts – in German. The well-known call sign (. . . –, taken from Beethoven's Fifth Symphony) exposed us to danger by alerting an army major to the fact that we were listening to enemy radio. It nearly cost us our lives.

Through the Confessional Church, founded in 1934 by Pastor Martin Niemöller to oppose the pro-Nazi so-called *Deutsche Christen*, my mother also began to learn about the fate of the Jews. On 19 November 1941, at the age of twelve, I wrote in my diary 'We are hearing terrible things about the mass slaughter of the Jews.' The Frauenkirche was the Saxon headquarters of the Confessional Church until 1938 when the Gestapo expelled the Superintendent Minister, Hugo Hahn, from Saxony. The Confessional Church, unlike the so-called *Deutsche Christen*, consistently resisted all Nazi blandishments.

Between 1938 and 1942, the Frauenkirche was restored from top to bottom, whilst the bombs were falling on other cities. Everyone *simply knew* that the destruction of Dresden by Western powers was unthinkable, which meant that both the Saxon Church authorities and the Berlin 'State Curator' had no worries about approving millions of Reichmarks for the restoration work. From the age of thirteen, when I heard the famous boys' choir of the Kreuzkirche sing Bach's Christmas Oratorio, I heard many great works in the church. Tickets were cheap for the fourth-floor gallery and the view across the huge rotunda was unique.

In the early dawn of 14 February 1945 we stood on our balcony again, but this time in stunned bewilderment: everything was ablaze in the firestorm. A Nazi woman, who lived above us, kept on calling out: 'Well, Frau Hoch, that's the English and the Americans for you! Göbbels is completely right, isn't he? Well isn't he?' My mother remained completely silent. We had never before known her lost for words. The following day the smoke lifted for a moment. It was unbelievable. I shouted to my mother: 'the Frauenkirche is still standing!' We stared again and again and saw through reddened eyes that it was so. Yet shortly afterwards it collapsed as if not wanting to survive the insanity. The disaster was now complete. Only the barracks area, the largest in Europe, remained intact. On 8 May 1945 its new occupants, the Red Army, marched into Dresden.

Even as this was happening, Nazis living in Loschwitz appeared in our garden in order to throw their Party insignia, daggers, medals and pistols, and especially copies of *Mein Kampf* down our deep vineyard well. I similarly disposed of my dagger on which was inscribed the words 'everything for Germany', but I put a pistol to one side. Could there be any truth in what Göbbels had said: 'You will either get a bullet in the back of the neck or be sent to Siberia?' In my boyhood diary of 7 May 1945 I wrote: 'there is a cyclist riding like the wind over the meadows by the Elbe down to the shore ... the Elbe has a white edge to it, it is the end of the "eternal" Third Reich!' In the evening the liberating news arrived: it was the capitulation. At once the most tragic firework display that I have ever seen began: everywhere, stores of ammunition were blown up, tracer rounds flew past overhead in colourful cascades. All the fantasies of a deluded nation were exploded with them. It was all a lie!

On 8 May1945 I wrote:

> the Russians are marching into Dresden, and the rule of the Bolsheviks is beginning. The Americans are playing tennis on the motorway near Chemnitz – they are not going to come ... someone has seen the first Russian soldiers. The sun came up in a cloudless sky as though nothing was happening. In most of the neighbouring houses, looting is going on. In front of the garden of the draper's shop, the owner lies dead; he had tried to stop it. Our teacher Pflugbeil's daughter was raped and murdered. We hid many girls in the three turrets of our house and shoved furniture in front of entrances.
>
> The first Soviet officer to find our out-of-the-way house spoke to me in an almost friendly way. He wore the green cap of the GPU (the Soviet secret service). He kept asking me: 'where is Schiller?' and then after a long pause 'Don Carlos?' It is unbelievable: he turns out to be a so-called Cultural Officer, from Iwanow, on the far side of Moscow, and he is looking for the Schiller House in Loschwitz, where there might still be manuscripts. I show him the way.

There followed a difficult post-war period. But in spite of everything, the feeling of gratitude for having survived was uppermost. We were able to sit our 'Abitur' (roughly 'A-levels') in a half-destroyed grammar school. A degree course in the Soviet zone of occupation was out of the question, especially if one came from a conservative and Christian parental home. An ecclesiastical university was founded for students of theology in the city of Berlin. Only a few days after I had begun my studies and – more importantly – after the issue to me of a Berlin pass, the city was divided up into four sections, not yet by the wall of later years but administratively. Suddenly West Berlin existed, and I had quite legally become a citizen of the West while remaining a citizen of the

East. The course began. The first lectures were given by George Bell from Chichester, Paul Tillich from the USA and Martin Niemöller after his release from imprisonment.

During this time, I naturally remained 'always a Dresdener' and I often travelled to the beloved and broken city that was my home. The Russians had requisitioned our house, cleared it out and then given it back. It was ideal for the pleasures of dancing; lots of empty rooms, candlelight, and nothing to drink; but there was potato salad, which everyone brought along to eat. The 'ladies' came in long dresses, which they had run up with their own hands from curtains. And there was a gramophone with just a few records. To start with, we did the 'Sir Roger de Coverley', an English country dance.

The world still lay open before me: I visited – often hitch-hiking and practically without any money – the Western Zone of Germany. Everywhere there were refugees from Dresden or relations of some sort. When I had said goodbye to them again I would find bank notes in the food given for the journey. With a grant from the World Council of Churches I was enabled to study at the ecumenical Kerk en Wereld Academy in Holland and at the Chateau de Bossey, a similar institute in Switzerland. I was also able to hear lectures in Basel and Zurich and, in the vacations, to visit our relations in England. During an excursion by steamer, a letter from my home church in Saxony reached me by a roundabout route (for my travels had to remain a secret in Dresden) with words to the effect that I really should try an application to the University of Leipzig, as the situation was currently more relaxed. In a library housed in the basement of the Munich Consistory, a man in a shabby suit sat next to me. He was a famous theologian of the Confessional Church, Helmut Gollwitzer, who had only just recently come home after having been a prisoner of war in Russian hands. 'My dear young brother,' he said, 'go back. You are not needed here, but maybe you are needed there. And consider: only where the field is deeply furrowed can fruit grow – and that's not the case here!'

I have never regretted crossing the frontier back to my homeland. Yet the start was grim: in Leipzig, the attempted repression of the Church by the state was in full swing. Schmutzler, the students' chaplain, was arrested. During the popular uprising on 17 June 1953, shots were fired into the crowd. Later on, the beautiful Gothic University Church – the one in which I had given my trial sermon – was actually blown up, together with its organ, the biggest in Leipzig. This was the Stalinist period of the GDR under Walter Ulbricht. Even at this time, however, it was by no means all 'suffering'. A Shrovetide carnival celebration by the young people of our parish was denounced and court proceedings were instituted against me as organizer. I got away with a formal caution, but was nevertheless left with a 'previous conviction'. However, the attempt to build a socialist society had its positive sides for Christians too. After all, it is stated in the Acts of the Apostles II, 4 about the early Christian community that 'they had all things in common'. And the separation of Church and state gave rise to a degree of liberalization within the Church community, although these relaxations were limited in scope.

The great watershed in the history of the GDR was the Helsinki Conference. Erich Honecker succeeded Ulbricht. Although the new party boss wanted a watertight separation of the two German states, neither the interests of the occupying power nor the economic situation in fact permitted it. On the contrary, the shameful Berlin Wall, erected in 1961, very gradually became leaky – not for the inhabitants of the GDR but certainly for visitors from 'capitalistic foreign countries'.

In 1983, the Central Committee of the World Council of Churches was even allowed to have its sittings in Dresden. I organized the cultural activities. The most important personalities of world ecumenism rounded off their visit with a trip on the big pleasure steamer, *Karl Marx*, to that beautiful chain of mountainous rocky cliffs, the Sächsische Schweiz. I wrote to all parishes along the Elbe to ask if, to express their thanks and their joy, they could ring their bells and wave from the shore. The church bells resounded along the narrow valley.

Everyday life in the GDR is difficult to describe. There was a little of everything, from the very bad on the one hand to the beautiful on the other. There was also very little crime as everyone was closely watched. Tragically, a former confirmation candidate of mine, Wolfgang Schumann, tried to escape to West Germany and died an agonizing death in the attempt. Under such circumstances people draw more closely together and there was much solidarity. There was also an amazingly rich cultural life. The rebuilding of the Semper Opera in Dresden, in the teeth of economic decline, was the cause of amazement throughout the world.

The basic question among middle-aged people expressed itself as 'adaptation or denial?' One could say what was on one's mind about such existential questions only in church circles, even though one knew that, even there, the Stasi might well have an eavesdropper present. The Church became a cover for numerous, and indeed very varied, protest groups. There was a wise thought circulating at that time: 'The Church is there for everybody, but not for everything.' It was clear that the continuing existence of the GDR was guaranteed by the many Soviet atomic rockets – some of them in a circle around Dresden – and that any thought of the reunification of Germany was an illusion. Any uprising would be crushed flat, as in Peking. I too was a coward. I still had the gunfire at Leipzig during the popular uprising on 17 June 1953 in my ears, and in my memory the catastrophes of 1956 in Budapest and 1968 in Prague.

In these circumstances the ruins of the Frauenkirche acquired great significance, not only as a memorial, a warning against war and the use of force, but also as a symbol of a collapsing system. Its two surviving stumps rose out of the rubble like two arms raised to Heaven to pray for mercy and peace. Every 13 February, in the late evening, at the same time as the first bombs had started to fall, thousands of people silently placed their candles on the fallen stones of the Frauenkirche or on the square in front of it, in the shape of a cross. There was, in this action, a yearning not only for peace but also for freedom.

Freya Klier, an obdurate critic of the regime, has recorded the following account of the events on 13 February 1982.

> Dresden. My native city. We go to the Kreuzkirche, as always. But what takes place today is indescribable. Crowds of young people stream in through the great portals. They seem to have come from all over the GDR. They have brought sleeping bags and personal belongings – a place to sleep is sure to turn up from somewhere, even in February. After the service, the crowds make their way over to the ruins of the Frauenkirche. Almost all have brought candles, and they pass on the light from one to the other. The deep tones of the Kreuzkirche's bells boom out. This silent procession is taking place without permission. The trams are forced to a halt. I am scared and I ask my mother to go home instead of going on. But there are no arrests. It almost looks like a first sign of tolerance from the State.

By the time the crises came, in the autumn of 1989, a new generation had grown up, and it set all our reservations aside. Its cries were 'now or never!' 'We are the people!' The Church nevertheless provided one of its most influential spokesmen in Superintendent Minister Christoph Ziemer, an intelligent and level-headed man for whom the key thing was certainly not the transformation of a politically based society into a profit-based society, but, quite simply, liberation from the intellectual and political dictatorship of the state. This vision was mightily encouraged by Gorbachov's *perestroika* and *glasnost*, and events rapidly acquired their own momentum. At the beginning of October 1989, five or more express trains were scheduled to take those GDR citizens who had fled into the West German Embassy in Prague to the West via Dresden. The Prague-to-Dresden railway line was soon lined with people (I personally saw many prams between the rails) who kept on shouting 'we want out!' I witnessed in the Wiener Platz the fury of the younger element, which expressed itself in smashing nearly all of the windows of the main railway station with paving stones. Even cars were set on fire. There were many arrests. Units of blood for transfusion were distributed to the city's hospitals and everything pointed to a Peking-style outcome. During the night I visited the families of people who had been indiscriminately committed to the notorious prison in Bautzen (the 'Yellow Misery'). These included the chairman of one of our parish councils, who was imprisoned for nothing more than his refusal to put out his candle.

If things had become critical, our two sons could have confronted each other on opposite sides. The younger one had been obliged, willy-nilly, to report for his compulsory military service and in his barracks, not far from Dresden, batons were issued. The older one, however, was with us among the demonstrators. Then there happened what has been called the 'Dresden Miracle'. On the wide square by the Prager Strasse, thousands of townsfolk and the lines of security police were standing facing each other, dangerously close – only a matter of a few metres apart. Two Catholic priests, with Frank Richter, the Chaplain of the Catholic Hofkirche in the lead, approached the policemen. So did the Lutheran Bishop of Saxony, Dr Hempel – at that time one of the presidents of the World Council of Churches – and Superintendent Minister Ziemer. They asked for the responsible commander and for a sign of goodwill. The command 'shields down' rang out. It was an historic moment. The spontaneous election of a 'committee of twenty' by the people on the street was made possible and there was agreement on negotiations. At this moment – around 11 p.m. – the murmur of the water in the many fountains stopped. Superintendent Minister Ziemer was able to call out, through a police megaphone, 'please go home. The result of negotiations will be announced tomorrow evening in the four largest churches in Dresden.'

A decisive factor in the 'peaceful revolution' was to be the journey of a courageous Dresden man, Frank Neubert, who drove in his little Trabi by a roundabout route to Leipzig. On the day after the 'Dresden Miracle', at the intercessions for peace in Leipzig's Nikolaikirche, he was able to announce, in the name of Bishop Hempel, that negotiations were already under way in Dresden. A wave of encouragement and relief surged through the crowd, both inside and outside the church, and set events on the wonderful and peaceful course that now belongs to history.

This turn of events, known everywhere by its German title of the *Wende*, almost inevitably turned people's minds not just to the preservation of the ruins but to the *rebuilding* of the Frauenkirche. A number of Dresden people had never abandoned the hope that this might one day be possible – notably Dr Fritz Löffler and Dr Hans Nadler. Over the years, I myself gave lectures with slides in many parishes, under the title 'A Walk through the Frauenkirche', to the accompaniment of its Silbermann organ, the aim of this being to keep memories alive and, in the case of the younger generation, to raise awareness. On 28 October 1989, in the *Haus der Heimat*, in the course of a very emotional discussion, a youngish dentist from our congregation, Dr Günter Voigt, asked me whether the time had not come to try to raise a citizen's movement to campaign for the rebuilding. He wrote to the Bishop of Saxony and, within a month, on 23 and 24 November, I found myself drawing up an 'Appeal from Dresden', which, on 25 November, somewhat toned down, was endorsed by a group of Dresden citizens. A 'citizens' initiative' was founded, which at the start held its meetings in the lounge of our vicarage; its biggest piece of luck was Professor Ludwig Güttler's willingness to become its spokesman and president; what he has done for the good cause since then is incalculable. In 1992, Her Majesty Queen Elizabeth and His Royal Highness Prince Philip visited Dresden and, in a gesture of reconciliation, drove slowly around the perimeter of the ruins (given the size of the mound of the stones that had fallen from the Frauenkirche, the security forces were unable to guarantee their safety had they stopped). In the Kreuzkirche, Prince Philip read slowly and with emphasis, the Beatitudes from Jesus' Sermon on the Mount: 'Blessed are the peacemakers, for they shall be called the children of God.' It made me think of a day in London in 1950. The taxi driver, taking me from one station to the other noticed that I was a German. 'Do you have some time? I'll give you a free ride around the area near St Paul's Cathedral.' And so I saw the countless craters made by German V1s and V2s. 'You have to see them!' he said, emphatically but in a friendly way. How right he was!

Three years later, on the fiftieth anniversary of the destruction of the city, His Royal Highness the Duke of Kent, Bishop Simon from our twin city Coventry, and the representatives of Britain's own Dresden Trust came to Dresden. They joined in the already legendary candlelit procession to the Frauenkirche and in the Kreuzkirche the Duke and the Bishop movingly expressed their deep regret for the suffering of, among others, the people of Dresden.

The Trust's work goes on and thanks, tinged with admiration, are due to all those who contribute to its work, for their devotion to a worthy cause, and especially to our friend Dr Alan Russell – *Der Vater des Dresden Trust* – who often comes to our city and whose heart, like my own I think, is now 'always in Dresden'.

Dresden: its Destruction and Rebuilding, 1945–85

John Soane

Ideology versus Conservation; the Fight for Dresden's Civic Soul

On 12 February 1945, when the *Manchester Guardian* expressed the hope that Dresden would be spared military attack, the city was still the great baroque *Gesamtkunstwerk*, or 'artistic whole', universally admired throughout Europe. A day later it was reduced to a heterogeneous collection of outer neighbourhoods surrounding a totally devastated inner core. Its outstanding baroque townscapes around the Royal Palace, the Altmarkt and the Neumarkt had been reduced to broken fragments of wall, and where the Frauenkirche had stood as the city's indisputable symbol for over 200 years, there was only a massive, brooding pile of stones. In a shattered wasteland of over 12 square kilometres, there were 10 million cubic metres of rubble, which eventually took 15 years to clear. Thirty nine per cent of the housing stock had been totally destroyed and 36 per cent seriously damaged, leaving only 25 per cent fully habitable (see Plate 3).

Not only did Dresden experience greater damage and physical suffering in relation to its size than almost any other major German city – it also had to endure the traumatic desolation of a long-familiar lifestyle in circumstances of increasing military chaos and political uncertainty. In retrospect, the end of old Dresden in 1945 can be seen as the most poignant footnote to the dissolution of the familiar old, pre-1914 European political order, when imperialism led to war, war to reaction, and war again to unimaginable destruction.

The ethical dilemmas surrounding this cataclysm were quite different from those facing the shattered cities of the Flanders region, such as Arras and Ypres, at the end of the First World War. There the instinctive reaction of their inhabitants was to restore, as quickly as they could, the aesthetic and social harmony of well-established civic traditions. A generation on, however, the moral confusions that had arisen from the general degradation of the integrated, liberal world order of the Belle Époque by the catastrophe of the First World War, would make the task of rebuilding ruined European cities after 1945 a much less straightforward undertaking.

In Germany, with its long tradition of devolved administration, based on moderately sized, but culturally distinctive, regional centres, the rapid growth of large cities after c.1870, appeared to many as a betrayal of German traditional values. Radical intellectuals such as Herman Bahr and Peter Behrens argued that only a total break with the past could enable Germany to come to terms with industrial urbanization. This was a concept that was further developed by the environmental visionaries of the Bauhaus School during the period of the Weimar Republic; they sought to use the austere, primitivist forms of the new modernist movement to create townscapes appropriate for a completely new, utopian society.

At the other extreme, many of the urban developments that appeared on the outskirts of large German cities by the early 1930s, were strongly criticized by populist commentators such as Alexander Schwab as having debased national civic virtues by being too symmetrically planned, too utilitarian and above all too anti-communal. Moreover, the Great Slump of 1929 had, especially in central Europe, encouraged a further distancing from what was considered the 'tainted' urban cosmopolitanism of the Atlantic capitalist world, a process hugely accelerated by the distinctly anti-urban, vernacular-orientated housing policies of the Third Reich.

Paradoxically, the sheer comprehensiveness of the Nazi state's new housing policies unwittingly laid the administrative foundations of the bureaucratic state-planning structures that spawned the modernist rebuilding frenzy throughout large parts of Central and Eastern Europe during the post-war era. Indeed even by 1940, for fascists and communists alike, the main purpose of significant historic urban centres was to serve as areas for cultural propaganda purposes. In pre-war Dresden, artistic spiritual alterations on the edge of the Old Town were planned to enhance the symbolic role of the Nazi party within civic life. Consequently, the subsequent destruction of Dresden was seen by a wide spectrum of politicians and planners of every political persuasion, as a unique opportunity for rebuilding the place on more rational, lower density, materialist lines, which would not only ensure a healthier lifestyle but would also allow a more effective degree of social control.

That such an uncompromising attitude was adopted from the beginning towards urban renewal in Dresden was not so surprising. Not only did the city now lie in the new Soviet zone of occupied Germany, but the final destruction of the political and physical structures of pre-1945 Saxony also brought into the open the still-festering social tensions that had come about when, during the nineteenth century, this German state had become one of the most rapidly industrializing and urbanizing regions in the whole of Europe. The first post-war Mayor of Dresden in 1945, Walter Weidauer, a former carpenter and long-time communist, imprisoned by the Nazis, greatly detested the vanished baroque magnificence of central Dresden because, for him, it had always represented the exploitation of working people by the bourgeois ruling elite. Speaking in 1946 he enunciated the basic principles that would guide the rebuilding of Dresden.

1. In order to prevent what was considered to be the unregulated, over-crowded, urban speculation of the past, the social and spatial structure of the new townscape would be subject to integrated public control in order to achieve a lower occupational density and more public open space.
2. The greater part of central Dresden would be rebuilt on modernist lines for residential purposes and also to facilitate better traffic movement and a more egalitarian lifestyle.
3. The baroque heart of the city would become a non-residential administrative and service area with access to all, but with only the most important historic buildings – such as those that made up the world-famous silhouette along the Elbe – being reconstructed.
4. To complete these intentions as quickly as possible, destroyed property would be confiscated. (Private and commercial sources would be invited to contribute up to 15% of the cost but the majority of funding would come from public agencies and municipal rents.)

Dresden's Chief City Planner, Herbert Conert, strongly opposed these ideas. They were in stark contrast to the rebuilding plans for Munich (a city in the American zone of occupation) that were presented to the City Council there by Karl Meitinger in 1945/6. The Bavarian capital, still surrounded by a non-industrialized, traditional rural hinterland, was not to be revived according to a set of imposed and abstract principles but, on the contrary, would be deliberately recreated to resemble its original architectural and spatial form, as far as possible. Every opportunity would be given to personal initiatives directed towards reconstituting a healthy civic culture, to ensure the preservation of the organic integrity of pre-war Munich. The comparison between the initial rebuilding proposals for Munich and Dresden – where municipal loans were deliberately refused to private owners anxious to repair their property – is very significant. It demonstrates how, in an era of highly divergent ideas on the ways in which cities should be rebuilt and replanned, the additional problems of the cultural division of Central Europe by the

Iron Curtain could make all the difference to the final appearance of cities on either side. The basic issue was the extent to which the radical planning philosophy (Modernism), which had originally evolved to alleviate the problems and deficiencies of the modern industrial city, could be used as a complete substitute for organically evolved and architecturally distinguished townscapes originally built to express totally different civic values.

Irrespective of the expansive rhetoric of politicians and the immediate desire of a traumatized population to have a modern, clean and efficient city as soon as possible, no rebuilding plan for Dresden could ever have completely replaced the residual longing for the unique work of art that had been lost; a sense of psychological alienation was now borne by practically every inhabitant. In a city that had so recently been a great centre of international culture and was so closely associated with a leisured and cosmopolitan lifestyle, it was scarcely feasible to create an environment expressing the totally contrary ideological values of the promised socialist millennium, whilst respecting the remains of a splendid eighteenth-century past. Thus the very concept and soul of Dresden were at stake.

Even the most conservationist-orientated planners realized that certain measures, such as the widening of some of the narrow streets and the hygienic improvement of many of the tenements, were urgently needed. The problem that they faced was the extent to which such 'necessary' improvements could be ideologically exploited to justify such drastic alterations in the historical fabric of central Dresden as to render the overall setting aesthetically and socially untenable for surviving or eventually reconstructed historic buildings. In effect, between 1945 and 1950, opposing groups of planners played out a battle for the heart and mind of the city. The traditionalists believed that the restoration of the pre-war shape of Dresden – irrespective of its former social connotations – was still a truer representation of how the majority of inhabitants felt their city should be. The modernists endeavoured to prove that, as the destroyed townscape of Dresden was closely associated with persistent inequality and the power structures that had been responsible for the catastrophic defeat of Germany in 1945, the construction of a radically new urban structure was the only way forward.

The more conservative planning lobby was led by Eberhard Hempel and Wolfgang Rauda from the Department of Planning at Dresden's Technical University. They argued that, irrespective of essential modern improvements, it was vital that the rebuilt city and its setting on the Elbe should not only regain their unique harmony of appearance, but should reaffirm the close relationship that had long existed between the physical environment and the citizens' daily and working lives. This, they agreed, could best be done by the retention of the greater part of the original street plan. By such means,

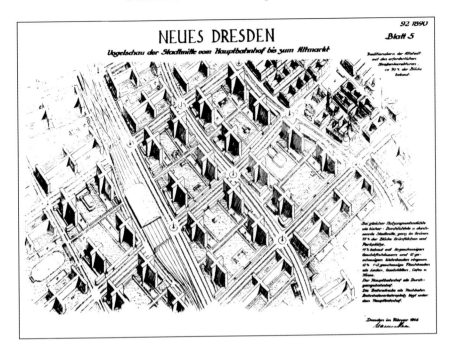

Figure 19. Hans Hopp's 1946 plan for the rebuilding of Central Dresden. Courtesy of the Stadtplanungsamt, Dresden.

not only would buildings be automatically related to the appropriate scale but the unique layout of the Old City – the series of interrelated squares and streets of differing dimensions and appearance – would also be recreated. Only in this way, they suggested, could the centre of Dresden regain its cultural distinction in an era when the uniqueness of historical cities was being increasingly eroded by the forces of economic determinism.

The modernist response was set out by the architects Hans Hopp and Mart Stams – the latter being a prominent Dutch follower of Le Corbusier. They, too, believed in an overriding concept of harmony, but not one based on the organic synthesis of aesthetics and slowly evolving functions. Instead, their vision of the new city was directly related to satisfying the social and utilitarian needs of the working people of Dresden within a contemporary industrial context – irrespective of particular historical considerations. Accordingly, the designs of both architects envisaged the reconstruction of the whole of the central area in the form of uniformly designed, high-rise residential blocks with only token remains of the destroyed baroque townscape. Enormous areas of open space would be created for leisure and demonstration purposes for which the former historic areas would become a mere backdrop rather than an integrated, urban entity.

The absence of sophisticated planning criteria that could successfully combine such sharply differing urban visions, a virtual non-starter, was the principal cause of the indecision and delay in preparing a viable rebuilding plan for Dresden between 1945 and 1950. Moreover, with the establishment of the Communist German Democratic Republic in 1949, whatever degree of independence that Dresden and other East German cities may have enjoyed in formulating their own reconstruction, was now lost to the centralized policy directives of the Ministry of Reconstruction in East Berlin.

The basic aim of this government department was to create residential and administrative districts that emphasized, as much as possible, the political, social and cultural role of the *Sozialistische Einheitspartei Deutschlands* (Socialist Unity Party) or SED. Furthermore, because the new regime feared the free opinions that had hitherto always been an integral part of German civic life, the rebuilding of towns and cities would be carried out in ways least likely to recreate genuinely integrated communities. Each neighbourhood was required to meet a comprehensive range of material needs as laid down by the Party, without any special provision being made for assisting the enterprising artisan or small business man – the social groups that had previously been the most vigorous upholders of city liberties.

The Imposition of the 1950 and 1967 Structure Plans

Dresden had no choice but to bow to such unrelenting influences and, by 1949, proposals for its future role were just beginning to emerge. Since the main function of the city was to become a showpiece for the new socialist Utopia, it was assumed that this aim could only be achieved by the elimination of the existing structure of private land ownership. This would prevent the re-establishment of middle-class behavioural patterns that had cemented the myriad domestic and commercial activities within the high-density townscape of the pre-war city centre. Thus, irrespective of the unique evolution of Dresden over the preceding 200 years, the main proposals of the 1950 Structure Plan (see Plate 9) amounted to a complete abrogation of the distinctive bourgeois character of the city. Except in the centre, which would be reserved for more specialized propaganda and commercial requirements, the old pattern would be replaced by a series of decentralized linear settlements of single, double or grouped apartment houses containing standard-sized flats of functional design, together with adjacent services and surrounded by considerable areas of green landscape. Every residential neighbourhood would consist of about 5,000 people and would make up an urban district of 30,000 persons. Within each district, there would be administrative, social and educational facilities including savings banks, schools, libraries, medical centres, swimming baths and old peoples' homes. In the pre-supermarket era, essential retail outlets would be allocated in strict proportion to the population, one shop generally serving between 1,500 and 5,000 persons depending on what was sold. Together, the urban districts would be combined to create a built-up whole of about 500,000 people, with a devolved and strictly controlled lifestyle and laid out – in accordance with the 1950 Structure Plan – in the form of a gigantic garden city of blocks of flats.

The Plan envisaged imposing such self-supporting residential units on the heavily damaged, but part-intact, inner suburbs, while beyond the Inner Ring, a series of large residential extensions to existing centres, together with small parks, and a modest industrial extension would also be built. Its most radical proposal was a huge increase in public open space from the existing Grosser Garten, across proposed new exhibition grounds (between the Garten and the city centre), through the northern half of the devastated Old Town, and on to the old Elbe docks north of the Friedrichstadt. While the greening of this decrepit part of Dresden was to be welcomed, the idea of turning what had recently been the magnificent centre of the city into a kind of cultural theme park – where only a few restored buildings would be left standing, caused the greatest controversy. The hidden political agenda was of course well understood, namely the prevention at all costs of any resurrection of the grand bourgeois centre of pre-war Dresden around the Neumarkt. In the same vein, but disguised as a means of easing the traffic flow across the town centre, the Neumarkt area was to be separated from the southern part of the Old Town by a huge boulevard or Magistrale – the Ernst – Thälmann – Strasse – now the Wilsdruffer Strasse, 50m wide. The adjacent area between the Altmarkt and the main railway station, as well as containing the principal shops and hotels, would also be available for political demonstrations and would become the principal showplace of communist Dresden.

In the face of demands by the central authorities in East Berlin that a start should be made on building the central Magistrale and a new monumental Altmarkt by 1953, the conservationists fought back by preparing an initial list of conservable buildings. But even as a townscape utterly at odds with the original character of the Old Town was about to be imposed, the political ramifications of the Cold War helped to save central Dresden from complete banality. In a frenetic attempt to assert its shaky legitimacy, the German Democratic Republic formulated new building laws (discussed at several Party conferences in the 1950s) in which Western modernist planning was denounced and architects were urged to build in a distinctive 'German' national style. On account of the close relationship that now existed between East Germany and Soviet Russia, this meant, in effect, adapting to German

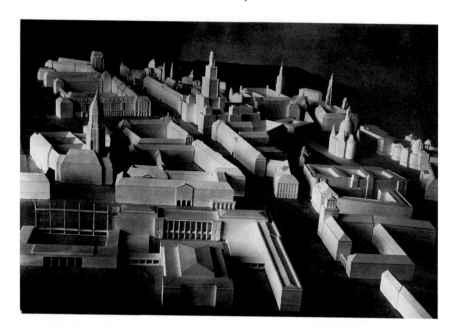

Figure 20. 1953 model showing the proposed new Altmarkt and the wide Magistrale. Courtesy of the Stadtplanungsamt, Dresden.

Figure 21. Aerial view of the new – and enlarged – Altmarkt, 1953. Courtesy of Siedel and Kruse, Weinböhla.

conditions, the huge neo-classical ensembles of urban planners such as Igor Fomine and Boris Iofane that had been built in Moscow during the 1930s in order to legitimize Stalin's dictatorship. Although much reduced in scale, the massive shape of the seven- to eight-storey blocks proposed for the new Altmarkt still appeared monotonous in comparison with the more varied shapes of the pre-war square. Nevertheless, the elaborately sculptured architectural decoration on the main facades – replete with ornamental pediments and triple oriels – bear some superficial resemblance to the aesthetic conventions of Saxon baroque. However, neither the more conservative architecture of the new Altmarkt nor the 1949/51 reconstruction of blitzed inner suburbs such as the Pirnäische Vorstadt and the Südvorstadt, in the form of relatively traditional four-to-five-storey residential apartment blocks, could hide the immensity of the symbolic and spatial changes that were envisaged for the city centre. Along the Wilsdruffer Strasse, with the exception of its Landhaus (now the City Museum), nothing would survive, whereas on the south side a greatly enlarged Altmarkt, a new People's Palace of Culture (first envisaged as a multi-storey Ziggurat loftier than the old Frauenkirche) would be built in a politically symbolic position on the site of some of the finest town palaces that had ever been built in the city.

And yet amidst the unstoppable momentum that was forcing the planners of central Dresden to adopt radical concepts, doubt still remained. Hatred of the Ancient Regime was inevitably tempered by the knowledge that the imminent creation of huge, simplistic vistas would remove, for ever, the distinctive silhouette of many familiar streets and squares. Small wonder that the principal entries in the competition for redesigning the Old Town – by H. Schneider, J. Rascher, W. Rauda and G. Funk – found it difficult to reconcile the monumental demands of the Communist authorities with the more human scale of the original buildings. On the one hand Rauda's entry was criticized as being too reactionary as it proposed the near-archaeological reconstruction of the original streets in the Neumarkt area. At the other extreme, Schneider's plan – which was eventually adopted in modified form – was first considered too radical because, in addition to the new Altmarkt, it advocated a vast extension of the Neumarkt, behind the Palace of Culture, that would have stretched right across that part of the Old Town, practically to the old Ständehaus on the Brühl Terrace by the Elbe. Even the most resolute of Communist planners were intimidated by the lingering urbane ambience of the ruined Old Town, and shrank from rebuilding their principal showplace for socialist Dresden on the former royal and aristocratic heart of the city between the Royal Palace and the Frauenkirche. But they sought to lay this ghost, by adopting a rebuilding plan for the centre that involved the demolition – ostensibly on hygienic and traffic management grounds – of over 80%

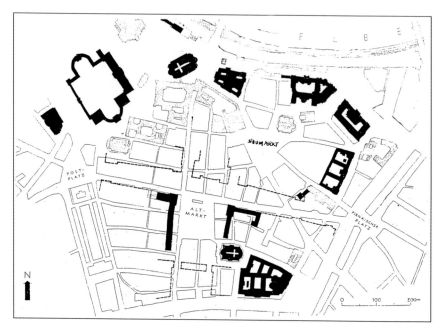

Figure 22. Main elements of the new building lines proposed for central Dresden. Courtesy of *Deutsche Architektur.*

of the surviving restorable ruins and, in this context, by bringing forward proposals for the redevelopment of the Neumarkt area. (These proposals were as deficient in spatial originality as their plans for a greatly enlarged Altmarkt were in their grandiosity.) They finally put paid to any remaining hopes of a sensitive recreation of the original townscape.

By 1960, despite some particular examples of good moderate design – as for example between the Gewandhausstrasse and the Weisse Gasse – the worst fears of conservationists such as Fritz Löffler and Hans Nadler, were being realized. The wide new central thoroughfares and the primitive spatiality of the new townscape that was soon to arise, would permanently exclude the possibility of regaining of those elements of order, shape and proportion that had defined the built and the unbuilt spaces of central Dresden until 1945 (see Plate 4 showing Dresden's pre-war and present street plans). Indeed, as the philosophical maxims of the East German government were translated increasingly into finite achievements, not only was less public discussion tolerated over future proposals but fewer attempts were made to conceal the radical transformations desired by the régime. There was, consequently, widespread sequestration of all small and medium-sized properties in the heart of the historic city, ruthlessly carried out to achieve the new planning objectives. This was one of the heaviest blows to the essential social and spatial continuity of Dresden that the city had ever suffered.

That such changes did not lead to the complete metamorphosis of the organic structure of a substantial portion of the Old Town was due to a combination of official attitudes, chance and the often courageous attempts of concerned individuals to retrieve what little of value there remained. As the new East German regime strongly equated many historical monuments with what it considered to be the inequalities of pre-1945 German society, official policy towards their conservation was often ambiguous and uncertain. While fully accepting that there were buildings representative of the cultural evolution of Eastern Germany, their significance was expressed in rather vague terms, which meant that only monuments that could be transparently associated with the widest possible aspects of regional culture would be given adequate protection and generous financial support. The artistic, craft and intellectual traditions of past ages were deemed to be of value only in so far as socialist society could be enriched by closer association with them.

Even before this policy had been formulated, reconstruction work had begun on the Zwinger – the most famous baroque building in Dresden – as early as October 1945, using the same workmen who had been employed on its last major restoration between 1924 and 1936. By 1949, at a time of continuing extreme scarcity of building materials, 2.5 million Marks had been spent on the Zwinger and reconstruction was virtually complete by the early 1960s. It is also greatly to the credit of the municipal authorities that, after much wide-ranging discussion, it was decided that the original layout of Dresden's most outstanding urban open space – the Theaterplatz – would be kept in its original form. The burned-out ruins of the famous Semper Opera were consolidated for further rebuilding and the exquisite Court Church that formed such an important element of the skyline of the Old City from the Elbe was largely restored by 1962. There was little co-ordinated effort by the Communist authorities to rebuild other areas of integrated historic townscape in the heart of the Old Town. Faced with antagonistic official attitudes, the conservation agencies were reduced to searching the huge piles of rubble for surviving pieces of architectural ornamentation that, even then, sometimes mysteriously disappeared during the night. Irrespective of an official policy on the conservation of historic monuments, restorable buildings had often to be vigorously fought for. Their preservation was often only possible if a suitable 'socialist' use could be suggested; and, as Dr Nadler relates (on pp 91–92 below), the fight to keep open the mere possibility – no more – of rebuilding the Frauenkirche was long and arduous. (It is said that the ruins of the Royal Castle and the Taschenberg Palace were only saved when it was suggested that, once rebuilt, they would be perfect for the new

Figure 23. The Rampische Strasse – pre-war, and in 1950. Courtesy of the
Sächische Landesbibliothek, Deutsche Fotothek.

People's 'Palace of Culture', and the Japanese Palace was preserved when it was suggested that it would be a suitable location for the Young Pioneers.)

However, the prohibitive cost of rebuilding, and continuing disagreements over the future social role of key areas such as the Neumarkt, prevented any significant conservation work there for a generation. The ruins of the Frauenkirche continued to rear up out of an enormous pile of rubble and were declared an anti-fascist war memorial by the Communist Party. In this way the void that used to be the Neumarkt was preserved for later rebuilding by a more enlightened generation. The nadir of the ideological desecration of historic Dresden came in the late 1950s and 1960s with the deliberate destruction of damaged but restorable ensembles, such as the Sophienkirche, the Rampischestrasse and the Grosse Meissner Strasse, as well as with the clearance of the sites of many smaller homes and shops west of the Altmarkt, all points of focus that would have more easily facilitated a general reconstruction of the Old Town. Of over 2,000 restorable facades, only 200 were eventually saved.

What was happening to the Saxon capital symbolized, in extreme form, the unremitting struggle for the souls of German citizens, to determine the moral and cultural values that would prevail in the new urban environments of the post-war era. In Dresden the most stalwart proponent of humane and organic town planning in place of the increasingly utilitarian achievements of the Ministry of Reconstruction was Fritz Löffler, distinguished art historian friend of the leading intellectuals of Weimar Berlin, and author of the key book on Old Dresden, *Das Alte Dresden*. He bitterly criticized the City Council of Dresden and in particular the Mayor, Walter Weidauer, for, as he put it, prostituting the cultural heritage of Dresden by claiming to be its defender but, in reality, impeding on ideological grounds its proper rehabilitation by substituting a sterile, social consumerism for free artistic endeavour. In more specific terms, Löffler accused the Communist authorities of effectively completing the initial destruction of Dresden by the Allies by deliberately attempting to obliterate every surviving remnant from the 'bourgeois era' and trying to justify this official vandalism with political propaganda. When Löffler was accused of putting the form and appearance of the townscape of Dresden above Marxist interpretations of the social and economic priorities of modern urban life, he responded by refuting his accusers' claim that exceptional historical buildings were part of the common accomplishments of past societies and therefore worthy of no exceptional consideration. Instead, he saw these structures as the creation of particular individuals whose singular talents had helped to create a distinctive and integrated urban environment for the free use and enjoyment of all classes of society for all time.

This conflict over the relative worth of particular visions of urban culture vividly demonstrates the tragic fragmentation of the formerly more integrated, aesthetic and social values across German society during the first half of the twentieth century – a fragmentation partially responsible for the destruction and subsequent degradation of the original concept of Dresden. That Löffler and the conservation authorities could still be accused of political disloyalty to the regime (which resulted in conservationists being forced to attend compulsory lectures on dialectical materialism) is dramatic evidence of the climate of mutual distrust and hysteria that continued to pervade aspects of East German civil life. A mirror of this cultural instability may be observed in the new plans of 1965 for the reconstruction of the Neumarkt. It was proposed that the Frauenkirche should be left as a quaint ruin adrift in a sea of uncompromisingly modernist blocks of which, thankfully, only one, the police headquarters extension, was actually built.

By the 1960s, however, the limited toleration of historic monuments in the Neumarkt was due more to influences coming from the Federal German Republic than to policy directives coming from East Berlin. The economic power and international prestige of West Germany was increasing by leaps and bounds and the growing acceptance in the GDR of modernist planning and architectural modes in place of its spurious 'German national style' was in no small measure due to its wish to emulate the architectural achievements, if not the social policies, of the West. At the same time, the building of the Berlin Wall in 1961 gave the Communists an inflated sense of confidence in the enduring ideological and institutional structure of their state. The government in East Berlin found it politically desirable to appear aesthetically progressive in Western terms and socially progressive in Soviet terms at one and the same time. With the development of industrialized building methods by which whole sections of a structure could be lifted into position on site, the Ministry of Housing, actively encouraged by Walter Ulbricht (the SED Chairman), began to exert ever tighter central control over the purpose, size and detailed layout of new urban development. This ever more politically motivated planning policy fell increasingly hard on Dresden, where it could be seen in the modernist designs and ever greater massiveness of later buildings in the Ernst – Thälmann – Strasse, in the construction after much delay of the People's Palace of Culture (1966/1969) and in the extensive residential/hotel/leisure complex in the Prager Strasse. The People's Palace, now arrayed in severe horizontal guise, instead of the originally planned multi-storey Ziggurat, was intended to embody the ideals of the new socialist society. The Prager Strasse development, an immense pedestrian precinct consisting of three huge parallel hotel blocks, each 17 storeys high, opposite a truly gargantuan 12-storey block of flats with shops beneath, was supposed to represent the triumph of populist values over private speculation.

Figure 24. The new Prager Strasse in the early 1970s. Courtesy of Dr John Soane

The official 1967 Structure Plan of Dresden represented the peak of this self-confidence and expressed enormous political enthusiasm for the symbolic importance of the new central Dresden in relation to the rest of the city. Against all professional architectural opinion, the SED considered the unfolding huge disparities between built and unbuilt space and the complete alteration of former visual relationships throughout the Inner City to be the final triumph of an integrated community over the more divided social hierarchies of a previous age. The fact that the great distances between buildings would tend to isolate people from each other far more effectively than the more closely built-up, pre-war townscape had ever done only showed how far from reality East German planning policies were becoming. The official line was that the wide East/West Magistrale, the longitudinal North/South pedestrian mall (the Prager Strasse) and planned improvements at other central intersections, were highly efficient measures in achieving the separation of essential services from designated residential, commercial and public sectors. Moreover, the Communists believed that relatively short distances between large open spaces enhanced the political and social control of the population, and this priority weighed heavily in the planning of further new developments in all parts of the city.

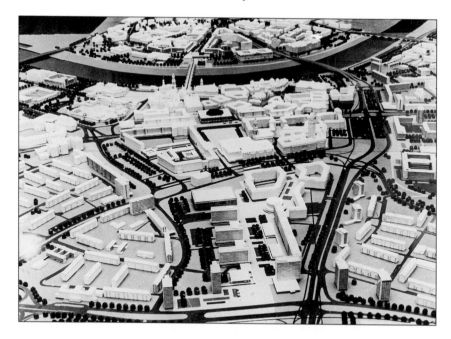

Figure 25. 1982 Planning Model of the whole city centre, showing (top centre with the black roof) the Palace of Culture with, beyond, the site of a fully-razed Frauenkirche. Courtesy of the Stadtplanungsamt, Dresden.

Thus in the early 1970s, entire self-contained neighbourhoods began to appear in increasing numbers quite close to the Old Town – in the Pirnaische Platz and the Leningrader Strasse (now the St Petersburger Strasse), in the Dr Otto Nuschke Strasse, in central Dresden, along Juri Gagarin Strasse towards the Technical University and, a decade later, in the blitzed area of the Neustadt across the Elbe around the Strasse der Befreiung (now the Hauptstrasse). Further out, entirely new high-rise settlements were built in the near vicinity of the existing suburbs of Zschertnitz, Seidnitz, Leuben and Prohlis, often on land taken from local farmers at a fraction of the fair price. Between 1967 and 1982 alone, a total of 60,000 new apartments were built; even more elaborate schemes would have followed in the Seevorstadt and in the Antonstadt had funds allowed. Not surprisingly, this led to a new and abrasive, vertical skyline becoming visible, not only on the south-western and south-eastern outskirts of Dresden, but, most damagingly of all, in the near vicinity of the Old Town, on its eastern side. These new buildings also seriously impinged on the Carola Bridge, near the previously inviolate, riverine landscape of the Elbe near the Brühl Terrace.

The ruling SED saw no particular discrepancy between the very different spatial structures and architectural forms that now existed in the city. To the

Figure 26. A recent aerial view of central Dresden, 1992. Courtesy of Müller Verlag, Cologne.

party faithful, as each segment of townscape was a perfect and finite example of human socialist perfection, the sum of these individual segments must fit perfectly into a complete urban cosmos. That the very limited changes in plastic facade treatments that were possible in industrially produced buildings were considered to provide sufficient variations in design was graphic evidence of the degree of aesthetic philistinism that gripped the party elite. Entire sections of post-war Dresden could now be dated by decade according to the varying policy directives of the central government in East Berlin.

Within the totalitarian vagaries of Eastern Europe, what had once been a revolutionary urban tradition had now been reduced from a means to a better end to a self-serving end in itself. The utter lack of any social animation and the unremitting ugliness of these massive mono-class residential ghettos made them totally inadequate for the emerging more individualistic life-styles of their occupants. Dresden artisans sorely missed the small premises and intimate spaces that, prior to 1945, had been readily available to small business enterprises. Many of them were increasingly forced to operate as members of large, forcibly created, state firms (*Kombinate*), where, apart from being unable to make any personal profit, they were subjected to regular bouts of meaningless political propaganda. As in most cities throughout communist Europe, free time for the ordinary citizen was closely monitored through the almost compulsory attendance of most wage earners and their families at the numerous political demonstrations and parades in the large new open spaces around the Altmarkt.

The Impact of New Planning Ideas from West Germany 1975–85

By the 1970s, of course, the general inadequacies of modernist planning were becoming increasingly noticeable in Western European countries. But whereas in East Germany and other Russian satellites, it was impossible to curtail a system of urban development now increasingly out of control, democratic institutions west of the Iron Curtain enabled more pluralistic attitudes to emerge, which would eventually effect a radical change in the perception and use of modern townscapes. After nearly three decades of vigorously imposed, modernistic hegemony and with post-war reconstruction now completed, many fundamental questions, buried since the early 1930s, began to be posed – especially in West Germany. To what extent should the evolved historic townscape of cities be valued according to purely materialist or utilitarian criteria and to what extent should it be valued in absolute terms according to its enduring cultural significance? To what extent should the political and technological imperatives of the modern state be allowed to have a significant impact on the quality of life in particular towns? Werner Durth, a leading German urban environmentalist pointed out that every reasonably sized place is a distinct entity, and that politicians and town planners must respect the particular characteristics of urban environments independently of perceived planning theory. As the internal social stability of Western Germany continued to grow during the 1970s, a greater interest in older building traditions and a steady retreat from modernist planning influences swept the country and culminated in the leading role played by the Federal Republic in the very successful, and influential, European Architectural Heritage Year of 1975.

The vernacular origins of many German towns were now no longer so readily associated with the planning policies of the Third Reich. Well-restored organic townscapes now allowed for the interplay of aesthetic, social and economic considerations within which urban conservation and town planning would again become fused into complementary disciplines. A spontaneous new planning movement, *Neue Urbanität* (New Urbanity), campaigned for the abolition of functional and architectural zoning divisions in towns and cities and their replacement by multi-functional streets, a better and more intimate balance between built and unbuilt space, and an improvement in

Figure 27. A recent aerial view of central Munich. Courtesy of Schöning Verlag, Lübeck.

the design of houses and apartments that should be affordable for a wide cross-section of the population. By the 1980s comprehensive measures to restore the morphological equilibrium of dilapidated neighbourhoods were being undertaken in many towns and cities. Two of the most successful were at Augsburg and Mainz, where lesser residential and artisan districts were rejuvenated by a most skilful mix of restoration and sympathetic new building. In Frankfurt the Römerberg and at Hildesheim the Market Places were reconstructed as counterbalances to adjacent urban environments that had been more radically rebuilt after 1945.

The resulting considerable regeneration of civic pride not only brought back into greater favour more traditionally rebuilt cities such as Freiburg, Münster and pre-eminently Munich, but it also began to display the sterile planning policies of the German Democratic Republic in an ever more negative light. Faced with increasing popular discontent, the Communist regime belatedly realized that an improvement in the basic design of its future urban schemes might enhance its fading political authority. New apartment blocks in the centre of East Berlin began to be clothed, somewhat self-consciously, in the modulated facades and mansard roofs of early West German post-Modernism. The main problem that faced the SED, however, was that a more visually appealing and socially integrated townscape would be closer in spirit and appearance to the buildings of bourgeois liberal epoch of the early twentieth century. As its unrestricted spread could eventually undermine the ideological beliefs on which the very existence of the state was based, the reluctant but increasing use of these 'subversive' forms of planning had to be vindicated on materialist and economic grounds alone.

Thus in Dresden, in the early 1980s, higher density use of the central area was justified on grounds of lower cost, improved amenity value and as an improvement of the general quality of the built environment. At the same time there was a tardy recognition that, on strictly practical grounds, considerable parts of the surviving outer nineteenth century suburbs of Dresden – as in the Neustadt – could, after rehabilitation and reconstruction, help ease the continuing housing shortage. However, quite apart from increasing difficulties of financial liquidity – mainly as a result of continuing exclusive reliance by the state and municipal authorities on public funds for major building projects – architects and planners also faced considerable problems in breaking free from nearly 30 years of rigid control from the Ministries of Reconstruction and Housing in East Berlin. Not only had the instinct for good, natural, organic design been considerably weakened, but the concept of integrating new buildings into existing historic ensembles in a sympathetic manner had been largely lost. These deficiencies are painfully apparent in the rigid massing and uncoordinated facade details of infill architecture put up on the corner of Bautzner Strasse and Martin Luther Strasse in the Neustadt. Such weaknesses were even more obvious in many of the designs submitted in response to a competition in 1981 for a more comprehensive reconstruction of the Neumarkt, as the social and cultural centre of the inner city. A fair number of proposals anticipated eventual rebuilding of the Frauenkirche by respecting its original built form. However, most of the entries to the competition, in attempting to restore the high-density character of the area, found it impossible to create well-designed structures that were architecturally compatible with, and proportionally respectful of, the general pre-war townscape.

The fact that ideas on the improvement of Dresden's urban surroundings, even in the Old Town, could still fall so far short of what the vast majority of the inhabitants wanted, was symptomatic of the approaching political crisis of an East German state that was increasingly losing touch with reality. The average citizen had become alienated, in surroundings that, according to Professor Jürgen Paul, many found 'banal, aesthetically boring, even downright dull'. In the second half of the decade, the missing impulse that would combine the surviving elements of the past with new urban development to create a proper sense of contemporary vitality, historical continuity, and above all revived civic pride, would hit Dresden along with the rest of East Germany with the speed of a whirlwind.

The Battle to Conserve – Securing the Ruins of the Frauenkirche

Professor Dr Hans Nadler, Head of the
Department of Conservation 1949–1982 and
Professor Emeritus at the Technical University, Dresden

Towards 11am on 15 February 1945, in the midst of the still smoke ridden city, the great dome of the Frauenkirche fell in upon itself with a loud sigh. The church's outer walls fell in a great pall of dust which, black as night, covered the whole area as with a shroud. Within a month investigations into the ruins had begun and, with a view to preserving them for future rebuilding, they were intermittently pursued over the next fifteen years.

In March 1945, Senior Church Inspector Hermann Weinert reported that, following penetration of the walls by means of tunnels and explosive charges, many drawings, photos, plans and statistics had been found, which – prepared by Baumeister Pinkert and by Architects Kiesling and Rüth during the 1930s and 1940s – were to prove especially valuable. During the months that followed Kiesling led a more detailed examination of the Neumarkt and Frauenkirche site, under the guidance of an expert Commission set up by the Saxon State Government to decide what stabilisation measures might be needed; and the recommendation was made that at the very least a partial removal of the rubble would be required to establish with any reliability whether rebuilding was conceivable.

In November 1948 further investigations began on the northern side of the church and, despite the hard weather, about 600 cubic meters of re-useable rubble were cleared, carefully measured and recorded, and taken on hand barrows to the nearby Salzgasse. The old folk who did this work deserved the highest respect and Arno Kiesling – whose services were retained by the conservation Department for around 11 years – produced an extremely useful description of the situation, indicating how the fallen monument might be restored.

On 6 September 1950, the GDR adopted new laws concerning the rebuilding of its war damaged town, which forbade the removal of material for use elsewhere, but – nevertheless – opened the way to systematic clearance of the centre of Dresden. With the help of a small rail transporter system leading to the Elbe side at Blasewitz, this promptly began. Conservationists quickly realised that stones likely to be needed for the eventual rebuilding of the Frauenkirche might easily be lost and campaigned for the retention of the huge pile of rubble where it lay,

Figure 28. The *Trümmerhaufen* – the ruins of the Frauenkirche as they remained until 1992. Courtesy of the Sächsische Landesbibliothek, Deutsche Fotothek.

until rebuilding of the church could begin. These efforts were on the whole successful but some of the less identifiable stones already taken to the Salzgasse were lost to work on strengthening the river walls.

Throughout this time, the Conservation Department concentrated its attention on the Zwinger and the Theaterplatz and spasmodic attempts were made by both Party and City Authorities to rule out the rebuilding of the Frauenkirche for good. Hints were dropped about the danger to traffic of falling stones and the removal of preservable ruins elsewhere, such as those of the Sophienkirche, in the Rampische Strasse and in the Grosse Meissner Strasse, boded ill. Fortunately funds were simply not available either for clearance or for rebuilding on the Frauen-kirche site and the Conservation Department's suggestion of simply stabilising the rubble mound by planting wild roses on it was finally agreed.

It was not however until the 1960s that the mound finally achieved formal recognition in the Structure Plan, as a monument. In later competitions and plans on the future of the Neumarkt area the rebuilding of the Frauenkirche became an accepted part of the briefs, with all this implied for the proportions of the buildings that would give it back its setting and for the restoration of the old street plan.

In this way the *possibility* of rebuilding the Frauenkirche was kept alive. But no-one thought that it would take a further forty years to begin to realise the dream!

The Renaissance of Dresden after 1985

John Soane

The Last Years of Communist Rule

Up to the early 1980s, profound changes in attitude towards the urban environment in West Germany were as much part of the country's long-term healing process after the travails of the Nazi era as its first attempts to re-establish a more benign German cultural presence within Central Europe. After about 1985 however, the accumulated momentum of nearly two generations of democratic evolution, together with a very considerable resurgence of civic pride, enabled *Neue Urbanität* and the Urban Conservation Movement to exercise a significant influence in their own right outside the Federal Republic. The revival and blending of regional vernacular traditions, the better regulation and control of property developers and the creation of more civilized, socially integrated city centres in which people felt more obviously at ease – these could all be seen and digested in Dresden, despite poor reception of West German television there, as well as in the remainder of the German Democratic Republic (GDR). These images inevitably had a considerable destabilizing effect on the political authority of the SED, a situation that Dresden's politicians and planners made one last fruitless attempt to combat.

Thus, in 1986, Dresden's last Communist planner, Heinz Michalk, announced fresh planning proposals for the coming five years in which he tried to blend centralist planning concepts with new measures designed to create a more aesthetically pleasing and more integrated city. He made much play with the historic concept of Dresden and promised new residential developments in the inner areas that would better reflect the architectural and spatial proportions of the pre-war town. However, the GDR's rigid, centralized structures still precluded any constructive dialogue between government and citizens, and the people's sense of alienation remained pronounced. Any real power of initiative was denied to the reformers and, against the advice of every senior civil servant in the Ministry of Housing, the Politburo still refused to accept that substantial changes to its official planning policies were needed.

As a result, the Dresden city planning authorities remained incapable of finding any *modus vivendi* that would satisfy the deeper psychological feelings of its citizens and, for reasons of financial expediency, concentrated on improving hotel and other tourist facilities within the central area. In addition to the successful reconstruction of the Opera House, the Bellevue Hotel was recreated on the Neustadt side of the Elbe, incorporating at its centre the one surviving magnificent eighteenth-century town house that conservationists had managed to preserve, in the Grosse Meissner Strasse. The Dresdner Hof, now the Dresden Hilton, followed soon after on the plots of several destroyed buildings in the Töpfergasse, opposite the Frauenkirche ruins, between the Brühl Terrace and the Neumarkt. Neither construction can be said to be an architectural masterpiece but in their general respect for the basic shape of the structures that they replaced, they were a distinct improvement on most previous schemes and clear evidence of the greater influence of Western urban design over the political taste of East German planners.

However, while particular building projects in Dresden and other East German cities appeared to give some glimmer of hope for the future, most promises of environmental improvement were not honoured by a regime that, by the late 1980s, was visibly losing its authority month by month. Amongst a whole host of political and social grievances, the ongoing desecration of organic townscapes in the name of party ideology continued to oppress the urban populations of East Germany. The massive demonstrations against the government that took place in Leipzig and East Berlin, as well as in Dresden, in the autumn of 1989, were prompted as much by planning issues as by more fundamental considerations. And yet even during the final months of the existence of the East German state following the fall of the Berlin Wall on 9 November 1989, a desperate attempt was made to prove that in Dresden, at least, hopes of a better city would not always founder on the rocks of socialist realism.

The last General Structure Plan of the communist era was prepared in the spring of 1990 by the Department of Planning at the Technical University, just when the population of the GDR was voting in their first free election for 68 years. In comparison with the earlier more didactic proposals of Michalk, an approach that had included all the received concepts of modernist and historical rationalization, the new 1990 proposals allowed for greater plurality and enterprise and for a less doctrinaire synthesis between private and public participation. They also reaffirmed Dresden's exceptional artistic heritage and regional identity and sought to encourage a greater variety of

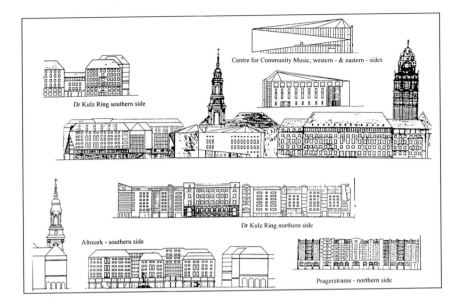

Figure 29. Design proposals for the re-building of the central area, prepared, in the last six months of communist rule, by the Department of Planning in the Technical University. Courtesy of the Department of Planning Technical University, Dresden.

clearly identifiable rôles for the city. Better cultural and leisure facilities were foreseen and these were to be matched by well-planned residential districts on a more human scale – both within and outside the central area. Improved designs for the rehabilitation of newly built neighbourhoods and greater flexibility of land use on the basis of specific social and economic priorities were promised.

Yet even this scheme, promoted by Hans Modrow – the last Prime Minister of East Germany – could not gloss over the basic ineptitude of 40 years of failed planning policies. With its overblown rhetoric, its continuing insistence on a fair degree of functional zoning and, above all, its inability to produce a design concept that effectively synthesized high-rise buildings, post-modern architecture and urban conservation, it appeared to the average citizen as yet another variant of socialist realism, albeit heavily disguised in more vernacular form. Most of the inhabitants of East Germany now knew that the utterances of their politicians were no longer prompted by trust and confidence but by a desperate need for self-preservation. In truth the people had always known instinctively what was best for their communities, though the SED in its arrogance and ignorance had never listened to them. Now, architecturally as well as politically, the game was up.

The Origins and Principles of the Post-Communist Structure Plan, 1990–5

According to a survey into attitudes of the inhabitants towards their city, carried out by the author in 1992 when a member of the Department of Planning in the Technical University, an overwhelming majority (80 per cent) were completely dissatisfied with what had been achieved since 1945 and professed a strong preference for the older forms. The survey came out in favour of the preservation (or recreation) of as much as possible of the ambience of old Dresden and singled out for special criticism the unsatisfactory spatial relationships created all over the city, but notably in the central area. Most respondents wanted the city to make the best possible use of the technological improvements of modern urban life but their attachment to the idea of Dresden as a *Gesamtkunstwerk* was shown to be remarkably strong. Disillusion with the past was, however, balanced by a new sense of hope for the future. Indeed the survey confirmed that opinions in the GDR on conservation, planning and rebuilding had closely followed contemporary opinion in West Germany. Moreover, with the ending of communist rule, it expressed the need that was urgently felt in Dresden to evolve a new planning concept that would balance aesthetic, social and economic considerations in place of the moribund belief that the city should symbolize an absolute idea, be it the utilitarian fantasies of Marxist Socialism or, indeed the baroque magnificence of Augustus the Strong.

It was now necessary to fundamentally rethink Dresden's unique position. It was a city that had been universally compared with Florence before the war, but it had been devastated in 1945 and then deplorably mutilated over the successive 45 years. All the questions that Dresdeners had wanted to ask for decades rose to the surface. In what way might a new concept of Dresden be expressed? How could it be at once believable and flexible enough to accommodate the greatly changed priorities of the modern world? How could the necessary moral and political will of the city's population to achieve these objectives, be mobilized? And how could the inexorable pressures of free market capitalism – which could all too easily impose an urban environment as unwelcome as anything that was created in Dresden between 1945 and 1990 – be resisted? Irrespective of the many different plans for renewal that had been brought forward during the communist era, no properly coordinated and fully endorsed plan for the orderly reconstruction of the city,

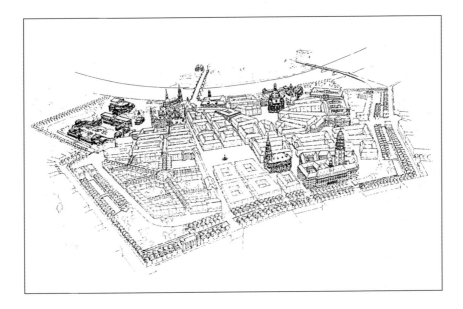

Figure 30. First proposals for the centre of Dresden produced after German reunification in 1991, underlining the return to more traditional concepts and values. Courtesy of the Stadtplanungsamt, Dresden.

existed. To obviate therefore any risk of a chaotic, unplanned reaction to the old centralization, the City Council abrogated all the development policies of the old regime and called a complete halt to all future planning activities for several months, immediately after German reunification on 3 October 1990. It then embarked on a most intensive programme of analysis and discussion to ensure that maximum consensus would be achieved prior to the finalization and publication of a new Strategic Plan.

Many people feared that their new-found hopes might prove to be no more than an unrealistic dream. Might it be, as Paul Kulka, the neo-modernist architect of the new Saxon Landtag (situated by the Elbe to the rear of the Opera House) has suggested, that the instinctive yearnings of the population at large to recreate the vanished historical magnificence of the *Gesamt-kunstwerk* merely perpetuated a myth that could appear all the more beguiling because the destruction had been so total. He felt it necessary to ask how, therefore, the myth of Dresden could be connected with present day realities. Should it be replaced by more normative perceptions of modern city life or did the future destiny of Dresden lie in the perpetuation of this myth by drawing as much on the past as on demands of the moment? Many architects and planners, strongly influenced by modernist orthodoxies and unnerved by the superficiality of the post-modernist Age found it hard to understand the remarkable persistence in Dresden of the belief that the visual qualities of its townscape held a deeper ethical significance than simply aesthetic gratification. In a city where a certain perception of urbanity could still appear timeless, it was essential, before rebuilding could take place, to ascertain just what was the abiding image of Dresden and then to determine how it would be preserved, enhanced and reinterpreted.

Eventually, after much discussion by leading planning and architectural specialists including Walter Jörn, Michael Kaiser, Anke Krüger and Ingolf Rossberg, it was decided that the criteria for shaping the ultimate visual appearance, social significance and economic viability of Dresden should be directly related to one basic idea. The city should be regarded as a stage set in which the fusion of its built environment and the activities of its inhabitants were intricately and unequivocally related to each other, so as together to recreate the indefinable atmosphere that had been Dresden. This concept could only be sustained by an harmonious synthesis between the natural riverine landscape of the Elbe and the spatial order, perspectual originality and architectural beauty of the central area as it had evolved during the eighteenth and nineteenth centuries. Although a very considerable proportion of this achievement had been destroyed in 1945, its recreation was considered essential for the reassertion of the true identity of the city, both as a general aesthetic idea and as a functionally working entity. Here was a complete vindication of the view that a conservative reconstruction of the city – a policy that had been so often rebuffed since 1945 – should be attempted. Probably in no other city but the Capital of Saxony has there been such a *volte face* from a rigidly imposed, anti-historicist, planning philosophy, to the opposite vision of one integrated, all-embracing artistic ideal.

Other factors lent urgency to the need for such a vision. Over 40 years had elapsed since the reality of old Dresden had been personally experienced by much of the population. After the enforced austerity of the communist era, the rapid material improvements now offered by Western investors could appear tempting indeed. Therefore if the original concept of Dresden was to be preserved, it was essential that protection be given against poorly designed buildings in the centre and rapidly built satellite settlements beyond the city limits. This would involve not just a recreation of former patterns of built and open space, but also the re-establishment of a much more integrated mix of commercial, service, leisure and residential uses over a considerable proportion of the inner historic area. Apart from serving as a general pattern for all building activity throughout the city, these precedents would also act as a guide on linking structures between surviving buildings, on the reintegration of isolated elements of the original townscape and on the reduction, through strategic positioning, of the visual impact of poorly integrated high rises. Only in circumstances where no amount of perspectual disguising could improve the situation, would out-and-out demolition be considered.

A unique opportunity now presented itself to undo much of the alienation of neighbourhood communities that had come about by the functional rebuilding of Dresden – and indeed many other German cities – after 1945. It would, however, not only be necessary to establish new guidelines to ensure that old and new were fused in a more plausible fashion; it was also essential that both the indigenous inhabitants and potential entrepreneurs were better informed about the enduring value of Dresden's unique architectural legacy. Ongoing public debate was therefore initiated between city planners and the people of Dresden through meetings, newspapers, radio and television, all culminating in the Dresden 2000 Exhibition held in 1995. At this event, information on every possible aspect of the rebirth of the city was on display, including an enormous scale model of how the city is likely to appear in the early twenty-first century. Out of this continuous educational process, a new civic pride is emerging that will not only give Dresdeners a reborn sense of place, but will also enable a better *modus vivendi* to be established between the legitimate aspirations of investors and entrepreneurs and the broader responsibilities of the city authorities.

This is the background to the City Structure Plan for Greater Dresden that emerged between 1992 and 1994 (see Plate 10). Unlike similar documents written between 1945 and 1990 – full of ideological ranting but short on practical application – the new proposals take a long-term holistic view of the city's future evolution in terms that relate directly to the unique characteristics of Dresden alone. This strategy, hopefully, offers a flexible working compromise between what is historically desirable and what is practically necessary. It makes precise connections between different areas of the city while recognizing that they will not always require exactly the same treatment.

The central assumption of the Structure Plan is that, because for both practical and financial reasons, it is impossible to re-establish the *Gesamtkunstwerk* of old Dresden, a more harmonious urban environment of complementary visual segments should be created as a fitting substitute. The shape and dimensions of each building block (generally as part of an integrated ensemble and averaging about 25 m high and 60 m long) will take precedence over the particular uses to which it will be put. A median scale of acceptable dimensions will thus be established that will be as applicable to the more traditionally replicated townscapes in the central parts of the city as to the more loosely planned outer areas, beyond the Inner Ring. Certainly, the recreation of more architectural and spatial forms will be facilitated by the revival, wherever possible, of the original balanced

Figure 31. The Great Model exhibited at the Dresden 2000 Exhibition in 1995; the darker colour denotes those parts of the centre that are being or will be restructured. Courtesy of the Dresdner Ausstellungsgesellschaft.

relationships between buildings and the streets and squares in which they stood up to 1945. In this way, it is likely that fully one third of existing open space in the centre will be built up again by the early twenty-first century.

The Plan therefore also envisages a significant restoration of the original road network of the inner city and, where this is not possible, a considerable narrowing of the Wilsdruffer Strasse, of the Inner Ring Road, and of other principal thoroughfares laid out during the communist era. The existing major intersections on the eastern, western and southern fringes of the Old Town, the Pirnaischer Platz, the Postplatz and the huge Wiener Platz between the Prager Strasse and the main station will be completely restructured. In addition, other long-forgotten squares; the Strassburger Platz, the Sachsen-platz and the Ferdinandplatz between the Inner Ring Road and the Wiener Platz will be recreated – along with the missing south side of the Altmarkt and the original, more intimate shopping streets between the West side of the Altmarkt and the Wallstrasse. The remaining open spaces will be linked to each other by means of green walks and strategically located small gardens, and access to the centre will be better controlled by means of a re-location of the main arteries leading through and out of the city.

While the original streets around the Altmarkt, Neumarkt and the Royal Palace are eventually to be more accurately rebuilt to contain a wide variety of more specialized facilities, the Plan envisages a considerable enlargement and improvement of the principal commercial and retail heart of the city as defined by the Inner Ring, the Railway and the Grosser Garten, and concentrated mainly on either side of the Prager Strasse. In comparison with the greater freedom allowed in restructuring outer Dresden, ensuring the recreation of a more integrated townscape in this area is obviously even more significant. Here the proposed higher density urban development must effectively soften the aesthetic differences between the more traditional remodelling of the Old Town and the modernist residential and commercial ensembles built during the 1960s and 1970s. Moreover, by greater use of pedestrian malls and better public transport, it is envisaged that not only will the new commercial centre become a more congenial place to visit, but it will also be possible to re-establish a better balance between shops (50 per cent), general leisure and other services (25 per cent) and apartments (25 per cent). The benchmark for the ultimate general character of central Dresden, its regional economic revival and the regeneration of a more tangible sense of civic well being will depend on the successful achievement of these goals. These sentiments have been fully endorsed by local politicians, city planners and property developers alike.

First Achievements of the Structure Plan

It is of course one thing for the City Council to lay down detailed guidelines and quite another to ensure that they are everywhere respected. In the process of coping with the flood of development projects that came in – some of which promised quick economic revival – the planners inevitably made some mistakes. Thus, irrespective of the general rule that more design restraint would be applied the nearer the building site was to the Old Town, several projects such as the over-large World Trade Centre (complete with 14-storey tower) on the western edge of the Old Town and the rather ungainly seven-storey Art Hotel, near the Zwinger on the Ostra – Allee, have to be numbered among them. In other cases, as in a new office development at the Rosa Luxemburg Platz in the Neustadt, the building may be the right shape for its surroundings but is spoilt by insensitive construction materials. These mistakes notwithstanding, the emergence of the detailed Structure Plan, the appointment of Gunter Just, a local architect, as the Deputy Mayor responsible for planning, and the introduction of an Internet/virtual-reality scenario of how Dresden will look by the twenty-first century have given the planning department increasing confidence in handling property entrepreneurs and their schemes. In the outer suburbs such as Klotzsche and the Südvorstadt, which contain an eclectic mix of detached and high-rise housing as well as many industrial/research complexes, the visual compatibility of future buildings will be judged as much according to their variety of forms and facade treatments as by their strict adherence to the dimensions and modulations of the standard Dresden building block. Thus, while at Waldschlösschen, on the north bank of the Elbe, a huge new mixed development of flats, small industrial ateliers and offices is a good example of a combined restoration/post-modernist development, at Niedersedlitz an informal residential ensemble of terraced/courtyard houses will be based on the best principals of German, pre-1914, garden suburb planning. In Johannstadt-Blasewitz, poorly designed residential high rises are being reconstructed and improved.

In the commercial centre of Dresden, either side of the Prager Strasse, however, it is the scrupulous respect for the new regulations on building sizes that will do most to establish a more liveable architectural scale and – in conjunction with the existing, widely spaced, high-rise buildings – to create

Figure 32. Effective Synthesis of old and new buildings in Waldschlösschen (between the Neustadt and Loschwitz). Courtesy of the Stadtplanungsamt, Dresden.

better perspectives by a lessening of the overpowering mass of the 1960s urban developments. All the principal German department store chains are now building in this area on sites averaging about 25,000 to 30,000 square metres. Some of the larger concerns will have interior garden courts, and the majority of new retail premises will make provision for smaller rentable shops, artists' ateliers and public exhibition spaces. Sheltered pedestrian passages, often tracing the lines of former narrow lanes, are to link up each separate complex and an enormous underground car park will be shared out proportionally at basement level.

An examination of the completed seven-storey structures along the present Prager Strasse – now reduced (at its northern end) to its original 18m width – reveals a general return to its pre-1945 proportions but also a much greater variety of facade design. Given the exceptional circumstances surrounding the destruction and total clearance of this part of the city, the use of extensive sandstone facing to enhance the facades of the emerging new retail townscape is probably the best compromise that can be had between historical traditions and the economic realities of modern commerce. In the Wiener Platz, a greater variety of large irregular and smaller, free-standing building blocks will be introduced to make this large open space more manageable and urbane. At other key points around the perimeter of the Inner City, major demolition and very large-scale redesigning, based on public competitions are taking place. They include the areas between the Pirnäischer Platz, the St. Petersburg Strasse and the Bürgerwiese, which contains the Robotron site opposite the City Hall; and the Postplatz with the adjacent Marienstrasse and Wallstrasse In accordance with the proposals of Professor Joachim Schürmann, the long boulevard between the two streets will be rebuilt on a more human scale and will include a water feature, which, as it approaches the Postplatz, will echo the moat of the Zwinger beyond.

The Reconstruction and Conservation of the Old Town

The fact that such drastic restructuring has to be carried out in large parts of central Dresden after the radical changes of the previous 50 years amply demonstrates how important the latest plans will be for the reconstruction of the historic core of Dresden – the Altmarkt and Neumarkt areas and the Southern Neustadt – in facilitating the recovery of this area's original urban form. As the Old Town will set the ultimate standard of townscape design for all other reconstructed streets, its recreation has to be carried out with a convincing degree of cultural continuity and legitimacy.

Figure 33. The re-modelled northern end of the Prager Strasse 1997. Courtesy of Dr John Soane.

Figure 34. Design proposals for the Postplatz (above) and the Wiener Platz (below). Courtesy of the Dresdner Ausstellungsgesellschaft.

Figure 35. Aerial view of the Neumarkt, 1994. Courtesy of Mr Jorg Schörner.

Fortunately most of the famous surviving buildings in Dresden – the Zwinger, the Royal Castle, the Taschenberg Palace, the Opera, the Court Church and the Frauenkirche – are situated in this area. Together with the ornate nineteenth century structures along the Brühl Terrace and other, older adjacent townscape elements, these important remnants of old Dresden provide exceedingly valuable strategically situated points of reference for the new construction. The survival of considerable parts of the original townscape of Dresden outside the central core give added weight for a conservative reconstruction of the Old Town. The continuing existence of over 600,000 m² of unrebuilt land in this exceptionally important area provides a splendid opportunity to ensure that the new developments not only positively enhance the Neumarkt-Schlossstrasse area – the heart of the Old Town – but also ensure that the Altmarkt eventually provides a much more acceptable visual and cultural bridge between the historic and business sectors of central Dresden. The fact that the neutralization, remodelling or even outright demolition of some of the unsuitable modernist buildings put up here in the communist era is considered a serious option, is an indication of the close co-operation between conservationists, planners and developers in seeking to ensure that the delicate balance between aesthetics and commerce will not be forgotten in the final appearance of the new townscape.

In the Altmarkt, the large Stalinist baroque buildings on the eastern and western sides are to be complemented by a well-proportioned but somewhat pedestrian scheme for the missing south side of the square. The basic intention is that the narrow streets on either side of the Schreibergasse, between the Altmarkt proper and the Inner Ring, are to be recreated by a variety of appropriately uniform blocks to be put up for medium-sized enterprises, with a choice of apartments above. Given the location, is is to be hoped that the buildings will be more traditionally designed with hipped roofs, arcades and symmetrically integrated fenestration. At the northern end of the Altmarkt, the uncompromisingly modernist Palace of Culture is to be given sympathetic extensions to its southern and western facades, both to match the new buildings to the south and as part of a more appropriate contribution to the much-narrowed Wilsdruffer Strasse. At a later stage the remainder of this thoroughfare might be remodelled, if the general momentum of reconstruction in the Old Town eventually leads to the removal of the three blocks of flats constructed during the 1960s. Even more likely to go will be the police headquarters extension in the Rampische Strasse, the modern commercial building erected on the site of the Sophienkirche, the two high-rise blocks that now dominate the Elbe in the Johannstadt, on the eastern edge of the Old Town, and large stretches of modern flats and commercial property between the Hauptstrasse and Albertstrasse in the Neustadt, where Saxony's governmental centre is being extended.

Figure 36. Model of the southern side of the Altmarkt, opposite the Kreuzkirche (buildings now nearing completion). Courtesy of the Stadtplanungsamt, Dresden.

However, many leading planners and environmental specialists believe that if a considerable proportion of the Old Town, the spiritual and cultural heart of Dresden, is eventually brought back to life, it must again become a properly balanced community and not merely a collection of opulent retail outlets, expensive restaurants, professional offices and luxury apartments. The unremitting gentrification of the Neustadt, especially between Albertplatz and the Königstrasse, splendid as it is, well demonstrates what can happen if the full rebuilding costs have to be borne by the future users of such premises alone. Consequently, the acceptable recreation, not only of the unique townscape of the historic Old Town but also a reasonable amount of its distinctive character, can never be left to the exclusive interplay of modern market forces. Arbitrary decisions will have to be made with respect to the size, exact proportions and types of shops, service facilities and apartments to be contained in the new buildings. More sensitive entrepreneurs will have to be sought because the emphasis on appearance and social cohesion will tend to limit the full earning potential of the new developments.

In order to facilitate these aims, a special committee of architects, in association with city planners, is establishing a practical plan for returning a viable sense of aesthetic and social place to the Neumarkt and adjacent areas. Accordingly, the renaissance of the pre-1945 urban elements of this world-famous square and its immediate surroundings will be facilitated by the restoration of the former street pattern, by the reconstruction of most buildings on their original plots and by the coherent harmonization of the principal facade elements – roofs, doorways and windows – in every building that is put up. It is to be hoped that the accurate reproduction of the more outstanding vanished structures such as the Dinglingerhaus, the British Hotel and the Cosel Palace, will give a sense of historical continuity and precise scale to the new urban scene. With the aid of much surviving documentary evidence, Saxon conservationists hope eventually that up to 80 original structures will be rebuilt. Indeed in the case of the northern half of the Schlossstrasse, the Jüdenhof and most of the Rampische Strasse, the artistic significance of the overall appearance of these ensembles makes their recreation indispensable for the final recreation of this key area.

Indeed, just what a difference a fully reconstructed piece of historical townscape can make may be seen in the complete rebuilding of the Taschenberg Palace, adjacent to the Royal Castle. Between 1992 and 1995, this large and famous building, the centre of so many fruitless schemes during the Communist era, was restored as a luxury hotel, with full archaeological reconstruction of its external walls, and the dramatic impact of its wonderful, ornamental facades has hugely improved the quality of its general surroundings and has exerted a powerful indirect influence on the final replanning of the western environs of the Old Town.

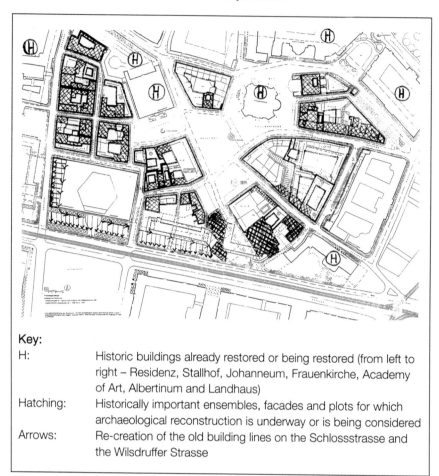

Key:

H: Historic buildings already restored or being restored (from left to right – Residenz, Stallhof, Johanneum, Frauenkirche, Academy of Art, Albertinum and Landhaus)

Hatching: Historically important ensembles, facades and plots for which archaeological reconstruction is underway or is being considered

Arrows: Re-creation of the old building lines on the Schlossstrasse and the Wilsdruffer Strasse

Figure 37. The planned re-shaping of the Neumarkt to restore old building lines. Adapted by Dr Alan Russell from material in the Dresdner Frauenkirche Jahrbuch and the Dresdner Hefte.

But, whilst it is relatively easy, given sufficient resources, to reconstruct Dresden's principal architectural masterpieces, the exact appearance of many more modest buildings is less well documented. Many are known only from old photographs and from surviving basements; over the years moreover, many of them were subject to significant change in height and mass as gables and windows were altered and extra floor space created. The total eradication of the old street patterns again made matters infinitely worse. The way in which the restored architectural masterpieces of the lesser buildings should be related to each other is therefore very problematic. If the Frauenkirche is taken as the defining yardstick for the Neumarkt area, then the shape and

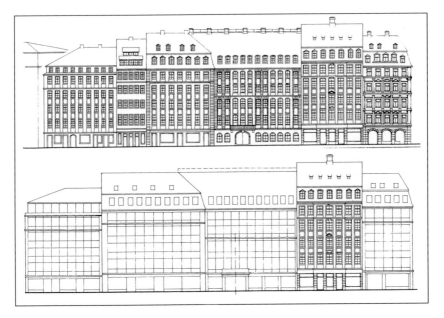

Figure 38. Design guidelines (below) proposed new buildings in the Neumarkt, showing how they will in some cases reproduce, in other cases mimic and in all cases respect the proportions of the original Baroque ensemble (above). Courtesy of the 1996 Dresdner Frauenkirche Jahrbuch – Hermann Böhlaus Nachfolger.

mass of the buildings that stood around it in the nineteenth century probably provided the best balance, and precise design guidelines on mass, shape and design are needed if they are, in some shape or form, to be replicated.

Accordingly, the city planning department has drawn up legally binding design guidelines, based on key original buildings, which will be applied to all future new construction. These take the form of blocked-in elevations, which indicate the general proportions of the roof and external walls and the approximate positions of the main elements of the facade. Developers will be free to submit detailed designs based on these precise criteria, but it still remains to be seen whether the interior planning arrangements of these new structures will fully reflect their exterior dimensions. What is certain, however, is that, provided sufficient investors can be persuaded to participate in this unique piece of urban regeneration, then by the early twenty-first century, a new Neumarkt will have brought back the original sandstone coloured walls and massed red tiled roofs of the Old Town, which will again stand in dramatic contrast with the stronger vertical shapes and domes of the adjacent Royal Castle and Frauenkirche.

These two edifices, once they are fully restored, will become again the finest surviving examples of Saxon artistic distinction in respect of architecture and the applied arts for the period c.1550–1914. Quite apart from the stimulus that their continued reconstruction gives to the general rebuilding of Dresden, it has given fresh impetus towards the revival of the long-neglected handicraft traditions for which Dresden is renowned.

The recreation of the Royal Castle after decades of scandalous neglect will enable one of the finest Renaissance palaces in Germany to revive the distinctive cultural significance of Dresden in relation to other famous Central European centres of art. Serious conservation work on the Castle, which is mainly state-funded, did not gather momentum until the re-establishment of the Free State of Saxony after German reunification; but now precise objectives have been defined and steady progress is being maintained. Since it was decided that the Castle should, in the main, be restored to its appearance before destruction, the famous series of eighteenth century state and museum rooms known as the *Grünes Gewölbe* or Green Vault, together with the sixteenth-century Court Chapel, are some of the interiors that will be recreated. Between 1990 and 1992 the greater part of the main structure was roofed and made structurally secure and with much artistic effort, a considerable proportion of the outstanding late Renaissance/Baroque griselle exterior ornamentation has been recreated in the Great Court. The intense research work generated by this exceptional enterprise has allowed the long-standing artistic connection between the former baroque Court cities of Munich and Dresden to be enhanced by the expert assistance of many conservators from southern Bavaria and other old 'Residenz' centres such as Würzburg and Schwetzingen. But if the restoration of the Royal Palace demonstrates the renewal of an accomplished cosmopolitan tradition, the ongoing rebuilding of the Frauenkirche is a much more personal affirmation by the people of Dresden of their general optimism for the future prosperity of their city.

This famous and unique building, a remarkable combination of Italianate architectural form and German linear virtuosity, has always been the tangible symbol most closely associated with the historic civic culture of Dresden. Not surprisingly, the Communist authorities, largely for ideological motives, repeatedly delayed serious consideration of its reconstruction until mounting public indignation took matters out of their hands. In February 1990, nine months before German reunification, a group of concerned citizens met informally to gather support for the rebuilding of the church; they were successful and their endeavours led to the establishment in 1991 of the Society for the Promotion of the Rebuilding of the Frauenkirche (see Appendix II). A unique feature of the reconstruction is the use of many of the 60,000 sandstone building stones that have been retrieved from the rubble. The original

1. The new Orb and Cross for the Frauenkirche, presented by the British people to the Dresden Foundation, through the Dresden Trust, on display in Windsor Castle on 2 December 1998, on the occasion of the State Visit of the German President. Courtesy of Carolyn Jordan.

2. The original Orb and Cross being salvaged from the ruins of the Frauenkirche, 1994. Courtesy of Dr Karl-Ludwig Hoch.

3. Plan of Dresden showing the scale of destruction in February 1945. Courtesy of the Stadtplanungsamt, Dresden.

4. Dresden's pre-war street plan (yellow) and its 1991 street plan (black). Courtesy of the Stadtplanungsamt, Dresden.

Four as yet unpublished pictures of the raid, as seen from Waldschlösschen,

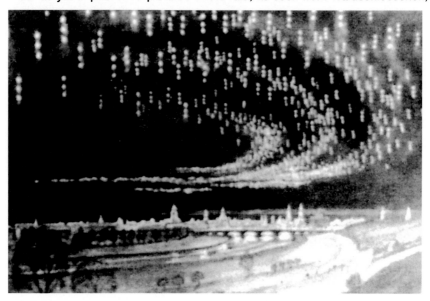

5. The lights – so-called Xmas trees – are dropped.

6. The fire takes hold as the explosives fall.

passed to the Trust, through Karl-Ludwig Hoch, by a 90 year-old Dresdener.

7. The inferno, at its height, with the flames leaping 500 metres or more into the sky.

8. The lingering fire, the morning after.

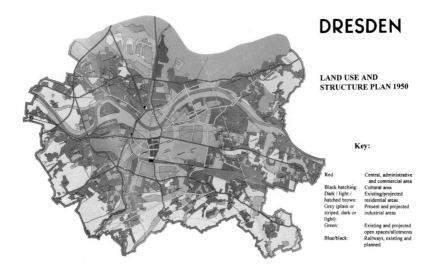

DRESDEN

**LAND USE AND
STRUCTURE PLAN 1950**

Key:

Red — Central, administrative and commercial area

Black hatching: — Cultural area

Dark / light / hatched brown: — Existing/projected residential areas

Grey (plain or striped, dark or light): — Present and projected industrial areas

Green: — Existing and projected open spaces/allotments

Blue/black: — Railways, existing and planned

9. The 1950 Land Use and Structure Plan. Courtesy of the Stadtplanungsamt, Dresden.

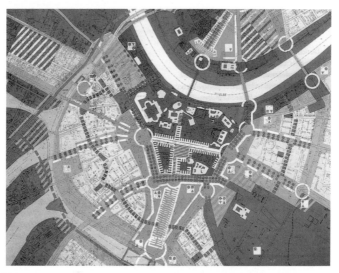

Key

Light Blue — General Structural Elements e.g. Railways

Dark Grey — Essential Open Spaces

Red — Principal Road Network

Black — Significant Historical Value, Intensive Use

Orange — Business and Commerce

Yellow — High Density Residential

Green — Meadows, Parks, Green Ways, Avenues

10. Dresden's 1994 Structure Plan. Courtesy of the Stadtplanungsamt, Dresden.

11. The Royal Household at Delhi on the Birthday of the Great Mogul by Johann
    Melchior Dinglinger and his brothers Georg Friedrich (enameller) and Georg
    Christoph (jeweller 1701–1708, in the Grünes Gewölbe. Courtesy of the
    Staatliche Kunstsammlungen, Dresden.

12. Schloss Pillinitz, home of much fine Chinese and Japanese porcelain as well as
    of ceramics, wood carving, textiles and furniture. Courtesy of the Sächsische
    Landesbibliothek, Deutsche Fotothek.

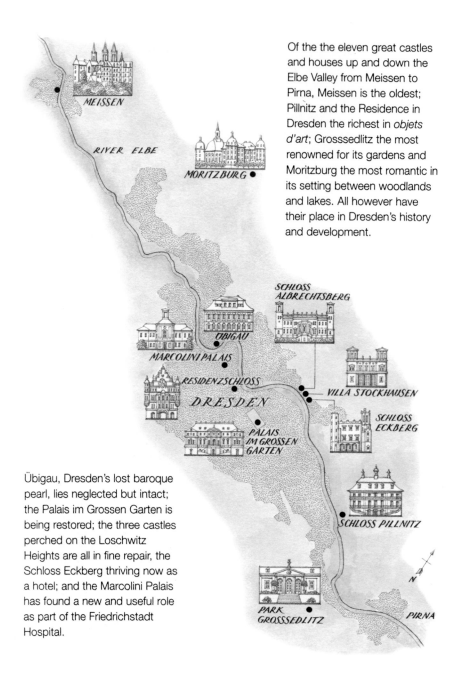

Of the the eleven great castles and houses up and down the Elbe Valley from Meissen to Pirna, Meissen is the oldest; Pillnitz and the Residence in Dresden the richest in *objets d'art*; Grosssedlitz the most renowned for its gardens and Moritzburg the most romantic in its setting between woodlands and lakes. All however have their place in Dresden's history and development.

Übigau, Dresden's lost baroque pearl, lies neglected but intact; the Palais im Grossen Garten is being restored; the three castles perched on the Loschwitz Heights are all in fine repair, the Schloss Eckberg thriving now as a hotel; and the Marcolini Palais has found a new and useful role as part of the Friedrichstadt Hospital.

13. The Castles of the Elbe from Meissen to Pirna. Courtesy of Stephen Conlin.

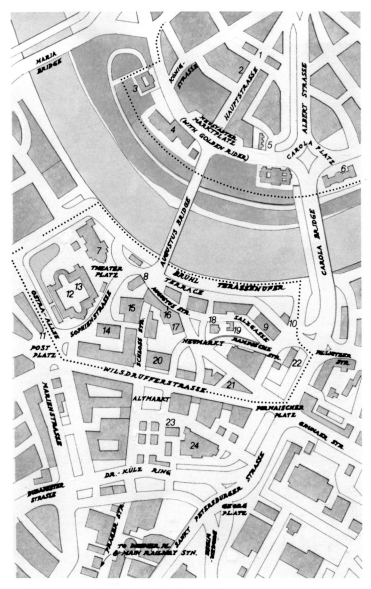

1. Dreikönigskirche	9. Albertinum	17. Johanneum
2. Kügelgenhaus	10. Casemates/fortifications	18. Frauenkirche
3. Japanese Palace	11. Schauspielhaus	19. Cosel Palais (ruins)
4. Bellevue Hotel	12. Zwinger	20. Kulturpalast
5. Museum of Folk Art	13. Gemäldegalerie	21. City Museum
6. Chancellery	14. Taschenberg Palais	22. Courland Palace (ruins)
7. Opera House	15. Royal Castle	23. Kreuzkirche
8. Hofkirche	16. Fürstenzug	24. Town Hall

14. Dresden: Principal Places of Interest in the City Centre. Courtesy of Stephen Conlin.

15. The Landhaus, a trace of old Dresden in the Wilsdruffer Strasse. Courtesy of the Dresden City Museum.

16. Bernando Bellotto – *The Neumarkt from the Moritz Strasse*, 1749–55, Gemäldegalerie Alte Meister. Courtesy of the Staatliche Kunstsammlungen, Dresden.

17. Exterior view of Gemäldegalerie Alte Meister (the Semper Gallery) seen from the courtyard of the Zwinger. Courtesy of the Staatliche Kunstsammlungen, Dresden.

18. Bernando Bellotto – *Dresden seen from below the Augustus bridge*, 1748. Courtesy of the Staatliche Kunstsammlungen, Dresden.

19. The Rüstkammer, ie the Armoury, in the Gemäldegalerie Alte Meister. Courtesy of the Staatliche Kunstsammlungen, Dresden.

20. Raphael's *Sistine Madonna* (c. 1513) – acquired for Dresden in 1745. Courtesy of the Staatliche Kunstsammlungen, Dresden.

21. Lucas Cranach the Elder – portrait of *Henry the Pious*, 1514. Courtesy of the Staatliche Kunstsammlungen, Dresden.

22. *Das Schokoladenmädchen*, Jean-Etienne Liotard's much-loved mid 18th century painting of an unknown girl serving chocolate, 1743–1745. Courtesy of the Staatliche Kunstsammlungen, Dresden.

23. Caspar David Friedrich – *Two men contemplating the moon*, 1819. Courtesy of the Staatliche Kunstsammlungen, Dresden.

24. Otto Dix – *War Triptych*, 1929/32. Courtesy of the Staatliche Kunstsammlungen, Dresden.

location of these pieces of masonry has been determined both by their fallen positions and by a computerized reconstruction that shows every stone *in situ* throughout the entire building. Otherwise, all construction is carried out by traditional methods and should be finished by 2004–5; the new crypt having already been dedicated in August 1996.

The new Frauenkirche will give back a vital element of the original town-scape to the Old City. It will again complete the world famous skyline of Dresden seen from across the Elbe and it will also set the scale against which the entire reconstruction of the central city will be measured. Its renewed presence will help to ensure that the restored townscape of the adjacent Neumarkt will be kept to widely accepted parameters of traditional design. At a deeper level, it is hoped that this great church, by recreating a strong sense of historical evolution and identity, will become a potent symbol of peace and international reconciliation.

Conclusions

The re-animation of the Commercial Centre, the humanization of the Altmarkt area and the archaeological reconstruction of the historic core will help Dresden to again become a cosmopolitan and civilised place in which to live, a major tourist mecca and a European centre of international cultural significance. Along with the revival of the Neustadt, the restoration of other interesting areas close to the centre such as the Friedrichstadt, and the careful preservation of the remaining parts of Dresden's once great Villadom area near the Elbe similarly give substance to the ardent wish of population and planners alike to restore some sense of artistic unity to the city as a whole.

Present day Dresden is probably unique amongst modern cities in manifest-ing such strong determination to create an urban entity fit for the emerging lifestyles of the coming millennium, whilst drawing, as deeply as circumstances and finances allow, on its historical evolution to reinfuse its streets and squares, old and new, with a distinctive aesthetic ideal. Through its cycle of degradation, neglect and eventual renaissance, Dresden has dramatically demonstrated the dilemmas faced by the ancient urban traditions of Europe during a period of unremitting industrial and post-industrial change. How Dresden responds will certainly help other well-established towns and cities to meet, in visual, and moral as well as in practical terms, the challenge of new technological and materialistic pressures.

Given the tension between opposing perceptions – organic and utilitarian – of urban renewal, all attempts made in the post-war period to achieve some balance, albeit precarious, between these two points of reference have been fraught with immense difficulties. During the communist era, the main task of conservation was always that of limiting the iconoclastic impact of the radical planning concepts imposed by a regime fundamentally at odds with everything that Old Dresden represented. After 1990 the problem became at once more complex and more open to resolution; for with German reunification and the collapse of ideological Modernism, the reinvention of democratic and civic life made it necessary to rediscover and recreate the true spirit of Dresden amidst a welter of contending ethical influences. The lack of widely accepted town planning criteria in the contemporary world is probably an advantage for the city. At the risk of unfair accusations by some experts of creating a 'Disneyland by the Elbe', the Dresden authorities are now freer to re-establish the city's unique sense of place than at any time in the last half century. But this will only be successfully brought about, according to the art historian Professor Jürgen Paul, when potential developers better appreciate that the main requirements for rebuilding the central area – a more socially orientated multi-functional, urban environment – are indeed the only way forward for the majority of large cities in the developed world.

Gunter Just believes that Dresden now has a last chance, not only to learn from the mistakes of other German cities that were rebuilt too rapidly after 1945, but to create a new, more lasting identity that will actually be close to the wishes of the majority of its citizens. As a result of their tragic history, its citizens have learnt not only that senses of continuity run deep but that they cannot easily be set aside with the promise of earthly utopia by radical forces of the right or left. Provided the correct accommodation can be made between the visual and functional characteristics of the historical and contemporary parts of Dresden, there is no reason why the Saxon capital should not aspire to again become a many-sided arena of humane and pluralistic activities.

In 2006, on the occasion of the 800th anniversary of its incorporation, the city will, hopefully, present a successful synthesis of continuity and innovation through the partial recovery of its past (poignantly symbolized in the appearance of retrieved fragments in its restored monuments), no less than by the general impact of its new buildings. Not only a tribute to the resurrection of civic enterprise in Central Europe, but also a vital symbol of the remarkable urban civilisation which the European continent has given to the world.

The Rebirth of Dresden, as Conceived by the City Council

Gunter Just, Deputy Mayor with special responsibility for development

Throughout its history, Dresden has repeatedly suffered severe setbacks through fires, wars and other events, which have in turn led to new planning and to programmes of reconstruction. None of these events, however, was as grave as the destruction in 1945 and the lack of continuity in the development of the town during the following decades. The wounds of war and mistakes in urban development are everywhere to be seen, even today.

In spite of this, Dresden's reputation remains high and it is a popular destination for tourists. Its appeal radiates from its lovely surroundings, from the several significant buildings like the Zwinger and the Opera House, which have been reconstructed, and from the attractive new townscapes on either side. The hopeful visitor who expects to find a lively, compact urban centre will, however, be bitterly disappointed because it has no such thing. It was totally destroyed in the Second World War and huge gaps remain even today. Built-up areas, which are anything but urban, spread out like over-extended housing estates, lacking any attraction that might make one want to linger.

In the new development strategy, its implementation and planning, unequivocal priority is being given to steps to remedy this situation. If the centre of Dresden is to promote the identification of its citizens with their own city and to become more attractive again as a place for residents, investors and tourists alike, it needs a density, quality of urban form and a liveliness that only small structures can create.

The quality of life and experience that the city centre can offer will be progressively improved as the sought-after variety is restored, along with the density of commercial, gastronomic, cultural, artistic and other service facilities. The public spaces between buildings and the architectural and artistic excellence of the facades that enclose them, the quality and uses given to premises at street level, the development of recreational spaces and the right proportion of residential accommodation in inner city areas – all these will play an important part in making the centre of Dresden worth living in again.

This rebuilding and reshaping is rooted in the historic and organic basic structure of the city, which is proving to be highly appropriate to the need. The Inner Ring, which follows the line of the one-time fortifications and encompasses the old and new market places, the

Frauenkirche, the Residence, the Zwinger and the Opera, can still be traced. This core area is to be characterized, as it was before the Second World War, by a high concentration of sites of architectural and cultural interest. The most important construction projects in this enterprise are the rebuilding of the Frauenkirche, the Academy of Arts, the Cosel Palace and, above all, much of the old, and virtually all of the new, market place.

This immediately raises the question of how best to handle Dresden's tragically decimated heritage. Through the historic reconstruction, for future generations, of the old baroque style? Or through the systematic rebuilding in a modern style, with the risk of alienation that it implies? The yearning felt by many, and in particular the older Dresdeners, to see their city rise anew in its old historical greatness does, of course, reflect their search for a lost identity, for a recognizable and under-standable cityscape, of world-wide repute as well as of local importance, which some remaining fragments still express.

In 1910, Erlwein, the city architect to whom Dresden owes a great deal, wrote as follows:

> There has been so much experimentation with so-called 'modern' art in Dresden that I have no desire to contribute in my turn to a mutilation of this beautiful city. For me, the concept 'modern' is a continuation and a development of what is good from the past, taking into account the needs and the means of our own time. Just as we speak modern German today, so I want to practise modern German art. I want nothing to do with the creation of a new artistic language which must inevitably lack the depth of feeling and the maturity of the past.

Our task, therefore, is to create something new, but to set it in its historical context. Renewal thus goes hand-in-hand with authentic restoration, as a building operation of equal importance. Incidentally, not only the source but also the direction of the flow has to be authentic. It is in this spirit that the planning group, set up by Dresden's Chamber of Architects with a strong complement of top-class conservationists and planners, has submitted an outline plan that is as unusual as it is audacious. Nothing with its combination of scientific reconstruction and of new building projects has been tried elsewhere on a comparable scale.

Appropriate scale, as defined by the roads and pedestrian ways that constitute the Inner Ring, is to be restored to the city centre and important spaces within it, such as the Pirnaischer Platz and the Post-platz, are to be laid out as town squares. Building will also continue along the basic structure provided by the radials, which, like the spokes of a wheel, lead out from the core and the Inner Ring to the Outer, so-called 26th Ring, and beyond, and which, at their intersections, form a chain of notable squares, each of which has lost its character and its quality. The most important spoke of this wheel is certainly the Prager Strasse, meeting Ring 26 at the Wiener Platz, which lies in front of the main railway station. This important square is now, after a successful competitive tendering exercise, beginning to take shape again. Similarly, large areas in the Lennéplatz and Strassburger Platz, on Ring 26, call for equally responsible schemes.

Dresden is renowned for its position on the Elbe, for its striking skyline, so often painted by Canaletto, and for its bridges joining the old town on the left bank and the new town on the right, which are together encircled by the 26th Ring. The exceptional quality of this river scene calls for very special attention. Kulka's building for the Landtag, the legislature, sets a standard for new construction affecting the skyline of the old town, as does the projected new Congress Centre immediately adjacent to it, which will ensure the integration of Erlwein's bulky warehouse on the Ufer Terrace.

It is, however, not only the physical appearance of the city centre that gives Dresden its special character. Charming district centres like the Körnerplatz and the Schillerplatz by the bridge, known as the Blue Wonder, the carefully developed slopes above the Elbe with their strong covering of green, splendid large residential areas, parts of the town going back to the late nineteenth century, and the centres of many attractive old villages – all these give character to the structure of the city. To preserve this character and its variety, whilst nevertheless allowing freedom to builders wherever possible, is an important part of the city's urban development strategy. Here, too, there is an area of tension, leading time and again to conflict between, on the one side, the sometimes unscrupulous investors who bring pressure to bear, and on the other side, the planners, conservationists and landscape architects who advise caution.

With its situation in the valley of the Elbe, Dresden calls for particular care in the formulation of its development strategy. A specially created Planning Staff for Strategic Urban Development is taking an overall view of the landscaping of the town, ensuring the integration of the wider city into its setting in the upper Elbe Valley. Important conclusions with regard not only to land utilization and landscape but also to smaller scale planning should flow from this.

The fields of work vary widely and the build-up of problems at every level is formidable. We must hope that Dresden's wounds can be healed and that it will stand again among Europe's greatest cities.

Dresden's Architectural Traditions and its Surviving Heritage

Alan Russell

The Origins of the *Gesamtkunstwerk*; Dresden as a Work of Art

For a city whose name became a byword for great architecture, Dresden was a latecomer. Compared with the other Electorates into which the Hohenstaufen Empire was divided in the early thirteenth century – the great ecclesiastical centres of Cologne, Mainz, Trier and the secular Electorates of Prague, Vienna and Berlin – Saxony was of small account. Four centuries elapsed before Dresden became Saxony's royal capital and during this time it regularly lost whatever notable buildings it had in the fires that ravaged the city every five to 10 years. In the great fire of 1491, indeed, it lost over 50% of its timber and mortar houses and it was never counted as one of Germany's leading medieval cities (such as Nuremberg, Rothenburg and Lübeck). Apart from its fortifications and Castle, the only significant buildings that it carried into the modern age were its twelfth-century Gothic Kreuzkirche with its unusual oblong tower, the original Romanesque Frauenkirche with its fifteenth-century Gothic choir (which stood outside the city walls until 1547); the Franciscan monastery whose chapel survived the Lutheran revolution as the Sophienkirche; and a few stone-built Gothic houses, like the single survivor that stood on the corner of the Wilsdruffer Strasse and the Schlossstrasse until 1945.

From the start, however, the city had huge natural assets in its setting alongside the broad stream and meadows of the Elbe and in its mild summer climate, which, under what Heinrich von Kleist described in 1813 as its 'Italian sky', allowed the grapes and clematis to thrive. As anyone who has

Figure 39. Dresden's medieval fortress, transformed in the sixteenth century into an Italianate Renaissance Castle with its exceptional s'graffito decoration, as shown in models displayed in the Residence. Courtesy of the Staatliche Kunstsammlungen, Desden.

walked the Elbeside meadows under the summer sun will know, something of the warmth and generosity of the Mediterranean is present there and nature has consistently exercised a powerful influence over the city's life, culture and thought. When the Italian Renaissance arrived, along with the new independence of mind wrought by Lutheranism and the combination of firm governance and aesthetic sensitivity that characterized so many of the Wettins, its basic ideas of beauty, harmony and form found a receptive environment in Dresden.

The city's sixteenth-century development was not as dramatic as in some other contemporary cities such as Augsburg and Würzburg; it was steady and above all incremental. Georg der Bärtige, George the Bearded (1500–39) built the Georgentor and Moritz (1541–43) embellished it; Moritz built the Castle tower and Christian I (1586–91) did further work on it; Christian I and Christian II (1586–1611) erected the elegant Lustpalast or Belvedere, in effect a House of Pleasure, which, with its tall windows and flowing concave roof, anticipated Pillnitz; and Georg I (1611–56) retained the services of Wilhelm Dillich to complete the Riesensaal, the Great Apartment, in the east wing of the Palace with an exceptionally fine timbered ceiling.

Creativity and continuity thus enriched each other – and the city. The elaborate s'graffito decoration of the Castle's inner and outer walls was among the best to be seen outside the warmer climes of Italy; the Stallhof, with its Tuscan columns and beautiful arcades, was by any standards a fine Renaissance building, and the mere fact that the Belvedere rose on the top of the newly fortified Bastei (where the city's fortifications, or Casemates, can now be visited) aptly symbolized Dresden's transformation from a defensive trading outpost into a city in which culture played a significant role. By the early seventeenth century it was well on the way to becoming a noteworthy Renaissance city and, although the Thirty Years War (1618–48) constituted a long and grievous interruption in its development, the creation of the *Gesamtkunstwerk* had most certainly begun. As the Dresden cultural historian and post-war conservationist Walter Hempel has observed 'the art of the Renaissance was the direct forerunner of baroque and rococo and formed one continuous sequence with them' – and this should never be forgotten.

This continuity was assured both by the encouragement that the Wettins gave to Saxony's Craft Guilds and to architects and artists from outside. The Elector, Moritz, for example, brought in Breslau sculptor Christoph Walther to add the Totentanz (Dance of the Dead) and other ornamental sculptures to Hans Schicketanz's worthy but homespun Georgentor. Christian I similarly summoned the first Italian architect – Giovanni Maria Nosseni – to help his Surveyor of Works, Paul Buchner, with the Stallhof and the Belvedere. During the Thirty Years War more artists left than arrived but, within months of the signing of the Treaty of Westphalia (1648), a whole company of talented Germans who – like their great musical contemporary Schütz, had studied, lived and worked in Italy – made tracks for Dresden. The most notable were the architects Wolf Caspar von Klengel and Johann Georg Starcke, the Court sculptors Paul Heermann and Jeremias Süssner and the painters Samuel Bottschildt and Heinrich Fehling.

During the consecutive reigns of Georg II, III and IV (1656–94), when knowledge of Italian achievements and literature (for example, Serlio's great Compendium of Classical Architecture, *All the Works*) became far more widespread and taste turned increasingly to the freer, more exuberant and more individualistic baroque style, Dresden acquired its first real baroque interior in von Klengel's Comedy Theatre (1656–67) and its first great baroque palace (1679), designed by Starcke, in the Grosser Garten where the young Augustus the Strong watched it rise. Dresden also acquired its first planned district following the great fire of 1685 in Altendresden, where – inspired by the Piazza del Popolo in Rome – von Klengel laid out three wholly new axes leading to a central square. These linked the Neustadt, to the Elbe Bridge, to the Castle and to the Old Town beyond. The new streets were lined with baroque houses, which, combining German assurance with Italian elegance, marked a radical departure from the older Renaissance houses which until the 1660s had still betrayed (notably in their gabled roofs) the influence of Gothic form and tradition. In this period, also, the Royal Hunting Lodge at Moritzburg, and the chapels there, and in the Residence, were remodelled in the new style. The trend towards the baroque was clear and it took a decisive turn when, in 1690 and 1691, the two Italian-educated Germans reached Dresden, whose great 'north–south' double act of outstanding and complementary talents did so much for the 'Augustan Age', namely the Salzburg sculptor Balthasar Permoser and the Westphalian architect Matthäus Pöppelmann.

When Augustus the Strong ascended the throne in 1694, therefore, the lines of Dresden's architectural and cultural enrichment had already been sketched. The new Elector was however his own man and his impact was immediate. He was never afraid to bring in new architects and artists – such as the Frenchmen de Bodt and Longuelune, the Italian Mattielli and Dresden's own George Bähr of Frauenkirche fame – and to have them competing against each other. Despite his frequent absences in Poland and elsewhere, little escaped his eye. He had stringent new building regulations brought in (in 1708 and 1720) to lay down strict plans and built dimensions and to make the use of slate and stone obligatory; he insisted that the new houses built in the Friedrichstadt should be neither too high nor too close to the city walls; and when, for example, he discovered that Pöppelmann and Bähr's recently

Figure 40. Dresden's first great baroque palace, in the Grosser Garten. Courtesy of the Stadtplanungsamt, Dresden.

re-built Dreikönigskirche (Church of the Epiphany) straddled the line of the Neustadt's central axis, he instantly overrode both City and Parish and (at huge cost) had it moved. In similar vein, to satisfy his taste and to accommodate his Collections, he insisted that de Bodt add four corner towers to the Japanese (formerly Holländisches) Palace; he directed that the new bridge over the Elbe should be modelled on the Charles Bridge in Prague; and he had mile posts installed all over his land.

In central Dresden his influence made itself equally felt. When fire destroyed the eastern wing of the castle, he resisted the pressures brought to bear on him to have it not only rebuilt but enlarged. In the adjacent buildings of the Taschenberg Palace and the Zwinger and in the Frauenkirche, however, he gave an energetic lead, which his aristocratic and wealthy subjects were quick to follow. The 1720s were particularly fruitful: they saw Bähr's wonderfully inventive Palais de Saxe and the elegant British Hotel go up in the Landhausstrasse, the Wackerbarth and Courland Palaces rise nearby and the completion of Count Brühl's Palace on the Terrace that was to bear his name. Each one of these was a mini-masterpiece of baroque styling, yet each one individualistic in its design details. Even the less opulent private residences, such as the Dinglinger house that Pöppelmann designed for his friend and collaborator's family, contained pleasingly offbeat features like the unexpected adaptation of the classical orders. In so small and compact a city, their juxtaposition, in the shadow of the Castle and near the rising Frauenkirche, was striking indeed.

Conflict, Change and Growth in the Second Half of the Eighteenth Century

By the middle of the century the baroque impulse was waning. Augustus II was more interested in fine arts than in buildings. He dutifully completed the Frauenkirche with its Lantern and Orb and Cross (in place of the Obelisk that Bähr had originally planned) and he brought in Gaetano Chiaveri to design the splendid Catholic Hofkirche. His rapacious minister, Brühl, created a palace and a garden on the Terrace where at least his name survives. But Augustus II was unlucky. In 1747 a gunpowder explosion in the Bastei totally destroyed the Belvedere and 10 years later the Seven Years War broke out; this not only forced him into exile but brought unprecedented destruction to the city. The Prussian cannonballs mercifully rolled off the Frauenkirche's great Bell of Stone without doing significant damage to it; but three of the city's other great churches (the Kreuzkirche, the Annenkirche and the Dreikönigskirche) went up in flames and several of its palaces and public buildings (including the Guardhouse in the Neumarkt) were destroyed. Over 300 houses, mainly on the eastern side, lay in ashes. 'Dresden exists no more', wrote a contemporary reporter. 'Its greatest palaces and streets, where art and splendour sought to outdo each other are piles of rubble . . . its richest inhabitants have been impoverished and everything the fire left behind has fallen prey to thieves.'

The visiting Goethe was appalled but, as always, disaster and opportunity walked hand in hand. Friedrich August III (1763–1827) rapidly re-established the Academy of Art and was responsible for the appointment of Christian Ludwig von Hagedorn as Director, with other talented Germans – notably the architect Krubsacius and the sculptor Knöffel – in leading positions. Italian influence declined with the departure of Chiaveri but French influence (de Bodt, Longuelune and, most particularly, the young Blondel) remained significant and there were no abrupt changes of style. The Dreikönigskirche was rebuilt very much as Bähr and Pöppelmann had designed it and Bähr's influence could clearly be seen (though less since the nineteenth-century remodellings) in the designs produced by his pupil and successor, Johann Georg Schmidt, for the Kreuzkirche and the Annenkirche. In the few great or public buildings that went up, the pendulum swung this way and that – Schmidt's Kreuzkirche swung towards German solidity and simplicity, Krubsacius' beautiful Land-

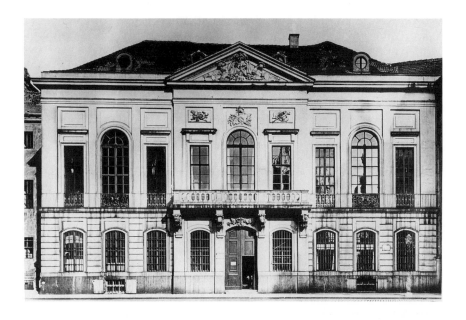

Figure 41. The Courland Palace, as built (above) and awaiting restoration (below). Courtesy of the Stadtplanungsamt, Dresden.

haus (see Plate 15) swung back towards a comfortable French baroque, and Christian Weinlig's Riding School stood somewhere between the two.

More important, however, than any question of style, was a significant change of patrons and therefore of priorities. With the Saxon Court and State being unable to spend with the profligacy of Augustus the Strong, matters of taste were determined more than ever by the aristocracy and the rising *haute bourgeoisie*. These provided the finance for the great houses that sprang up in the new streets that rose from the rubble to the east of the New Market, the Rampische Strasse, Pirnaische Strasse, Moritzstrasse, Kreuzstrasse, and others. Some brought older buildings back to life with new facades and gables but many more built from scratch on the ruins of war. Few of them were classical in any pure sense; traces of the baroque could still be seen, the influence of Blondel was especially strong, and flourishes of rococo ornamentation were not infrequently added to the exterior facades (even more it has to be said inside).

Yet there was a perceptible change, dictated no doubt by money as much as by taste, towards less ornamentation, quite often total abandonment of the orders, and greater overall simplicity. Number 10 Neumarkt, known as Stadt Rom (City of Rome) (1773), with its handsomely decorated corner balconies, is often cited as proof of continuity of style with the earlier more florid buildings; but it was indubitably plainer than it would have been if it had been erected 40 to 50 years earlier. Countless other houses had very little decoration at all, except around their rococo doors. The second half of the eighteenth century saw an increasing willingness to experiment and a greater eclecticism of style than had earlier been the case; but Dresden had to wait until 1833 before it acquired, in Karl Friedrich Schinkel's Altstädte-Wache (Old Town Guardhouse), a classical building of quality. By then socio-economic changes were rapidly altering the whole environment in which architects and their patrons lived and worked.

Enlarged, Industrialized Dresden

The Napoleonic invasions did not desecrate Dresden, as had the Prussian war, but Napoleon's edict that the city walls be demolished finally liberated it from its mediaeval constraints and meant that, with the arrival of the railways in the 1830s and the consequent growth in industry, the rapid and considerable extension of the city was inevitable. Gottlob Friedrich Thormeyer who gave the Annenkirche its tower (1823) and designed the steps leading to the Brühl Terrace, when the then Russian Governor, Count Repnin, opened this up for public enjoyment, was – perhaps – the last of the old school of architects. Instead of Italians and Frenchmen, the new architects – Schinkel, Semper and Nicolai – came from the north and were largely trained in Berlin. Gabriele Hoffman surely exaggerated when she wrote, in her novel *Constantia von Cosel* that 'in the 19th century everything that Augustus the Strong had created was forgotten or despised'. But the changes were certainly significant.

Gottfried Semper and Hermann Nicolai set the architectural pace and, indeed, created a robust northern Renaissance style that became known as the Dresden School. It can be seen in the surviving public buildings along the Brühl Terrace, in the governmental quarter across the river, and also in a number of villas. Elements of a gentler 'Palladian' style were still to be seen and, under the influence of Constantine Lipsius (Professor of Architecture at the Dresden Academy in the 1880s) the French mannerist style became more fashionable. A few Gothic Revival buildings went up (although fewer than in other German cities), the 1896 Old Town Exhibition generated a modest baroque come-back, and the end of the century saw (as in England but less markedly) the formalism and not infrequent pomposity of great houses give way to a more relaxed country-house style, pioneered by a number of architects and turned into a movement in 1907 by the *Deutscher Bund für Heimatschutz* (the German Association for the Preservation of Local Traditions). Even though the neo-Renaissance style of the Dresden School provided the period's leitmotiv, there was great variety of style.

In the twentieth century the Bauhaus School had its followers, but Dresden was never again at the forefront of architectural experimentation and development. Volkswagen's imaginative new glass-built factory – *das gläserne Manufaktur* – on the old exhibitions' site may mark a new beginning.

Dresden's Architectural Heritage Today

No one who knew, or knows, Dresden can be under any illusion about the extent of Dresden's architectural losses: hundreds of beautiful buildings of all periods, set within a cultured, cosmopolitan and balanced whole, have gone for ever. Given such losses, however, it is little short of astonishing that so much remains. A journey through the Castle, the Taschenberg Palace, the Zwinger Complex, the Opera, and the Catholic Cathedral; westwards to the Friedrichstadt; back through the Great Garden to Blasewitz, Loschwitz and the Villas; up and down the Elbe to some of the Castles and Palaces; across to the Garden Village of Hellerau; and finally to the site of the Frauenkirche will amply underline the point that, with the sole and grievous exception of the Old City's baroque houses, examples of all the influences that have shaped Dresden over the years can still be seen.

Figure 42. The Theaterplatz today – Hofkirche, Residenz and Altstädtewache. Courtesy of the Stadtplanungsamt, Dresden.

The Theaterplatz

The Theaterplatz is once more one of Europe's great architectural ensembles; and the Residenzschloss (the Royal Castle), which dominates it, is the oldest, most extensive and most representative of all Dresden's great monuments. Standing on the site of the twelfth century Fortress, its basic modern form was created in the mid-sixteenth century by architects Hans von Dehn-Rothfelser and Caspar Voigt von Wierandt, although it has been much extended and restored (1674, 1679, 1701, 1833 etc.). Its essential plan has survived unaltered: a large courtyard (containing the Great Apartment on its eastern side and crowned on its western side by the great seventeenth-century Hausmann Tower); a smaller courtyard to the south, connected in the later eighteenth century by a first footbridge to the Taschenberg Palace; a great gateway over the Schlossstrasse recalling the name of the sixteenth-century Duke George the Bearded (the Georgentor), which became part of the Georgenbau residence of the heir to the throne; and a long arcade and gallery following the line of the old moat in the Augustusstrasse, to link these to the old stables now known as the Johanneum (1588) with its later 'English' steps. One of Europe's great Renaissance palaces, it was at the same time an intimate part of the overall life of the city.

The total destruction in 1945 of everything except its outer walls nearly provided the perfect excuse for ideologically motivated demolition. Indeed,

Figure 43. The Stallhof in 1934, with the Frauenkirche in the background. Courtesy of the Sächsische Landesbibliothek, Deutsche Fotothek.

had the Hausmann Tower not stood so close to the Court Church, it would have been blown up as early as 1945 or 1946. Alerted by this threat, however, the Conservation Department found excuse after excuse to use and therefore to secure the ruins, until, slowly, the tide of opinion began to turn and some rebuilding work was put in hand. Restoration did not seriously gather momentum until the 1990s, when private sponsorships came to the aid of the public purse in raising the approximately £200 million that was needed (more, even, than the likely rebuilding costs of the Frauenkirche). Since then, the authorities have expressly sought to proceed on the basis of the principles laid down by the International Council of Monuments and Sites (Icomos) in its 1964 Venice Charter, namely that 'a monument is inseparable from the history to which it bears witness' (Article 7) and that 'the valid contribution of all periods must be respected' (Article 11).

The street facades have therefore been rebuilt as they stood in the 1890s, after their restoration during the so called *Gründerzeit* (in effect the late Victorian period) in the Germanized neo-Renaissance style; but the courtyard walls are being brought back to their original Renaissance brilliance. Much of the s'graffito work has been recreated and this provides a fascinating glimpse of the exuberance that once characterized the whole building. With the robust form of the Georgentor, the slender and delicately floodlit spire of the Hausmann Tower, the beautifully pargetted stucco of the Stallhof (stables) and the dignified, simple Classicism of the Johanneum, they make an impressive group. Inside, the state rooms, including the Great Apartment, have been restored for museum use, along with the succession of ground floor rooms on the western Theaterplatz side, to which the *Grünes Gewölbe*

Collection is being returned. The lovely seventeenth-century Court Chapel where Schütz once played and prayed (before it was secularized by Friedrich August II when the Court Church was built) is also being restored to its splendid baroque original.

Thus whilst the Saxon Court has for ever gone, its great Castle still stands and, with the Taschenberg, Zwinger, Court Church and Opera House, sets the tone for the whole area around. The Saxon Princes who still parade in Meissen Tiles down the outer wall of the Stallhof (the Fürstenzug or Procession of the Princes) would be well pleased.

Augustus the Strong had the Taschenberg Palace built for his mistress, Countess Cosel. Standing just to the south-west of the Castle it was his first great building initiative and, thanks to an outstanding feat of reconstruction (1990–5), it is again one of Dresden's finest baroque/rococo palaces. Its central section – the first to be built – replaced five houses that the Countess bought in 1705/6 (for 36,000 talers) and stood on the site of a small swamp that had been undergoing drainage and clearance over many years, first by the Augustinian house that had once stood on the western side and later by Johann Georg II. Its imaginative and original baroque was the work of the State Architect Matthäus Pöppelmann and of Baumeister Christoph Beyer and had been more-or-less completed by the time that work on the neighbouring Zwinger began in 1709.

Like the Villa Torrigiano in Lucca, on which it was largely modelled, it was built with three entrance doors opening into an inner space with a great baroque double staircase leading to the living quarters on the first floor. Unlike the Villa Torrigiano, each level of the street facade was given its own original style of pediment and each pediment was set sufficiently high above the fenestration to allow full play, above the windows, for the skill of Dresden's baroque sculptors. Inside, the Countess spared no expense, creating the famous Blue Room and bringing in many fine pictures, gilded mirrors, Flemish tapestries and Middle-Eastern and Oriental *objets d'art*. Perhaps because of the slightly oriental style of the pediments and of many of the contents, it became briefly known as the 'Turkish House', after the Countess was removed from it on 13 September 1713 – first to house arrest in Pillnitz and subsequently to imprisonment in Stolpen.

In 1719 the Taschenberg Palace became the official home of the heir to the throne, when Kurfürst Augustus moved in with his bride Maria-Joseph, the Emperor's daughter. Between 1727 and 1746 it became a kind of general annexe to the Castle in which distinguished visitors could be lodged and many Court artists and craftsmen – Torelli, Thomae, Kugler, Höse, Wöhler and Knöffel – continued to work on it. In 1746 it again became the heir apparent's official residence until the Republic was declared in 1918. The

Figure 44. The Taschenberg Palace today, seen between the Altstädte Wache (left) and the *Gemäldegalerie Alte Meister*. Courtesy of Dr Alan Russell.

eastern and western wings were built between 1756 and 1762 by architects Julius Heinrich Schwarze and Christian Friedrich Exner, along with a southern service wing in the Kleine Brüdergasse. The full facade, as it is seen again today, was complete.

The Taschenberg Palace had, however, seen its heyday. In the nineteenth century the crown princes lived quietly in it and gave over parts of it to provide a home for various artistic bodies such as Prince John's *Academia Dantesca* and the Saxon Heritage Union (the *Altertumsverein*). Late nineteenth-century restorations did it no favours and following the abdication it went into steep decline, becoming successively a jam factory, the administrative centre of the State Theatre and – during the Second World War – the Dresden Army Command. After the war, the site was considered for a number of rather more worthy purposes: as a palace of culture when, in 1949, the Theaterplatz was briefly conceived as the main new city centre; as an academy of music and theatre (1952) for which Hans Nadler pleaded strongly 'in the interests of Dresden as a city of culture'; as a student hostel when, in 1957, Wolfgang Rauda was asked to prepare plans; as a state hotel (1964–78); as an academy of music again in 1978; and as a trade union holiday home and/or as a cultural institute and youth centre, in 1985. In 1990, following an open competition, designs for its full archaelogical reconstruction as a privately owned hotel were prepared by Dieter Schölzel and the Berlin-Dresden Institute for Cultural Buildings.

In little more than four years the total reconstruction of the palace was triumphantly achieved. Adaptations inevitably had to be made, for example to accommodate the hotel reception in the west wing and to enable under-ground garaging to be created; but, here too, work was done according to the best Icomos principles. Thus: the great baroque staircase was rebuilt exactly as it was in 1707/9; the spatial proportions of the Chapel were recreated (though with other purposes in view); the Blue Room was reassembled as far as possible; the southern facade (i.e. of the original Palace, and of its eastern and western wings) was rebuilt as it stood in 1767 (that is, without the balconies added in the nineteenth century); the southern wing in the Kleine Brüdergasse was recreated as it was in the 1850s; the nineteenth-century hip roofs were replaced with original-type double mansards; Knöffler's exquisite fountains in the western Court have been fully repaired; and his equally wonderful sculptures of Mars and Minerva with cherubs between, have been put back where they originally stood, on the northern wall of the interior courtyard. Today, therefore, as in the late eighteenth century, the Taschenberg's sculptural reliefs present the evolution of Saxon (indeed of German) sculpture from early eighteenth century high baroque, to more disciplined later German romanticism. For both artistic and historical reasons, it is therefore, a building that merits rather more than a passing glance; and it wonderfully restores the view presented in Bellotto's 1758 painting – looking eastwards, across the Zwinger.

The Zwinger was Augustus the Strong's second great creation. His dream of creating a new complex of palaces and museums there failed to come to fruition, as surely as did Charles I's hope of making Wren's banqueting hall the first step towards a new Whitehall Palace. But the reality was perhaps nobler than the plan: a uniquely beautiful enclosed baroque garden – open to ordinary people for most of its existence – in which the arts and sciences were celebrated. Pöppelmann, who built it, found inspiration in Prague and Vienna for its impressive combination of discipline and exuberance; and if, as has been said, 'the stuccoed windows seem to come from France', its water motifs, including the nymphs bath, are surely Italian. Below the faded inscription 'ARP' (Augustus Rex Poloniae) on the Crown Gate, Polish eagles and two-headed Imperial eagles co-exist, and amongst the voluptuous sculptures of Permoser, Heermann and Kretzschmar, the Greek gods, Lithuanian knights and Solomon the Jew are to be found. Gottfried Semper's nineteenth-century gallery, which fills in the northern side (where the classically colonnaded but temporary wooden gallery that Augustus the Strong erected for the wedding of his son to Maria-Joseph once stood) may be heavy by comparison with Pöppelmann's eighteenth-century pavilions, but his rounded windows, with their Ionic columns, pick up the earlier rhythms, and the writers and artists who gaze out from their niches over the manicured lawns are worthy companions for the Putten (cherubs) and the shepherdesses so beloved of the Dresdeners.

It is hard to believe that so much of the beauty still to be seen in the Zwinger dates from the twentieth century. But today's visitors should reflect not only on Pöppelmann, Permoser and Semper but also on Hubert Ermisch who in the 1930s gave the Zwinger the steel and concrete foundations that kept at least some of the walls standing in 1945, when he once again took charge of rebuilding. They should also reflect on the architect and conservationist Hans Nadler who returned after the war, to the Conservation Department, to help him. And they should reflect on the many ordinary Dresdeners who, in extraordinarily difficult times, contributed generously to the post-war Zwinger Lottery. The advertising display that peeps over the top of the Town Pavilion, is scarcely an improvement on the lost nineteenth-century spires of the Church of St Sophia but the so-often altered views contrive, again, to appear unchanged. If Goethe called the Brühl Terrace the 'balcony of Europe', the Zwinger might justly be called its showcase.

The third great eighteenth-century baroque building in the Theaterplatz is the Catholic Hofkirche, built between 1738 and 1756. Augustus the Strong never gave his conversion to Roman Catholicism enduring expression in a new building. He contented himself with equipping Dresden's first Comedy Theatre/Opera for temporary ecclesiastical use, where Permoser's wonderful baroque pulpit was installed before being transferred at a later date to the Cathedral. Reasons of state prevented him from going further. It took his son, Friedrich August III, to overcome these and, six years into his reign (in 1739), to commission ' a great building between the Royal Palace and the Bridge'. Significantly, he did not dare to mention the real nature of the project and he chose to go not to any of Dresden's well-known, well-qualified and Lutheran-minded architects, (Knöffel, de Bodt, Longuelune, Schwarze and Bähr) who might have asked too many questions but to Chiaveri, the Roman with a proven track record in St Petersburg and elsewhere. Chiaveri brought with him the painter Torelli and the sculptor Mattielli and a half dozen other Italian artists who established the so-called little Italian Village (*das Italienische Dörfchen*), remembered to this day in the name of the nineteenth-century restaurant building that stands on the river side of the Theaterplatz (to the west of the pre-war Bellevue Hotel). Ironically, Chiaveri left for Italy in 1749 because he was unable to collaborate conveniently with anyone and two of the sidelined Dresdeners, Knöffel and then Schwarze, had to assume responsibility for the completion of the Hofkirche, for such it was. In the end the Dresdeners came to love their masterpiece of high Italian baroque; since 1980 it has been the Cathedral Church of the Dresden and Meissen Diocese and its bells, silent for the first 50 years to avoid offence to the Lutheran majority, rang out with those of 90 or more other churches when, on 13 February 1995, Dresden mourned its dead and celebrated its rebirth.

Nowhere is this rebirth more vivid than in the Cathedral itself. Many things of value were lost in 1945 – great Austrian late baroque frescoes (Maulbertsch) and important sculptures like Bernini's *John the Baptist*. But many more have been saved and/or restored: Permoser's superb pulpit, Mengs' wonderful painting of the Ascension, over the high altar, Hutin's *Crucifixion* in the Kreuzkapelle and even the superb organ designed by Silbermann. In the luminous, newly decorated interior these are shown off to outstanding effect. Indeed, the great 50m wide aisles and nave, with their interposed collonaded passage-ways, may never have looked as splendid as they now do. And the Cathedral's great bulk, which from the sides has an almost Palladian simplicity, makes a statement of great force from whichever angle it is seen – from the Brühl Terrace, from the Zwinger, from the Italian Village, or from across the bridge. Mattielli's 59 statues, each 3.5 metres high, look out again across Castle, Elbe and Theaterplatz and the cleverly sited oval tower, fortunately loftier than Chiaveri had originally sketched it, impresses with its strength from the front and with its slender elegance from the sides. With the increase in Catholic numbers wrought by successive migrations, the Hofkirche can truly be said to have come home.

Until Dresden's fortifications came down in the years leading up to 1829, it had looked out across open land, towards the Königliche Stalle, the Royal Stables, on the western side of the Zwinger's moat, and beyond to the Friedrichstadt and the then wild open spaces of Ostragehege. Unsurprisingly, therefore, when (in 1834) the renowned Berlin classical architect, Friedrich Schinkel, sent for Gottfried Semper, from Hamburg, to become Professor of Architecture in Dresden's Academy of Arts, his ambitious and talented young protégé quickly turned his mind to the preparation of an overall plan for the area. With courage and imagination, he proposed that the size of the Zwinger be doubled by considerably extending its eastern and western axes in the direction of the Elbe, by a museum building on the old theatre side, and by an Orangery close to the Taschenberg and Castle. His ideas were worthy of Augustus the Strong himself and were welcomed by the artistically inclined Prince Regent Johann (the future Dante scholar). It even implied the removal of Schinkel's ascetically elegant and newly erected Altstädte Wache (Old Town Guardhouse). It was however refused by the City Council and Semper turned his attention to other briefs: the Maternity Hospital, the Synagogue (1839) – which stood next to the Albertinum until the *Kristallnacht* in 1938, the new Court Theatre and Opera House (1841), the Gemäldegalerie (1849), a limited number of Villas and, for a second time following a fire, the Opera House, during the years 1871–8.

Semper's architecture was a conscious attempt to breathe fresh life into the early Italian Renaissance style and his influence in, and impact on, nineteenth-century Dresden was enormous. The synagogue, built in a kind of Roman-Moorish style, was original and impressive and his first rebuilding of the Theatre and the Opera House produced a severely classical, colonnaded building with a powerful semi-circular front facade which stood in no little stylistic contrast to the Hofkirche opposite it, yet complemented it well. In 1849 he helped man the revolutionary barricades and had to flee from Dresden whilst work on the Gemäldegalerie was still under way. His successors, Kruger and Hänel, failed to complete it with the high, fenestrated and sculpture-bedecked dome that he had envisaged and when it was rebuilt after the Second World War, it was (unfortunately) their squat little cupola that was reproduced (see Plate 17).

When Semper's revolutionary ardour had cooled and been forgiven and his services retained once more for the second rebuilding of the Opera House, he sought – perhaps to compensate himself for the damage done to his design for the Gemäldegalerie – by building the wider, more exuberant and more baroque Opera House that (rebuilt with near archaeological exactitude) can be seen today. The great auditorium where, in February 1995, Mahler's Resurrection Symphony was played to a spellbound audience, is breathtaking in its sweep and colour; and on the outside walls of the good modern extension built behind it to provide practice rooms and other support facilities, a much loved modern gargoyle, tongue-protruding, records a sense of political frustration that, until recently, the Dresdeners could not otherwise articulate. Visitors should look for it! They should also stand alongside Schilling's statue of King Johann Georg, 1854–1873, in the middle of a square to which Semper contributed so much, and reflect that although it was not completed as the young Semper would have wished, it is splendid nevertheless.

The Friedrichstadt

A much smaller, but nevertheless interesting ensemble had, meanwhile, been growing up just outside the city walls to the west, known since 1728 as the Friedrichstadt (after the then Crown Prince). In the seventeenth century it was a kitchen garden area, providing rich and titled Dresdeners with a combination of provisions and summer pleasures. Elector Johann Georg II (1656–80) tried to develop it as, in effect, Dresden's first suburban settlement, by offering artisans and traders freedom from commercial restrictions and a 10-year tax break. Defeated by the City Guilds, his idea failed to prosper and in 1720 there were still only 18 houses there.

Through his usual combination of patronage and the pursuit of women, Augustus the Strong again proved a more effective catalyst for change. 'Out of affection', it is recorded, he gave the Countess von Manteuffel permission (in 1720) to build one of the area's first industries – a brewery. Out of necessity, no doubt, he established Dresden's first Catholic cemetery in 1721 and, a little later, a Catholic hospital. Six years on, he acquired the plot in the Friedrichstrasse, next to the brewery, as a gift for his then mistress, the Duchess of Würtemburg and procured the services of architect Johann Christoph Neumann to design and build the fine baroque Summer Palace for her. In 1728 he commissioned Pöppelmann, of Zwinger and Taschenberg fame, to build a Lutheran Church, the Matthäuskirche; and in 1729 he had a complete building plan drawn up for the erection of several streets of three-storey stone houses, for which plot size, height and roof design were laid with some care: they were to be of good quality, but smaller than the city buildings and not too near the walls! A few more signs of industry came in – a glass and saltpetre works and a wax factory – but the rural idyll was little disturbed.

The Summer House, however, prospered. Following Friedrich August's death, it came into the hands of his minister, Count Heinrich Brühl, who, with his immense fortune, commissioned several well-known Dresden architects and artists (including Knöffel and Longuelune) and the Italian Mattielli (of Taschenberg and Hofkirche fame) to build an Orangery, enlarge the Palace and beautify the grounds. Mattielli's Neptune Fountain was perhaps the masterpiece. When Brühl fell from power and died in 1768, there was a period of decay. In 1774 however, the Palace was acquired by one of Brühl's ministerial successors, Count Marcolini who, this time, through Wiskotschele and Dorsch, had it further embellished. Significantly, the young Goethe chose to lodge in one of the nearby Friedrichstrasse houses (in fact the shoemaker's) when, in March 1968, he paid his first visit to Dresden. Some years later, in 1813, Napoleon selected the Summer Palace as his headquarters and as the venue for his famous meeting with Metternich; and the nearby Ostragehege, lying on the Elbe, to the north, provided a fitting location for troop inspections and reviews. At this time, the area was still as spacious and beautiful as Caspar David Friedrich portrayed it on canvas in 1832, with a fine view across the Elbe of the lovely Castle at Übigau, now Dresden's 'lost baroque pearl' – lost, that is, in a dilapidated and industrialized zone.

In the first half of the nineteenth century, peace, quiet and artistic endeavour resumed their sway. Master builder Ernst Julius Hänel chose the Orangery as his studio for work (1844–54) on the Gemäldegalerie and the Opera House whilst, two floors up, Richard Wagner completed Lohengrin (1849) and planned the Mastersingers.

Change, however, was in the air. In the same year the conversion of the Summer House into Dresden's first great research hospital began and with the arrival of the Berlin railway (1839), the progressive encirclement of the Friedrichstadt by a combination of goods yards, port facilities and factories began in earnest. The erection of Seidel and Naumann's huge typewriter and sewing-machine factory in the Hamburger Strasse in 1884, and of the Yenidze or tobacco factory in 1908 were symptomatic of a growing trend towards industrialization, and the covering or canalizing of the area's little river, the Weisseritz, seemed to state with some finality that the idyllic period was over. The combination of bombing in 1945 and of communist replanning thereafter nearly gave the Friedrichstadt its *coup de grâce;* the 1967 Structure Plan envisaged a wholly new quarter and, notwithstanding the repairs effected on some of the older buildings, notably the fine baroque houses at 29 and 33 Friedrich Strasse, the demolition of properties continued (for example in the Schäferstrasse) right up to 1989.

Miraculously, important elements survive. The hospital has been beautifully refurbished and its gardens restored. It contains significant segments of Augustus', Brühl's and Marcolini's work – including Mattielli's great fountain – and it must be counted among the two or three greatest surviving baroque palaces in the city. Pöppelmann's church has been faithfully rebuilt; the eighteenth-century schoolhouse in the appropriately named Seminarstrasse can still be seen and more baroque and nineteenth-century houses are being restored. The Seidel and Naumann factory has been converted into a Technical Institute, the once-despised Yenidze houses gastronomic and other leisure and business facilities under its colourful glass dome; and plans are afoot to extend the Elbe walks and roads westwards from the Theaterplatz past Kulka's fine Modernist State Parliament Building and Erlwein's *Speicher* towards the new Exhibition Halls being cleverly carved out of the old slaughter house complex (shades of Kurt Vonnegut!). The many and multi-national clientèle of the Friedrichstadt's Catholic Ceme-tery – German, Polish, Italian and other – can once more rest in peace.

Dresden's Villas, Big and Small

Many of the suburbs that grew up after the city's fortifications came down in the early nineteenth century displayed a bourgeois bravura that was, perhaps, very special to Dresden. The villas that sprang up (in the Wilsdruffer Vorstadt) between the Friedrichstadt and the Central Station, in the Südvorstadt (in the Swiss and English quarters), along the Wiener Strasse, in the southern Johannstadt (alongside the Grosser Garten), and through Blasewitz and beyond, were phenomenal in their number, splendour and scale. They were, moreover, set in generous individual plots and, however heterogeneous were their styles, typically effective Saxon building regulations ensured that the mass and proportions of the buildings were kept in scale. In Blasewitz in 1880, for example, 98% of all buildings were detached, in Loschwitz all except those around the Körnerplatz, and in the old spa town of Weisser Hirsch every single one.

Great swathes of Dresden's Villadom were, alas, destroyed in the firestorm of 1945 or were demolished to make way for the regimented social housing of the later 1940s, 1950s and 1960s. The English and Swiss quarters have vanished as surely as the thousands of foreigners who once lived in them; Semper's splendid Villa Rosa (in effect the Chiswick House of Dresden) and Nicolai's Villa Struve (which had been more influential than any other two single buildings) were lost and almost none of the beautiful baroque and German Renaissance villas that stretched from the Courland Palace to the green strip of the Bürgerwiese on northern and southern sides of Karcher's Great (once French-style) Garden have survived. It is hard now, if not impossible, to visualize the old splendour. All that visitors can do is to walk from the city centre, past the Hygiene Museum – one of the very few fine buildings put up in Weimar Dresden – into the centre of Dresden's great green area and allow their imagination to run riot. The baroque palace that Georg Starcke designed in 1680 for Johann Georg II was the first and perhaps the greatest of many and has been well described as the prelude to the symphony that followed.

Beyond the Great Garden, sits Blasewitz, an independent township until 1921, which was fortunately little damaged in 1945 and is now, in its entirety, an historic monument; beyond, on the Loschwitz Heights, many fine houses similarly survive, with scintillating views across the city. Down the Bautzner Strasse towards the dilapidated but partly surviving old Prussian quarter near the Antonstadt, Dresden's three great mid-nineteenth-century Elbe-side castles (in effect sumptuous villas) can still be seen. Two of these, the Villa Stockhausen (1853) and the Albrechtsberg (1854) were designed by one of Karl Friedrich Schinkel's pupils, Adolf Lohse, who clearly brought his Berlin training and influences with him. The Villa Stockhausen became known as the Lingnerschloss, after the founder of the Odol firm, whilst the Albrechtsberg recalls not only the Villa d'Este but also 19th Century Potsdam Classicism. The third, Castle Eckberg (1861), was the work of one of Dresden's few Gothic revival architects, Christian Friedrich Arnold, and is rather reminiscent of sixteenth-century English Tudor Gothic, or indeed of Strawberry Hill. Other villas that survive and deserve mention, in some sort of order of stylistic evolution, are: the Semper – influenced early (1835) Villa at 17 Bautzner Strasse – well preserved by the bank that occupies it; Theodore Lehnert's beautifully simple Italianate Villa Thorwald (1852) in the Schiller Strasse; one or two surviving villas in the University area (which bordered the English quarter), for example, the villa at 7 Liebig Strasse (1875); Oskar Kaiser's Rosenhof (1886) in Loschwitz, Gotthilf Ludwig Möckel's neo-Gothic villa (1878) at 18 Leubnitzer Strasse; Karl Scherz's Villa Rothermund (1897) at 34 Mendelsohn Allee with its splendid Jugendstil or Art Nouveau interior; the extraordinary Villa San Remo in Loschwitz (1900), from which American

Figure 45. Oskar Kaiser's Rosenhof in Loschwitz, built for and still occupied by the Hoch family. Courtesy of Dr. Karl Ludwig Hoch.

Figure 46. Gottfried Semper's fine Villa Rosa – destroyed in 1945. Courtesy of the Stadtplanungsamt, Dresden.

industrialist John Noble was (quite falsely!) said to have guided in Allied planes with a lamp; and Scherz's splendid example of the half-timbered English style (1901/2) at 18 Goetheallee. There are a number of others – some like the lovely Villa Eschebach (1901) in the Albertplatz that have been restored or rebuilt – and no-one interested in architecture and in historic Dresden should fail to explore them.

By the early twentieth-century the boom in villa building was clearly over; the economy was in recession and there was a change of mood. Just as in England, William Morris sought to promote craft, care and conservation, and Ebenezer Howard promoted his Garden City Movement as at once a planning concept and a philosophy of life, so in Dresden Karl Schmidt (1873–1948), Richard Riemerschmid, Hermann Muthesius, and others founded Hellerau on the north-eastern fringes of Dresden as an alternative to the utilitarian conditions produced by late nineteenth-century capitalism. Muthesius (one of whose descendents is, interestingly, the author of the classic work on English terraced housing) gave his houses an unmistakably English look, whereas his colleague Heinrich Tessenow gave the Festival Theatre a modern classical appearance: after decades of neglect by successive occupying armies this fine building is now being restored, with the help of the Getty Foundation and the University of Warwick. The little suburban village that once welcomed such great artists as Hauptmann, Kokoschka, Rilke, Kafka and Bernard Shaw is coming to life again. With the baroque palaces and the Villas it is, in its own small way, part of Dresden's contribution to Europe's architectural identity.

The Royal Palaces down the Valley of the Elbe

At the other extreme from Hellerau, with its vernacular and democratic roots, is the great chain of Royal Palaces and Gardens that stretches from Meissen's Albrechtsberg (1471–1525) to Moritzburg and Übigau, on to the Japanese Palace in the Neustadt, and through the city centre and the Great Garden to Pillnitz and Grosssedlitz (see Plate 14). As much as Dresden itself they express the history and taste of an era. Moritzburg takes its name from the Hunting Lodge erected in the sixteenth century by the Elector Moritz (1541–53) but it was substantially remodelled in the baroque style by Augustus the Strong and speaks volumes about the man. With its four powerfully rounded corner towers, it is masculine and strong and the waters in which it is reflected on all sides (and which separate it from the little town) seem redolent of Saxon absolutism. In the interior, dominated by antlers and leather wall hangings, there is little subtlety or femininity. Only Wolf Caspar von Klengel's baroque chapel (1661–1672) and Johann Daniel Schade's delicious *Fasananschlösschen*, the Little Castle of the Pheasants, (1769–1782) add a softer touch.

Pillnitz is the other side of the coin – artistic, oriental, delicate. The early von Loss palace (1610–1633) erected in the Renaissance style, the two new wings built in the 1720s – the *Berg*/Hill and *Wasser*/Water Palaces added elegance and fantasy. They represent some of Pöppelmann's and Longuelune's best work: a rich blend of baroque proportions, Chinese motifs and Saxon craftsmanship. The Chinese Pavilion, added in 1804, is said to be the best of its kind in Europe and the New Palace which replaced the late Renaissance building destroyed by fire in 1818, is a fine example of early neo-classicism in Dresden; its Catholic Chapel is well worth a visit. Around all of these buildings the gardens are a valuable history of landscape styles, from the pure baroque to the informal English. Together with the baroque gardens, and the house across the Elbe at Grossedlitz that Augustus the Strong acquired from Count Wackerbarth in 1723, they demonstrate the taste, harmony and design that overlay, and perhaps depended on, the absolutism of the eighteenth-century Wettins.

The Frauenkirche

In the case of Dresden's greatest building, the Frauenkirche, this absolutism can, however, be deemed to have been less important, if only because, since 1539, the living had been under the patronage of the city fathers. Augustus the Strong nevertheless took a very close interest in it. He played on the differences of view expressed by the major protagonists – the architects Johann Christoph Knöffel and Johann Georg Schmid, the Superintendent of Buildings Count Wackerbarth and (together with Johann Christian Fehre) George Bähr himself – and received Bähr an unprecedented five times to discuss design details with him. Along with the city council, Augustus also did all he could to keep costs down (the original estimate of 103,000 talers came down to 82,555 talers before rising – on the back of a beer tax and of funds extracted from Protestant refugees from Salzburg – to 288,510).

The designs prepared by George Bähr, which were finally agreed in 1726, were therefore of somewhat mixed provenance. Bähr was forced to set aside his early plans for a bell tower, or for twin towers, at the western end and to accept the square-shaped ground plan in the form of a Greek cross that has been attributed to Christoph Knöffel. However, in the face of persistent structural doubt, expressed inter alia by Schmid and Fehre, his preference for a stone cupola that would rise uninterruptedly from the walls beneath rather than a more usual copper-clad timber roof (of the kind seen at St Paul's, London, and on the Radcliffe Camera in Oxford) prevailed. It is recorded that Dresden's carpenters were displeased but the suppliers of the milk and quark used to mix the mortar no doubt saw their profits increase handsomely.

Schmid had his say after Bähr's death, when he had Bähr's design for a solid stone obelisk to top the roof set aside in favour of his own design for an open (and consequently structurally lighter) lantern with an Orb and Cross above, for the renewal of which the Dresden Trust has successfully raised the funds. Bähr, however, the undoubted genius of the project had the last laugh when the archaelogical investigations undertaken prior to beginning the rebuilding of the church in the 1990s revealed that the eighteenth-century foundations underneath the eight load-bearing columns had, in fact, been laid with considerably greater strength than Bähr's critics (contemporary and more recent) had been led to believe.

Bähr did not live to see his unique building finished but, in words that bring to mind the dedication that Elgar wrote on his Dream of Gerontius, his reflections are recorded in the following way on his tombstone in the crypt.

> Now I have lived, built, suffered enough,
> Struggled enough with Satan, sin and the world.
> Now I lie in the building that soars above.
> I have achieved complete victory and rest in peace.
> My loved ones, take God as your Husband and Father
> In whose faith no one can decay.

It is good to believe that these thoughts inspire the designers, managers and workers of today.

The rebuilding of the Frauenkirche will not be fully complete until 2005 or 2006; the baroque masterpiece cannot yet be seen. But the visitor to Dresden can be guided through the wonderful new sandstone vaulted crypt, where the British sculptor Amish Kapoor's marble altarpiece now stands a few steps from Bähr's re-assembled tombstone. The visitor can see, in the rapidly rising church above the galleries with their 48 prayer rooms, many of the 2,800 places that the church will provide for worshippers, music lovers and concert goers. In a few years' time, Silbermann's organ, Feige's pulpit and Johann Baptist Grone's fine ceiling frescoes will have been recreated and the greatest of baroque churches will grace the city again with, at its pinnacle, a recreation of Schmidt's Orb and Cross, manufactured in the United Kingdom, and given by its people.

It only remains to restore to the Frauenkirche as much as possible of its historic Neumarkt setting. The adjacent Cosel Palace is a good start and the city authorities have pledged themselves to recreate as many as possible of the old baroque houses that once graced the Salzgasse, the Rampische Strasse, the Moritz (or Landhaus) strasse and the Jüdenhof. A pressure group – the *Gesellschaft Historischer Neumarkt Dresden* – has been established to hold them to their word.

The Rebuilding of the Frauenkirche in Dresden

Engineer Eberhard Burger, Director of Construction

Since 1992, as Director of Construction, I have been responsible for the rebuilding of the Frauenkirche. This assignment has given a new direction to my specialist and professional development and has left its mark on my personal life. Many people live, like me, for the day when this wonderful edifice will be restored to Dresden, to Saxony, to Germany and to Europe as a House of God, contributing to peace and reconciliation in our world and giving us hope for the future.

The first task in 1992 was to make those parts of the ruin still standing safe. From 1993 to May 1994, during the archaelogical clearing of the site, some 20,000 cubic metres of heaped-up rubble were removed, of which about one-third was salvaged for re-use in the new building. The same month saw the symbolic beginning of the rebuilding with the laying of the first reclaimed and repaired stone as part of the door frame of Entrance A. At the same time, the constructional elements preserved under the rubble and now uncovered were renovated and strengthened to bear the load of the building to be reconstructed.

By the beginning of 1996 a start had been made on the collapsed vault of the basement and, by May of that year, about 6,800 vaulting stones had been laid. To make the western barrel-vault we refurbished stones taken from the pillars of the bridge at Torgau (dismantled in 1994) on which, just before the end of the disaster of the Second World War, Allied troops and Russian soldiers shook hands. And so, at every service and event that takes place in the crypt (consecrated in August 1996), we have around us a reminder of both guilt and friendship. It is very important to me that we are making immediate use of these former burial and basement areas below what will eventually be the church. Even during the construction period, full services of prayer and vigil are being held in which we can be grateful and give thanks to God for the years of peace and friendship that we have now had.

Concurrently with the work on the historical building, an outer construction of reinforced concrete was inserted around the ground plan of the building, enabling us to create underground technical and supply facilities. Then, in August 1996, we made a start on the outer walls at ground level and above, and thus on the visible part of the church.

This first stage involved about 2,100 m³ of sandstone masonry for the walls, the stair treads, and the building stones for the facade. During the winter we enveloped the entire building in plastic sheets and heated it so that the limestone mortar could set hard, as is necessary, at a minimum temperature of +5 °C (41 F). The stones that were to be laid in a given working day were stored in pre-warming containers at a temperature of +12 °C (54 F). They were then transported to the building, covered in its plastic sheets, from 4.00 in the morning till 6.30 in the evening, and were used up during the normal working shift. It was a hard winter, with temperatures down to –22 °C ; nevertheless, using radiant propane gas heaters, we were able to maintain the temperature and work every day. In this way a minimum of about 150 jobs were secured throughout, and this fact alone justified the extra cost incurred.

In this section (about 8m above ground level) we were only able to use 267 recovered and repaired pieces from the rubble heap into the outer face of the wall, as the degree of destruction was naturally greater in the lower levels than higher up. During this phase, we were nevertheless able to build in around one of the windows on the western side many of the sixty-or-so building stones that members of the Dresden Trust are enabling us to acquire through their Stifterbriefe or special donors' certificates.

The next phase of construction began in June 1997 and ended in August 1998. The outer walls, stairwells, drainage structures and inner pillars were taken up to a height of 15 metres. In addition, the prayer rooms, the main entrance on the ground floor, and the sacristy and baptismal chapel in the choir area were completed and the structural steel girders for the prayer room balcony and for the first- and second-floor balconies were put up. This entailed the dry setting or laying with mortar of around 2,700 cubic metres of sandstone and the mounting of 290 tons of structural steel.

Altogether, the cost of this phase came to some 25 million DM. The work has continued to progress rapidly, with optimal planning, preparation and execution of all building work and the subsequent phases have been able to begin ahead of schedule.

Restoration work on the altar moved forward simultaneously. More recovered pieces of stone were repaired and research was carried out on the interior colour scheme as it was in 1739. Work was also done

Figure 47. The Frauenkirche – building under way 1998 (it is now – 2000 – at nearly 50 metres about twice as high: eds). Courtesy of Jens Christian Giese.

on the specifications of the great main organ (originally a Silbermann creation), lists of doors and windows were drawn up and a plan was formulated to recreate the artistic and decorative work.

Everything is continuing to move forward well and good progress is being made: the main cornice level was reached in 2000, work on the inner dome above the main body of the church should be completed in 2002; and complete fitting out of the inner, and construction of the outer dome, in 2004. The construction of the lantern, the process of roofing and the mounting of the Orb and Cross will follow, so that by 2005–6, the Frauenkirche will have made the skyline of the city complete once more. It is estimated that the net building costs will be of the order of DM250 mln but that is not a mark too much for this jewel of Saxon baroque architecture.

I should say, in conclusion, that the Orb and Cross manufactured and financed by our British friends, through the Dresden Trust, presented by HRH the Duke of Kent on 13 February 2000, will be doubly significant: outwardly as the crowning and embellishment of the church and a sign of forgiveness and, inwardly, as a call to humanity and peace.

There could be no better symbol for our common endeavours and for the future.

We are always conscious that without reconciliation with one another and without the blessing of Almighty God none of it would have any meaning, for 'Unless the Lord build the house, they labour in vain that build it.'

The Art Collections of Dresden

Clare Ford-Wille

Dresden owes its importance to the discovery, during the twelfth century, of silver deposits in the Erzgebirge. Other important minerals were also found, including gold, tin, copper and semi-precious stones. Without these discoveries, the art collections could never have been started or built up to the extent that Dresden became, in the eighteenth century, one of the great artistic centres of Europe. The House of Wettin, the first dynasty to rule the area, first made its capital at Meissen, but moved to Dresden in the fifteenth century. During the sixteenth century the family divided. One branch began to rule territories outside Saxony, eventually emerging as the Saxe-Coburg line in Thuringia. The other line, known as the Albertines, remained to rule Saxony.

The Wettins established their residence in Dresden in 1464 when Dukes Ernst and Albrecht moved there and Dresden became the capital of Saxony in the following year. Dresden's development, from a fairly wealthy but minor trading town into a cultural centre of importance, began in the sixteenth century. It grew strongly after the battle of Mühlberg brought Weimar and Wittenberg under Albertine rule. If any one date were to be taken as its starting point, it should be the year 1560 when the Elector August I (1553–86), who was to become one of the greatest collectors in Europe, set aside two rooms in the Royal Castle, in which could be displayed the treasures that he and his brother (and predecessor) Moritz had begun to gather together.

The first of these was a room on the ground floor of the west wing of the Castle. Walls, several metres thick, gratings and iron shutters on the windows made the room very secure. The room was linked to the private apartments of the Elector's family by a spiral staircase, hidden within the thick walls. It was intended to be a safe deposit for jewels, documents of state and money; in effect a Treasury. The second room, on an upper floor, was the Elector's Kunstkammer or small private art gallery, which included a number of Cranachs (the inventory of 1722–9 lists 77). Together they evolved into what became known as the *Grünes Gewölbe* or Green Vault, possibly originating in the sixteenth century as a courtly nickname that reflected the

Figure 48. Jan van Eyck's Virgin and Child Triptych (1437), one of the Gemäldegalerie's earliest paintings. Courtesy of the Staatliche Kunstsammlungen, Dresden.

original colour of the walls. August I also had the first Albertinum, or arsenal, built on the site of the citadel, which much later in Dresden's history was to house an important part of Dresden's museum complex.

August I brought together not only paintings, sculpture, graphic art and the splendid Saxon crown jewels but also instruments, tools and precious metalwork, which formed an even more important part of the Collection: almost a small private university for the ruler, from which court mathematicians, architects, cartographers as well as artists, whom he had attracted to his court, both contributed and derived benefit from the instruments they borrowed for their work. The emphasis upon science was strong even in the early days of the Collection and a number of items were deliberately kept as examples of the latest technological developments. In the first inventory of 1587 (which comprises 317 double pages) almost all the objects listed are implements and scientific instruments. These included tools for gardening and hunting together with medical instruments and instruments for astronomy and music.

The Elector also developed the *Münzkabinett* or Coin Collection, founded by his predecessor Duke Georg of Saxony (1500–39), and initiated the

Rüstkammer or armoury (see Plate 19). This developed into a fine collection of guns, cross-bows, swords and armour, such as the tournament armour made especially for him between 1550 and 1560 by Hans Rosenberger and a beautiful sword made by Lorenz Trunk of Nuremberg. In addition to all this, he began to amass books and the library he created, already famous in his lifetime, today forms part of the Sächsische Landesbibliothek (the Saxon National Library).

August I's successors continued to build up the collections. His son, Christian I (1586–91), bought the panels of the *Seven Sorrows of the Virgin* and 200 prints by Dürer, whilst his grandson, Christian II (1601–11), acquired many objects carved from semi-precious stones. A century later the Kunst-kammer began to reflect the artistic tastes of the Electors and became a showcase for prestige purposes. Medieval artefacts, sixteenth- and seventeenth-century objects of gold, silver and semi-precious stones made by the gold-and silver-smiths of Nuremberg, Augsburg and Leipzig, as well as of Dresden, were collected. Typical of these is Elias Geyer's group of three ostriches crafted in Leipzig at the end of the sixteenth century, where the ostrich eggs form the bodies, whereas the legs, wings, head and neck were made from gilded silver (the heads being removable so that wine could be drunk through the necks). Another fine example is a casket for writing materials, decorated with a reclining female figure, representing Philosophy, holding a tablet with an inscription in praise of scholarship on one side and Pythagorean calculations on the other. High-ranking visitors were encouraged and the guest book of one of the earliest curators contains the autographs of many princes and nobles.

As mentioned elsewhere, the Thirty Years War (1618–48) was a period of terrible devastation for Saxony and, for a time, collecting all but came to a standstill. However, political and economic conditions had improved by the last third of the seventeenth century when a large number of acquisitions were made, heralding a new beginning for Dresden as one of the greatest cultural centres in Europe. Of inestimable importance in this was another August, Friedrich August I (1670–1733), known as Augustus II or Augustus the Strong.

Augustus the Strong

Augustus the Strong became Elector of Saxony in 1694, aged 24, and King of Poland from 1697. It was at this time that collecting became a symbol of the prestige and power of the ruler in Europe generally. Inspired by the example of Louis XIV of France, Augustus the Strong began a systematic founding and expansion of specialist collections. These were to become known throughout Europe and were a focus for study by artists and all kinds of visitors. He commissioned a grand scheme to combine the *Kunstkammer*, (the Treasury), the *Silberkammer* (the Silver Collection) and the *Grünes Gewölbe* (Green Vault) into one of the first museums in Europe to be opened to the public. He began the process of rationalizing and classifying the Collections that form the basis of their existence today. Augustus the Strong purchased the Roman antique sculptures that now form the basis of the *Skulptursammlung* (the Sculpture Collection) in the Albertinum. He had a passion for oriental porcelain and devised the Japanese Palace to house his Collection. Clocks and instruments were separated from the *Kunstkammer* and given their own museum, the *Mathematisch-Physikalische Sammlung* (the Mathematical and Physical Instruments Collection). Similarly, drawings and prints were catalogued and put together to form the *Kupferstichkabinett* (the Print and Drawings Collection). Augustus' enthusiasm was boundless and there was scarcely a field of knowledge with which he was not involved. He sent the first zoological expedition to Africa, commissioned a publication on Saxon Folk Costumes and founded an anatomy collection, a zoological museum and a collection of minerals. He was also passionately keen to unravel the secret of hard-paste porcelain (long known to the Chinese) and he finally brought together the two men, Tschirnhausen and Böttger, who solved the riddle.

The *Grünes Gewölbe* is, arguably, Augustus' most enduring legacy: it still represents one of the richest collections of late Renaissance, Baroque and Rococo objects in the world. It began in three rooms created for it, between 1723 and 1724 in the Royal Castle and, between 1727 and 1729 was expanded to include a further five rooms there. Even then, it was incomplete when Augustus died three years later (mercifully it was well protected during World War II and was subsequently displayed in the Albertinum pending its being returned to its original location in the Castle).

An eighteenth-century visitor would have first entered the Ivory Room in which hundreds of ivory objects were mingled with amber ones and were arranged against a background of panelling marbled in shades of brown. He would have marvelled at the early seventeenth-century amber cabinet, two metres in height, from the Königsberg workshop of Georg Schreiber. This reached Dresden in 1728 as a present from the King of Prussia. Beautifully restored by Polish craftsmen after World War II, it is the largest surviving artefact in that material. Exceptionally beautiful ivory sculptures, dating from the seventeenth century, and precious objects of Italian and German origin carved from lapis lazuli and rock crystal are an important part of the collection. One of the greatest craftsmen represented was Jakob Zeller, who came to Dresden in 1610. An example of his virtuoso skill is the ivory model of a frigate that has miraculously survived in good condition. Carved in 1620, the year of Zeller's death, it is an outstanding example of just that combination of art, science and technical ability so typical of an early seventeenth-century baroque *Kunstkammer* and still so admired by Augustus a century later.

The next room to be entered by the visitor, known as the White Silver Room, contained the King's plate and other items associated with state occasions. These were arranged against a contrasting crimson background. Since the room was also decorated with mirrors, the objects would have appeared far more numerous than in fact they were, in order to impress the visitor. The Silver-Gilt Room followed, with antique and modern objects arranged against a green background. These first three rooms culminated in the *Pretiosensaal* (Hall of Precious Objects) with an area twice as large as the previous rooms. Here an enormous variety of objects was displayed; Venetian glass, Bohemian ruby glass, mother-of-pearl shells, ostrich eggs, objects of agate, lapis lazuli, rock crystal and alabaster, dazzlingly multiplied in the mirrors behind. A small corner room led off the Pretiosensaal and on tables stood small figures and groups made up of pearls, enamel work, diamonds and other precious stones.

The Armorial Room that followed was of contrasting simplicity with oak cupboards, decorated with copper-gilt Saxon coats of arms. The Jewel Room was of dazzling richness containing the greatest collection of jewels ever amassed in Europe. The eighth and last room, the Bronze Room, contained a collection of bronzes arranged against sombre dark oak panelling. An inventory made in 1733, the year Augustus the Strong died, lists a total of 103 bronzes, amongst which survive Giovanni da Bologna's *Satyr and Nymph* and his pupil Adrian de Vries' *Woman Bathing*. They possess all the elegant, elongated grace and complicated poses so admired by patrons in the sixteenth century.

Much of this enormous collection has been lost. Most of the pieces in the White Silver Room were disposed of and probably melted down. Various items were given to the house of Wettin as compensation in 1924 and losses were suffered during the Second World War. It is to be hoped, however, that in the near future the remainder of the Collection that still survives will once more be revealed in all its splendour in its original setting in the Royal Palace.

If, however, any one single work has to be singled out, it would be *The Royal Household at Delhi on the Birthday of the Great Mogul* (see Plate 11), which took the court jeweller, Johann Melchior Dinglinger, and the sculptor Balthasar Permoser, who collaborated, eight years (1701–8) to create. It is considered the greatest work of its type in Europe made by any Baroque

Figure 49. Antoine Pesne's portrait of J.M. Dinglinger holding his famous sculptural group *Diana Bathing* (1721) which is on display in the *Grünes Gewölbe*. Courtesy of Manfred Lauffer.

court jeweller and it is the focus of the collection as it exists today. It is a miniature recreation of the court of the Mogul Emperor Aureng-Zeb in silver, inhabited by 137 gilded and enamelled figures made from gold, silver, enamel and 5,000 precious stones: diamonds, emeralds, rubies and pearls. Augustus the Strong adored such ostentatious displays of wealth. Another fascinating piece is the gold coffee service made for him in 1701 to celebrate the ceremonial consumption of this newly discovered beverage. A sculptural group of *Diana Bathing*, 38 cm in height, combines ivory, enamel, chalcedony, gold, silver and precious stones and is a masterly example of baroque design achieved by Dinglinger and Permoser working together. The figure of the goddess, in delicate ivory, by Permoser reclines in a chalcedony bath, mounted in gold and studded with precious stones; the bath is balanced on the antlers of a stag's head representing the hunter, Actaeon, a mortal who dared to gaze upon the goddess while she was bathing.

Figure 50. The Grand Turk by J.J. Kaendler 1741–42, in the *Grünes Gewölbe*
(Green Vault). Courtesy of the Staatliche Kunstsammlungen, Dresden.

If the Green Vault is Augustus the Strong's greatest legacy, the Porzellansammlung (Porcelain Collection) is, perhaps, the most original. Augustus
the Strong was an avid collector of porcelain from China and Japan, but it
was during his reign that one of the greatest discoveries was made by a young
alchemist working in the Elector's employ. Johann Böttger (1682–1719) was
a Prussian refugee who was for years held by Augustus in conditions of virtual
imprisonment and whose story has recently been excellently told in Janet
Gleeson's book *Arcanum*. He failed in his original mission to create gold out
of base metals but he finally succeeded in creating the 'white gold' or porcelain
that had, thus far, eluded all other Europeans. In 1708 he first produced a
high quality, reddish-brown porcelain, then, in 1713, he succeeded in making
white porcelain from kaolin, feldspar and quartz. At first Böttger was given
a workshop in Meissen's Albrechtsburg Castle. When this was invaded by
the Swedes, he moved to the fortress of Königstein, then finally to the vaults

beneath the Brühl Terrace in Dresden itself. The Castle in Meissen, which gave the product its name, then became Europe's first hard-paste porcelain manufactory before, in 1845, it moved to a new site in the valley below.

Augustus intended to fill an entire palace with his collection of over 20,000 pieces of Oriental and European porcelain. This was to be the Japanese Palace across the River Elbe in the Neustadt where, according to the architect's plans, the collection would be arranged by category, first Chinese followed by Japanese then Meissen. The porcelain would be displayed in formal patterns in groups of a single colour over the walls of thirty rooms. Augustus died in 1733 before his intentions could be realized. However, something of his original ideas can be seen in the arrangement of porcelain at present exhibited in the Zwinger.

A particular favourite with Augustus the Strong was underglaze blue and white porcelain, made during the reign of the Chinese Emperor K'ang-Hsi (1662–1722). In the first large room, bowls and plates are arranged in dazzling patterns on the walls of the curving room. Dating from the earlier Wan Li period (1573–1619) are the monumental Chinese cobalt Dragoon vases, acquired by exchange from the Prussian Royal collection. In 1717, Augustus the Strong gave 600 troops to the Elector of Brandenburg for his dragoon regiment in exchange for the vases. There then follows the largest collection of Japanese Imari porcelain outside Japan. It was made in the seventeenth and eighteenth centuries in the city of Arita, on the island of Kiusha, and exported to Europe. There are two further collections of Chinese porcelain, or *famille verte* as it was known in Europe because of its delicate green colour and the collection of white porcelain, known as *blanc de chine*.

Not surprisingly, the Meissen factory was soon able to produce copies of Oriental porcelains, often so convincingly that they can barely be distinguished from the originals. The Japanese Kakiemon porcelains were copied more frequently at Meissen than Chinese porcelains. The famous Meissen blue and white Zwiebelmuster ware, which has in turn been copied all over the world, was strongly inspired by Chinese design and technique.

In the second section there are fine examples of Böttger's stoneware, such as a coffee pot painted with enamel colours and decorated with gemstones and a small statuette of Augustus the Strong (1713) in armour, bearing a baton of power and draped in a cloak of swirling baroque folds. The statuette is only 11 cm high and yet has a swagger and physical presence that might be expected of such an extraordinary man.

Two of the greatest names to emerge from the anonymity of the Meissen factory were Johann Gottlieb Kirchner and Johann Joachim Kändler. They created figurines and animals of the greatest variety and of sizes varying from almost life size to only a few centimetres in height, in both white and painted porcelain. Sets of figures from the Comedia dell'Arte or charming personifications of the seasons or the trades reveal both artists' virtuosity in modelling and design.

Augustus' artistic endeavours did not cease with the Green Vault or with the collection and manufacture of porcelain. His energy and enthusiasm were indeed boundless and there was scarcely a field of knowledge or art in which he was not, to some extent, involved. He had clocks and instruments separated from the *Kunstkammer*, and classified and placed in the Collection of Mathematical and Physical Instruments, for which a home was found, in 1728, in the South West Pavilion of the Zwinger (completed on three sides for the wedding of his son in 1719). This includes a fine collection of more than 70 globes, the oldest of which is Arabic and dates from 1279, and a vast number of clocks and watches. Of special interest is the planetary clock created for Augustus the Strong by Eberhardt Beldewien and Hans Bucher. It has eight faces and can track the paths of the five planets then known – Mercury, Venus, Mars, Jupiter and Saturn.

In 1720, Augustus also had his drawings and prints made into an independent collection (the *Kupferstichkabinett* or Museum of Prints and Drawings), which was catalogued in the manner pioneered under the French King, Louis XIV. Some of its earliest works are 113 sixteenth-century woodcuts and 69 copper engravings by Albrecht Dürer, which reached Dresden via the estate of another important German Renaissance artist, Lucas Cranach. The 22 outstanding engravings by Lucas van Leyden and Hans Burgkmair's series of proofs for his *Triumph of Maximilian* were acquired in the seventeenth century. Other important acquisitions made in the eighteenth century included 21 works by the then little appreciated Dutch artist, Hercules Seghers, 134 prints by Master ES, a complete set of Piranesi's *Prisons*, and a large number of drawings (including 42 by Rembrandt). These and other works by mainly Dutch and German artists were systematically arranged during the reigns of Augustus the Strong and continued by his son, Augustus III. By the outbreak of the Seven Years War in 1756, the Collection contained a staggering total of 130,000 graphic works.

Augustus the Strong also purchased the Roman antique sculptures that formed the basis of a collection that, many years later, in the nineteenth century, was housed in the Albertinum. The core of the collection consisted of works acquired from the estates of Cardinal Albani and of Prince Chigi and purchases made in 1726 from Frederick William I of Prussia. Over the years, it developed into a fine collection of over 15,000 pieces covering all periods of antiquity.

Finally, Augustus set in motion the steps that led to the creation of Dresden's splendid Collection of Old Masters when, early on in his reign, he called for an inventory to be made of all the paintings in the royal collections in Dresden and the nearby castles. In 1707 he had many of these hung in the Festsaal or Hall of Festivities in the south wing of the Royal Palace and, after 1730, in the Great Hall and its adjoining rooms. It was, however, his son Augustus III (1733–56) who, with the time as well as the inclination and knowledge, expanded and enhanced these beginnings into something like the Collection which can still be seen today.

Augustus III and the Old Masters Collection

Augustus the Strong was succeeded by his son, Augustus III, a loyal son and heir who is remembered above all for ensuring the completion of the Frauen-kirche and the building of the Hofkirche, the Court Church. He was primarily interested in the visual arts and he was an enthusiastic and knowledgeable collector until his death in 1756, which coincided with the outbreak of the Seven Years War and any further collecting ceased. By 1745, when the collection moved to the Stallhof, the Stables of the Jüdenhof or Jews' Court-yard, which had been specially converted for the purpose, its international reputation was well established. By this time 268 paintings had come from the Wallenstein collection in Bohemia. A hundred of the finest paintings from the collection of the Duke of Modena, including important paintings such as *Portrait of the Sieur de Morette* by Holbein, Titian's *Lady in White,* the *Tribute Money* and four panels by Correggio, were purchased in 1745. The last and most important of the acquisitions in 1745 was Raphael's world-famous *Sistine Madonna* from the Church of San Sisto in Piacenza (see Plate 20). Always the most famous painting in the Dresden Gallery, this was commissioned by Pope Julius II for the main altar of the monastery church and is named after the beatified Pope Sixtus, who was martyred in the third century. The Pope nevertheless bears the features of Pope Julius II, whose *della Rovere* heraldic device of an oak tree is alluded to by an acorn placed on top of the papal tiara. By the mid-eighteenth century, at the time of a neo-Classical revival in artistic taste, the painting was seen as a model of perfection, as a symbol of the ideal and timeless quality of the Italian High Renaissance.

Augustus III also commissioned a remarkable series of 25 views of the city of Dresden, painted by Bernardo Bellotto, the nephew of Canaletto, after his arrival in Dresden from Venice in 1747. They are a wonderful record of the city and have already been, indeed still remain, of invaluable help in the rebuilding of Dresden. The view of *Dresden from the Right Bank of the Elbe, below the Augustus Bridge* (1748) represents the most characteristic and well-known view of the left bank of the Elbe, probably from the gardens of the Japanese Palace, dominated by the dome of the Frauenkirche in a central position, with, to the right, the Hofkirche, in front of the Royal Palace, and the sweep of Pöppelmann's Augustus Bridge forming the main horizontal focus of the middle ground of the composition (see Plate 18). This is not simply just an historical and architectural record, but a composition of shimmering refinement where the fitful play of light upon the surfaces of the buildings, the reflections in the water and the variety of subtle tones render this an outstanding work of art.

It was the taste of those years of collecting during the reign of Augustus III that determined the nature of the collection that we see today. Uniform rococo frames from about 1746 are still in use. There was a preference for the grand manner of the High Renaissance and Baroque as well as contemporary eighteenth-century works. Northern art of the fifteenth century, as well as the artists of the early Italian Renaissance, were less popular. Nevertheless there is a fine and representative collection of Dutch and Flemish painting of the late sixteenth and seventeenth centuries.

Count Heinrich Brühl, the ambitious and wily Prime Minister who served both King Augustus II and Augustus III, often acted as the king's representative aided by his secretary, Carl Heinrich von Heinecken, together with ambassadors and diplomats, acting as dealers in finding and purchasing paintings. Count Algarotti who, in 1742, provided a detailed programme for the building of a museum also advised him. Algarotti went himself to Italy and returned with the *Sisters* by Palma Vecchio, among others. He was also responsible for the acquisition of Liotard's *Chocolate Girl* (see Plate 22).

At the outbreak of the Seven Years War in 1759, the paintings were packed into crates and sent to the fortress of Königstein, where they remained during the unsettled latter part of the eighteenth century.

The Seven Years War proved to be politically disastrous for Saxony and the country never recovered. It ceased to play an important role of any kind in European politics. The Napoleonic Wars were to be even more detrimental for Saxony, increasingly overshadowed later in the nineteenth century by the rising power of Prussia. However, the prestige of Dresden as a cultural centre grew considerably, attracting talented artists and writers. Johann Joachim Winckelmann spent a year in Dresden and, in 1755, he published there his highly influential *Gedanken über die Nachahmung der griechischen Werke in der Malerei und Bildhauerkunst* (Reflections on the Imitation of Greek Painting and Sculpture). Goethe visited Dresden in 1768 and recorded some years later:

"with what delight even a daze did I roam through the shrine of the gallery! How many dim feelings came into clear view! How many gaps in my historical knowledge were filled here and how greatly my perception widened as I took in the splendid multi-layered edifice of the Arts."

Madame de Stael, writing in *De l'Allemagne* (1810), commented that 'various outstanding painters have settled in Dresden; the masterpieces in the Gallery encourage talent and stimulate competition'.

In 1836 the organization of Augustus III's collection of paintings was finally given a more professional foundation with the appointment of a Gallery Commission; the collections were catalogued and reorganized, gaps were filled with new acquisitions (including a number of seventeenth-century Spanish paintings from the estate of the French king Louis Philippe in 1853). Artists, writers and a burgeoning middle class visited in increasing numbers. New, larger buildings were erected to cater for the increasing number of visitors. A new building to house the painting collection was begun by Gottfried Semper and was opened in 1855, the *Gemäldegalerie Alte Meister* or Semper Gallery of Old Masters. It completed the fourth side of the Zwinger complex and was one of the earliest purpose-built galleries in the world.

The Gemäldegalerie Neue Meister (The Gallery of New Masters)

The important *Neue Meister* collection was built up, not by Saxon rulers, but by a retired Minister of State, Bernhard August von Lindenau (1779–1854). He devoted a substantial part of his pension to collecting contemporary art.

In 1843, when Lindenau retired, romanticism was the by-word for German culture. Dresden had become a centre for young writers and artists desirous of giving a new impetus to German culture. Romanticism had begun partly as a reaction to the traditions of the eighteenth century and partly to the constraints of neo-classicism. It gathered momentum and became strongly nationalistic as a result of the occupation of the German states by Napoleon. One of the first purchases financed by Lindenau was *Bridal Procession in Spring* (1847) by Ludwig Richter. This is a wholly German work inspired by a musical motif from Richard Wagner's opera Tannhäuser and contains references to many of the characteristics of German romanticism, such as a love of nature, in the careful and detailed depiction of a quintessential northern landscape of dark forest, limpid, tranquil mountainous distances and a late-Gothic castle. This is contrasted with the bridal group of fairy-

Figure 51. Portrait of Bernhard of Riesen by Albrecht Dürer, 1521, in the
Gemäldegalerie Alte Meister. Courtesy of Manfred Lauffer.

tale figures dressed in medieval clothes emerging from the edge of the wood
into the sunlit clearing.

An early product of these ideas was the group of young German painters
living in Rome, known as the Nazarenes. As with the slightly later English
group, the Pre-Raphaelites, the Nazarenes sought to return to the styles of
fifteenth- and sixteenth-century German art. One of these was Schnorr von
Carolsfeld from Dresden and he is represented in the collection by *The Family
of John the Baptist at the Family of Christ* (1817), painted in Vienna before
his departure for Rome. The meticulously painted details of brick, wood
and stone of the buildings and rose-covered fence, clear outlines and rich,
solid colours, are reminiscent of late Gothic artists such as Martin Schongauer
and Albrecht Dürer.

One of the most important artists of the early nineteenth century was the
German romantic painter, Caspar David Friedrich. Examples of his work in
the Dresden collection include *Two Men Contemplating the Moon* (1819)
(see Plate 23). This is typically romantic, in that the spectator is not involved

in the action but simply contemplates the back views of the two men who are distinct and separate in the middle ground of the composition. The moon spreads an eerie and mysterious light, isolating and emphasizing the knotted branches and trunk of the dead tree. There is peaceful contemplation but there is also tension and more is suggested. In 1921, Friedrich's daring and inventive *Cross in the Mountains* (1808) was acquired from Tetschen Chapel, for which it had been painted. With this painting, landscape had become the subject of an altarpiece of haunting beauty. The loneliness of the individual in the face of the overwhelming power of nature is also the theme of one of his last works, the *'Grosse Gehege' near Dresden,* the Great Enclosure (1832). Friedrich had made Dresden his home in 1798 and he attracted a number of pupils and followers whose works are well represented in the collection. The Norwegian, Johann Christian Clausen Dahl, Friedrich's most worthy follower and founder of the Norwegian school of painting, followed Friedrich in fusing romantic mood with realistic subject matter, as in *View of Dresden at Full Moon,* (1839) which must be one of the most evocative cityscapes ever painted. The naturalist, physician, philosopher and amateur painter, Carl Gustav Carus, was also drawn to Friedrich, and in his *Woman on a Balcony* (1824) adopts from him the icon of a figure, seen from behind, in quiet contemplation.

There is also an important collection of Biedermeier painting. 'Biedermeier' is used to describe paintings produced after the Napoleonic Wars up until about 1850; a typical example is *View of Salzburg from the Gaisberg* (1817). by Julius Schope. Some of the most important artists to develop new ideas in the mid-nineteenth century were Carl Spitzweg and Adolph Menzel. Spitzweg's subject matter is still romantic in spirit but more lighthearted and his painting technique is freer as in *The Angler* (1875). Menzel, on the other hand, heralds impressionism with his choice of contemporary subject matter and observation of light. *Afternoon at the Tuileries* (1867) was painted on a visit to Paris, too early as yet for the impact of French impressionism. During the later nineteenth century, romanticism continued in the works of Anselm Feuerbach and the Swiss painter Arnold Böcklin, whose *Summer's Day* (1881) with its strong contrasts and dream-like quality evokes an earthly paradise.

Despite this auspicious beginning, acquisitions were made slowly and this situation only changed when Karl Woermann became director of the gallery in 1882. He was an archaeologist and art historian and had a more objective view of purchases that was to make the collection a more complete and representative one. He announced his intention 'to illustrate the development of art history in the nineteenth century in its various movements and also to do justice to progressive contemporary art'. Contemporary German artists such as Menzel, Böcklin, Thoma and Leibl were added under his directorship.

Woermann also included works of French realism with such paintings as Gustave Courbet's *Stonebreakers,* tragically lost in the Second World War. Woermann's successor was Hans Posse and over the next thirty years, under his directorship, it became one of the most important collections in Germany. Works by nineteenth century artists such as Caspar David Friedrich, Carl Blechen and Ferdinand Waldmüller, who had been neglected earlier and who had reached public notice in the centenary exhibition (*Jahrhundertsausstellung*) in Berlin in 1906, were added to the collection. Similarly, works by German and French Impressionists were acquired during the first three decades of the twentieth century.

On 9 August 1931 the *Neue Staatliche Gemäldegalerie* (New Masters' Gallery) was officially inaugurated as a separate collection, although still under the direction of the Semper Gallery until 1945.

The number of French impressionist painters is small but representative, beginning with Manet's *Lady in Pink* (1881), painted two years before his death. Another portrait, by Auguste Renoir, of *Capitaine Darras* (1871) and Claude Monet's *Banks of the Seine near Lavacourt* (1879) are fine examples of the work of two major French impressionists. French artists of the 1890's, such as Gauguin, Van Gogh and Toulouse Lautrec are represented by powerful works; for example Gauguin's *Two Tahitian Women* (1892) and *Still Life with Quince* (1888/9) by Vincent van Gogh. Six works by Max Liebermann, one of the earliest and most important German Impressionist artists, show his consistent use of contemporary life as the subject matter of his work, together with a liquid and flowing brushwork with which he captures sunlight and water.

Examples of German Expressionism date from the last years of the nineteenth century and early twentieth century. One aspect of this was the group of artists known as *Die Brücke* (The Bridge) who came together in Dresden in 1905. They include Karl Schmidt-Rottluf, Emil Nolde and Lyonel Feininger. Schmidt-Rottluff's *After the Bath* (1912) with its strong, strident colours, vigorous brushwork and violent dynamism gives a feeling of erratic tension and revolt, characteristic of the 'freedom of life and action against established and older forces', which was in the background of the ideas *Die Brücke* aimed to achieve.

The Nazi Period and the German Democratic Republic

The period before the rise to power of the Nazis, in 1933, had been fruitful for the acquisition of works by German Expressionist painters, although certain of these were to suffer destruction at the hands of the Nazis' purge of 'degenerate art'. Fifty-six paintings were lost in this way; another sixty-three works were consumed by fire during the bombing raid on Dresden on 13 February 1945, and a further 106 paintings disappeared from deposits to which they had been evacuated. Further immediate and serious effects of the Nazi regime included the dismissal of modern artists from official positions at the Academy, the reduction or cancellation of purchasing funds and the destruction or sale in foreign auctions of much art seen as 'degenerate'. During the war the collections were dispersed and stored, sometimes in climatically unsuitable venues such as the Rotwerndorf sandstone quarry near Pirna and the Pockau-Lengefeld lime pit near Marienberg. Many were lost. For example, in the chaos at the end of the war many objects and pictures were removed from depots east of the Elbe to western depots and on one such occasion 200 paintings, including Caravaggio's *St Matthew and the Angel* and Courbet's *Stonebreakers*, were burned by a firebomb while in transit through the city.

In 1945 the Russian Army occupied Dresden and the Soviet authorities set up a trophy commission in order to trace the whereabouts of the evacuated works of art. Once items were found, they were removed for 'safe-keeping' to Moscow and Kiev while the museums in the bombed-out city were restored. On 25 August 1955, the art treasures of Dresden that had been taken to the USSR were returned by the Soviet authorities to a delegation from the German Democratic Republic. Later, in 1963, a catalogue was compiled entitled *War Losses of the Dresden Paintings Gallery* in which 206 paintings are listed as destroyed in the war and 507 as missing. Of these, only 44 have come to light in the meantime.

Despite these unfortunate statistics, much still remains. No doubt, in the future, gaps will be filled and the collection will continue to grow, but the present director and curators already have a superb collection to build upon.

The GDR authorities worked hard to restore the galleries. The Zwinger was rebuilt and many of the other collections were re-established, although not always in the same place as before.

Socialist realism was the only style of painting to be officially recognized during the days of the German Democratic Republic and so one does not expect to see any examples of abstract art, but this is not in any way to decry socialist realist art itself, of which there are some interesting examples. For instance *War Triptych* (1929/32) by the German expressionist, Otto Dix (see Plate 24), was acquired in 1968, long before the demise of the German Democratic Republic, and this is also the case with all but one of the other paintings by him in the collection. *War Triptych* portrays in powerful detail the ravages of war. The most important Dresden socialist realist artist of recent years is Hans Grundig, whose work is strongly influenced by Dix and earlier artists such as Dürer and Grünewald. A major example of Grundig's work is *The Thousand Year Reich* (1935/38). Hans Grundig survived four years in a Nazi concentration camp and in 1947, upon his return to Dresden, became Professor and Rector of the Hochschule für Bildende Künste.

Buildings continue to be renovated and new systems of lighting and display increasingly enhance the outstanding art treasures that make Dresden, once more, one of the great cultural centres of the world.

The Collections Today

At the present time Dresden and its environs have c.30 museums, mainly artistic and scientific, of which at least one third can be traced back directly to Augustus the Strong and his forebears. All those of concern here can be described under six geographical headings: 1. the Zwinger complex; 2. the Albertinum; 3. other museums in or near the Old Town; 4. museums in the New Town; 5. museums, mainly small, located on the fringes of Dresden, old and new; and 6. those situated outside the city boundaries (see Plates 13 and 14).

The Zwinger complex

The origins and development of the Zwinger, one of Europe's outstanding baroque buildings, have already been described (pp 15–16 and 130–131). This fine group of buildings now houses the core of the great eighteenth century collections, with the exception of those in the Green Vault. The south-eastern gallery houses the Porcelain Collection and the south-western gallery, the Collection of Mathematical and Physical Instruments. The eastern section of the Semper Gallery contains the Rüstkammer (Armoury), which the Dukes and Electors of Saxony developed not only for practical aesthetic reasons but also to preserve ideas of dynasty and lineage; it is unquestionably one of the finest in the world.

The fourth range of the Zwinger, comprising Semper's nineteenth-century gallery, contains the Old Master Collection. The historical development of this has already been described, but so great is its richness and span that it is worth recalling some of the major elements as they are presented to the public today. The Collection is arranged on three floors of the Semper building. The ground floor is mainly concerned with cloakrooms, ticket office and gallery shop and the main or first floor galleries, by and large, house the major core of the collection, beginning with the outstanding views of Dresden by Bernardo Bellotto. Six large rooms open into one another, three on either side of a central hexagonal space and, behind these, other smaller rooms provide greater intimacy for the smaller paintings. On one side of the hexagon is the collection of Italian paintings from the fifteenth to the late sixteenth century, whereas on the other side are northern works by Dutch, Flemish and German artists.

The third section of the Gallery on the second floor comprises small rooms with mainly eighteenth-century French and Italian oil paintings, together with a significant collection of pastels of similar date. Seventeenth- and eighteenth-century German and Spanish pictures are also to be found here, including a fine series of views of Dresden by Johann Alexander Thiele, who spent most of his working life in Dresden.

Despite the fact that the collections in Dresden have not been seen by anything like the numbers of Western European visitors who over the last 40 years, have poured through the portals of galleries in Florence, Paris, Vienna, or London the riches in Dresden have remained surprisingly familiar.

The early Italian Renaissance collection, although not large, has some outstanding works. Pinturricchio's *Portrait of a Boy* must have been an early acquisition, as it is first mentioned in the inventory of 1722–8. The boy gazes steadily and solemnly out at the spectator, his glowing red jacket set off against a luminous landscape. Mantegna's *Holy Family* (c.1495) was not acquired until 1876 and is a fine example of the master's later work, where the figures have all the sculptural, measured stillness of an antique relief. Another late work by the Florentine painter, Botticelli, *Scene from the Life of St Zenobius* (c.1500), is one of four panels which would have served as the interior decoration of a religious building. Two other panels are in the National Gallery, London and the fourth is in the Metropolitan Museum of Art, New York. The mysterious and rare painter, Antonello da Messina, is represented by a haunting *St Sebastian* (c.1475/6) standing calmly, pierced by the arrows of his martyrdom, against the lucid perspective of a Renaissance town square. One of the most famous of all sixteenth century Italian Venetian paintings, Giorgione's *Sleeping Venus* (c.1509), was acquired in the reign of Augustus the Strong. It is an enduring inspiration for artists and a model of the ideal concept of feminine beauty, derived from antiquity but transformed by Giorgione's ability to infuse the rounded forms of the figure and landscape with a soft, atmospheric unity that gives a dreamy, mysterious mood. One of the paintings acquired by Augustus III from the Duke of Modena in 1746 is the *Tribute Money* (1516) by Titian, originally painted for Duke Alfonso d'Este of Ferrara. The story is from St Matthew 22: 15–22. The Pharisees, wishing to plot Christ's downfall, tried to trick Christ by asking him if it was lawful to pay tax to Caesar. Seeing through the trick, Christ asked to see a coin and pointing to the head of the emperor, said: 'Render therefore unto Caesar the things which are Caesar's; and unto God the things that are God's'. Here Titian concentrates upon this moment by focussing strongly on the two half-length figures of Christ and the interrogator, which fill the composition. Christ's glowing pink gown and beautiful face contrast strongly with the angular, gnarled features and hand of the other man.

Later sixteenth-century developments are well illustrated in the work of Correggio and Parmigianino. Correggio's *Madonna with St George* (1530/32) is a large public altarpiece and Parmigianino's *Madonna of the Rose* (1528/30) was a private devotional work painted for the writer, Pietro Aretino, but then appears to have been given to Pope Clement VII. Parmigianino was greatly influenced by Correggio in Parma and both paintings exhibit that restless style and grace known as *maniera*, from which the term 'mannerism' is derived. There is an ambiguity about Parmigianino's Virgin and Christ Child, which might equally portray a Venus and Cupid.

Baroque painting of seventeenth-century Italy is well represented by large devotional altarpieces by Annibale Carracci, Guido Reni and Guercino. Spanish seventeenth-century religious works such as Ribera's *St Agnes in Prison* (1641) or Murillo's *Virgin and Child* (c.1648), both acquired by Augustus II before the Seven Years War, can be contrasted with an outstanding portrait by Velasquez, *Portrait of a Gentleman, probably Don Juan Mateos, Royal Master of the Hunt*. The direct, steady gaze and large, powerful form of Don Mateos fill the canvas. Velasquez's broad and varied brushwork suggests the rich but sombre costume, gleam of sword hilt and belt, but above all the hair, skin and fleeting emotions of the intelligent face.

Classical ideas of restraint and balance exemplify seventeenth-century French painting in the Dresden collection. The evocation of a classical world inspired Poussin's *Realm of Flora* (c.1630) in which Flora, goddess of Spring, dances in her garden surrounded by mythological figures who were turned into flowers after their death. On the right, the lovers Smilax and Crocus recline. She holds white bindweed while he has crocuses in his hair. Behind them is Adonis, Venus' lover, with a pheasant's eye springing from a gaping wound and, behind him, Hyacinth stands as hyacinths bloom from the wound in his head where Apollo's discus struck him. To the left of Flora, Narcissus gazes with lovesick intensity at his own reflection in a bowl of water, which the nymph, Echo, holds out to him. Behind them, Clytie shields her eyes while gazing at her lover, Apollo, in his chariot above. She becomes a sunflower. On the far left, Ajax falls on his sword, from which carnations spring. Claude Lorrain, Poussin's seventeenth-century contemporary, was the greatest exponent of the ideal, Classical landscape so admired in the eighteenth century. *Acis and Galatea* (1657) is a late-evening scene in which Claude uses the small Classical figures as a focus in the foreground for his observation of the light effects that drench the tranquil, timeless landscape that seems to stretch to infinity. Eighteenth-century painting is represented by the exceptional collection of pastels by French artists such as Maurice Quentin de la Tour, whose portrait of *Count Moritz of Saxony, Marshal of France* (1748) is refreshingly informal and a *tour de force* of technical virtuosity in the handling of textures and expression. The Swiss pastellist, Jean-Etienne Liotard, sold his *Chocolate Girl* (see Plate 22) to the Count Algarotti, the agent of Augustus II, in 1745 in Venice. There is also a *Self-portrait* by Liotard where he is dressed in 'Turkish' costume according to the current fashion for the exotic.

Northern paintings of the fifteenth century are not numerous, but they are outstanding in quality. Jan van Eyck's *Virgin and Child Triptych* (1437) is a luminous jewel of Flemish painting (see p 146). German art is represented by Dürer's early work of the *Seven Sorrows of the Virgin Altarpiece* and a late portrait of *Bernhard von Reesen* (1521) (see p 157). Two further portraits by Lucas Cranach the Elder of *Duke Heinrich the Pious* and *Duchess Katharina of Mecklenburg* are important early examples of full-length court portraits (see Plate 21).

The collection of Dutch and Flemish painting of the seventeenth century, on the other hand, is outstanding in its variety and importance. Major Flemish painters such as Rubens are represented by exceptional examples, such as Rubens' *Bathsheba Bathing* (c.1635). The Dutch collection is extraordinarily diverse with examples from almost every period and facet of Rembrandt's career, such as *Rembrandt and Saskia in the Parable of the Prodigal Son, The Rape of Ganymede* or *Samson Proposing the Riddle at the Wedding Feast*. There is a fine collection of Rembrandt's pupils, Ferdinand Bol, Aert de Gelder and Gerard Dou. A host of other fine quality examples by Dutch masters makes an exceedingly comprehensive collection. Genre painters such as Vermeer, Gabriel Metsu and Nicolaes Berchem demonstrate the development of that particular specialization, while the range of Dutch landscape painting is encompassed in the works of Jan van Goyen, Jacob van Ruisdael and Philips Koninck.

The Albertinum

The first Albertinum was built by Kurfürst August I, between 1559 and 1563, as Dresden's Arsenal but was largely rebuilt, for museum purposes, between 1884 and 1887 in a heavy but not unattractive neo-Renaissance style. It presently houses the Collection of New Masters and the Sculpture and Coin Collections. The Green Vault collection of silverware and other fine arts is also there, pending its transfer back to the Royal Palace. Like the Old Master Gallery these collections are also open six days a week, but the closure days vary and must always be checked. Across the road can be found the remaining sections of the city's fortifications, the Casemates, a series of old vaults situated directly under the Brühl Terrace, which can also be visited.

Other museums in the old town

The Museum of the City of Dresden (*Stadtmuseum Dresden im Landhaus*) is housed in the Landhaus, a fine and probably the first example of neo-Classical architecture built from 1770–6 by Friedrich August Krubsacius as a centre of administration and assembly for the Saxon provincial estates. The entrance hall is dominated by a double staircase with fine wrought-iron banisters.

The historical display of the City of Dresden begins on the fourth floor, at the top of the building, with the beginnings of the city in the early medieval period and further developments in the Renaissance and baroque periods up to the end of the Seven Years War in 1763. One of the most important objects is a series of ten panel paintings, dating from 1528/29, illustrating the Ten Commandments by Hans Johann of Dresden. Not only are these paintings rare examples of art produced at the time of the Protestant Reformation but they are interesting as examples of the secularization of art with their attention to details of everyday life and contemporary early sixteenth-century costumes, observation of northern townscapes and landscape backgrounds. For example the second Commandment, 'Thou shalt not take the name of the Lord thy God in vain', depicts a comfortable interior with three men in fashionable dress seated at a table playing cards. The man on the right has two fingers of his right hand raised and is obviously swearing.

The third floor deals with the history of Dresden from 1763 until 1918 and the remaining floors brings the visitor up to 1989 and the end of communism.

The *Kupferstichkabinett* (the Print and Drawings Collection). Following its huge expansion under Augustus the Strong, little was added to the Print and Drawings Collection save the private collection of King Frederick Augustus II (added in 1831 but lost when the Soviets arrived in 1945), some nineteenth-century posters and photographs and works by twentieth-century German and European artists. These include Käthe Kollwitz, Whistler, Ensor, Munch and the Dresden artist, Wilhelm Rudolph (1889–1982), whose cycle of 150 drawings describing the burnt – out city of Dresden were acquired in 1959. Thanks to its evacuation to the castle of Weesenstein, most of the Collection survived the Second World War and is now back at 34 Güntzstrasse.

Museums of the Neustadt

The Museum der Frühromantik (the Museum of Early Romanticism) in the Hauptstrasse comprises nine small rooms of a late seventeenth-century house belonging to the early nineteenth-century Dresden painter, Gerhard von Kügelgen (1772–1820). Of the old houses that survive in this part of Dresden relatively few have historical associations with leading cultural personalities and movements. Important figures, such as Goethe, Caspar David Friedrich

Figure 52. Dresden's Jägerhof before World War II: happily the main wing was rebuilt as the City's fascinating Museum of Saxon Folk Art. Courtesy of the Stadtplanungsamt, Dresden.

and Philip Otto Runge, however, visited Kügelgen here. Each room of this atmospheric small museum deals with various aspects of romanticism, including art, music and literature. The final room is laid out as Kügelgen's studio.

The *Japanisches Palais*, the Japanese Palace, was built for Count Flemming in 1715 by Pöppelmann and bought by Augustus the Strong two years later. His ambitious project, referred to above in the section on the Porzellansammlung, was to house the Royal collection of porcelain in sumptuous rooms. The sculpture that decorates the central pediment on the facade reinforces his intention. Here, Saxon and Chinese figures hand pieces of porcelain to an enthroned figure representing Saxony. In the inner courtyard statues of herms have obvious Chinese features. From the gardens of the palace can be seen one of the famous vistas of Dresden that Bernardo Bellotto painted. Although the porcelain was housed there briefly from 1729 to 1741, the completion of the project was cut short by the death of Augustus in 1733. Now it is the home of the Museum of Anthropology and Pre-History.

The *Museum für Volkskunst im Jägerhof*, the Saxon Folk Art Museum, is the oldest surviving building in Dresden, constructed on the site of a medieval monastery. A Renaissance gable and three staircase towers remain from the original Electoral hunting lodge, which was renovated and converted into a museum in the late nineteenth century. It opened officially in 1913 and became the first museum of its kind in Germany. It had served as a menagerie for exotic animals under Augustus the Strong.

The Collection concentrates primarily on Saxon folk art and illustrates the culture and way of life of the people from the sixteenth century onwards. The museum serves a very important function in preserving and describing regional handicrafts. Costumes, household furniture, tools, implements, and painted Easter eggs are some of the thousands of objects maintained by the museum. From the Erzgebirge region are displayed Christmas decorations of all kinds, pyramids, nutcrackers and animated models.

The *Militärhistorisches Museum* (the Military History Museum) lies to the north of the Neustadt in the Olbruchtplatz. It is housed in the former arsenal where the weapons and armour of the Saxon rulers were kept until the outbreak of the First World War. Today more than six thousand objects, from the Renaissance to the modern day, give a fine chronological history of warfare.

Smaller Museums located on the fringes of Dresden

The Kraszewiski Museum is the home of the Polish writer during the time of Augustus the Strong.

The Schillerhaus, the house where Schiller stayed as a guest of the Körner family between 1785 and 1787, lies just across the famous Blaues Wunder Bridge. Various mementoes and contemporary furniture can be seen. Here it was that Schiller worked on *Don Carlos* and Körner wrote the first musical setting of Schiller's *Ode to Joy*.

The Carl-Maria von Weber Museum is in the summer house that was used by the composer where he composed *Freischütz, Euryanthe, and Oberon*.

Museums outside Dresden

Pillnitz The Museum of Arts and Crafts in Pillnitz Palace, in the small village of Pillnitz, is set in magnicent gardens. The original late Renaissance palace belonged to Sibylla von Neitschütz and was given to her by her lover, the Elector Johann Georg IV. At their deaths, it passed to Augustus the Strong who gave it to his mistress, Countess Cosel, in 1707. When she fell from favour, Augustus began building a new palace in the 'Indian' style. By 1724 the Wasserpalais and Bergpalais had been completed by Matthaeus Daniel Pöppelmann and Zacharias Longuelune. The style is in fact closer to the exotic chinoiserie illustrations of temples and buildings on the Chinese and Japanese porcelain that Augustus the Strong so enthusiastically collected.

The old palace of Pillnitz was destroyed by fire in 1818 and the Neues Palais was built between 1822 and 1826. The gardens represent a complete history of eighteenth-century garden design. The Wasserpalais now contains a museum devoted to the decorative arts and it is part of the collections belonging to the city of Dresden. The most important part of the collection is a series of rooms arranged in chronological order, with furniture and wood-carving of all periods and a magnificent textile and ceramic collection.

Meissen   The *Staatliche Porzellanmanufaktur* (the State Porcelain factory), stands below Meissen's great Castle, the Albrechtsburg (1471–1525), once the royal residence of the Wettins.

The various stages in the process of manufacturing porcelain items are demonstrated by individual craftspeople in a series of five rooms. This a porcelain museum, built from 1912 to 1915 and opened in January 1916. Three thousand pieces are selected each year from a total collection of over 20,000 items and are exhibited to show the history and development of Meissen porcelain over three centuries.

It may be said, in conclusion, that Meissen's famous hallmark of two blue crossed swords is a familiar and graceful symbol of the artistic achievements and elegance that have characterized the City of Dresden over the centuries and for which, despite the ravages of war, it still deserves to be known and to be remembered.

Dresden: A Music Metropolis

Derek McCulloch

The Pre-Reformation Years; the Earliest Choirs and Places where they Sang

It is in one way a happy coincidence that the publication of this book, with its chapter on the musical aspects of the city's past and present, should coincide with the 450th anniversary of the founding of a *Hofkantorei* at the Saxon Court in Dresden in 1548. In English parlance we would talk of a Chapel Royal, although the title would be technically inappropriate in reference to a state whose ruler was not a king but an Elector of the Holy Roman Empire.

Prior to that, Saxon Electors had maintained *Hofkantoreien* at other residences, notably in Torgau, Altenburg and Wittenberg. Not until the accession of Elector Moritz in 1547, however, was Luther's exhortation to 'kings, princes and lords' to maintain quality musical establishments – 'for such is the duty of great rulers and lords; individual private persons cannot do so' – finally made reality.

Originally this *Kantorei* comprised but a score of lay clerks and boy choristers. The singers came under the direction of an organist and an overall director of music or *Hofkapellmeister*, the first person to hold this office being the famous Protestant musician Johann Walter (1490–1570), a close friend of Martin Luther. Indubitably, the founding of this *Hofkantorei* represents a significant milestone in the musical history of the city. The danger, however, is in thinking that there were no musical establishments before it, and that following its two golden eras under Heinrich Schütz and later as a Roman Catholic court at the time of Handel, music dried up in the Saxon capital. Nothing could be further from the truth. The evolution of music in Dresden shows a vigorous juxtaposition and intermingling of church, court, private and municipal institutions that survived the various calamities and political upheavals that have beset the city intermittently over the past centuries.

Dresden's first church was the Frauenkirche, meaning in shortened form 'Church of Our Lady', being dedicated *zu unserer lieben Frau*. The exact date of its consecration is uncertain, but is thought to have been in or about 1142. The records show that by the early fourteenth century masses – possibly polyphonic, that is to say sung in parts as opposed to the single line of 'monodic' Gregorian chant – were sung in the church. The rebuilding of the organ, both in 1559 and in 1616, provides further proof of serious musical offerings in the church. It was in the Frauenkirche that Heinrich Schütz, 'the Father of German Music', was interred in 1672, at the side of his late wife. The mediaeval building was replaced in 1726 by the baroque edifice known to us from numerous depictions and now in the throes of restoration to its former glory. Schütz's grave was obliterated during the rebuilding process in the early eighteenth century. It was here that, in 1736, J.S. Bach played the great Silbermann organ to members of the Court.

Throughout history, the Frauenkirche has vied for pre-eminence with the Kreuzkirche. The latter was dedicated in 1216 as a market church to St Nicholas, the patron saint of merchants, and was first known as the Nikolaikirche. When Dresden achieved municipal status and a city wall was built, the Frauenkirche was situated outside the city confines. It became *de facto* the church of the outlying villages, while the Nikolaikirche was *de facto* the municipal parish church. *De jure,* however, the older church retained its status as Dresden's senior place of worship, a situation that lasted until the overall upheaval brought by the Reformation. Some twenty years after the Nikolaikirche was built, Margrave Heinrich, or Henry the Illustrious, donated to the church a splinter from the Cross, and the chapel purpose-built for the veneration of the Cross, *Capella Sanctae Crucis,* acquired the name *Kreuzkapelle* and later *Kreuzkirche* – the name by which the Nikolaikirche has long been known. From the time the chapel was built in around 1260, it became a place of pilgrimage. Its function as a place of worship to which people flocked from near and far had wide-reaching implications for its musical life, for which subsequent centuries have good reason to be thankful. The elaborate musical provision expected of such a centre of attraction made necessary the setting up of a choir school to train choristers. The *Schola Crucis* or Kreuzschule was instituted, and in the latter half of the fourteenth century this now world-famous institution became a municipal school. The list of *Kruzianer,* as the alumni are known, who have made their mark on musical history as composers or performers, is too extensive to attempt here. At all events the impact of the Kreuzkirche and the Kreuzschule on the life of the city and beyond can hardly be exaggerated.

From the mid-sixteenth century to the end of the nineteenth century the choristers of the Kreuzschule also served the Frauenkirche, but the latter instituted its own boys' choir, which was itself superseded by a mixed choir in 1925. The wide range of duties required of the choristers of the Kreuzschule in the course of time ranged from the daily singing of *Salve regina* and *O Crux ave spes* at sunset, as instituted by trust in 1398, to acting as an opera chorus from 1717 to 1817. During the last twenty years of that time, the boy singers from the Kreuzschule were reinforced by the boys of the choir based in the Dreikönigskirche or Church of the Epiphany. Not until Carl-Maria von Weber took up office at the opera was a mixed chorus with female voices deployed. Church, State and Court have operated across blurred lines throughout the musical life of the city. A less exalted musical activity pursued by the poorer boys of the Kreuzschule was that of busking in the streets of the city, as a means of paying for their keep. Not until 1848, a year with a revolutionary ring to it, was this humiliating requirement brought to an end.

Originally the directors of music at the Kreuzschule were known as 'rector', the title of 'kantor' not being used until after the Reformation. An early rector to make his mark (from 1409–12) was Petrus Dresdensis. Scholars are no longer convinced that he composed the famous carols *In Dulci Jubilo*, *Quem Pastores* and *Puer Natus in Bethlehem,* or that he composed polyphonic motets for the Kruzianer to sing, but his biography has a certain fascination, not to say an element of sad irony for the director of music at an institution that was to become part of the bedrock of Lutheran church music. As a Hussite sympathizer he was forced to leave Dresden, finding asylum in Prague. He was finally held by the authorities and burned at the stake as a heretic in the staunchly Catholic cathedral city of Regensburg. A century later, with the Court firmly entrenched in Luther's reforms, Petrus would have been in his element.

Two further pre-Reformation churches made significant contributions to the sacred musical life of the city and continued to do so until they were devastated in 1945: the Sophienkirche (St Sophia's) and the church Zu den Heiligen drei Königen – the Dreikönigskirche. The former was a church of the Franciscan order, dating back to 1265 and rebuilt in 1351. The records make early reference to the organ in the church, and after a period of neglect in the second half of the sixteenth century (coinciding with the rise of the Hofkapelle), the musical life of the church blossomed again in the early seventeenth century, when the organist of the Frauenkirche served both churches. In 1695 the church was finally permitted to appoint its own organist, and under Christian Pezold (1677–1733), previously organist to the Court, a magnificent Silbermann organ was commissioned and consecrated in 1720. For the consecration ceremony Pezold wrote a festal cantata, performed by the choir of the Kreuzkirche. Pezold was a highly respected church musician and virtuoso organist, as records of recitals in Paris in 1714 and Venice two years later testify. Among his pupils was Carl Heinrich Graun, a prominent member of the musical establishment of Frederick the Great in Potsdam and Berlin in the mid-eighteenth century. His surviving compositions are all to be found in manuscripts in the Sächsische Landesbibliothek (the Saxon State Library) in Dresden, and include suites for the viola d'amore, as well as organ and harpsichord collections.

The presence of a Silbermann organ would have greatly enhanced the reputation of the church as a desirable post for organists. On the death of Pezold the shortlisted applicants included 'the king's harpsichordist' Christoph Schaffrath (1709–63). Though unsuccessful in Dresden, Schaffrath went on to become harpsichordist to Crown Prince Frederick of Prussia (later Frederick the Great) and subsequently to the King's sister, the cantankerous Princess Amalie, herself a talented composer. The post at the Sophienkirche was awarded to J.S. Bach's wayward eldest son, Wilhelm Friedemann Bach (1710–84). In the early years of Friedemann's tenure, the Sophienkirche was officially adopted as the Lutheran Court Church. At the end of the seventeenth century (1697) the Court itself, for reasons of political expediency, had forsaken the Lutheran cause, Elector Friedrich August I having seen conversion to Catholicism as a prerequisite to securing succession to the Polish Crown and with it the titles *in Personalunion* (two posts filled by one person) of Elector of Saxony and King of Poland. A similar case of 'personal union' existed in Georgian Britain, where the King remained also Elector of Hanover until early in the nineteenth century. Wilhelm Friedemann was to discover that the charms of Silbermann's organ wore thin with a part-time salary (coupled to his extravagant lifestyle) in a cultural climate where a Catholic – influenced Court was manifestly more devoted to opera than Protestant church music. In 1742 Bach tried to improve his situation by applying for the vacant post at the Frauenkirche, which still carried more status in Protestant circles than the Sophienkirche. By then both churches boasted Silbermann organs that had been put through their paces by Johann Sebastian himself. Wilhelm Friedemann's application was not successful, and four years later he moved on to the prestigious post of organist at the Liebfrauenkirche in Halle. Alas, it was a case of moving from a Catholic (and essentially ecumenical and liberal) frying pan into a Pietistic fire, and after nearly twenty stormy years that must have been insufferable for all parties concerned, Wilhelm Friedemann simply walked out without bothering to hand in notice to the church elders.

The last of the great pre-Reformation churches to enrich the musical life of the city was the Dreikönigskirche, founded in the early fifteenth century as a parish church for the settlement then called Altendresden on the right bank of the Elbe. It was rather radically renamed Dresden-Neustadt following its destruction by fire in 1685. Like the Kreuzkirche, this church, too, maintained a choir school to enhance the musical celebrations of the liturgy. The records first mention a schoolmaster there in 1431. In 1465 he and the choristers were bound by covenant to sing the *Salve Regina* daily. The organ was rebuilt in 1489, 1509 and again in 1606. Here, too, the city elders intervened at the Reformation to convert a church school into a municipal grammar school in 1539. The fire that destroyed the city in 1685 claimed the church as a victim. A new church with a new organ was built by 1711, and the rebuilt church was then replaced in 1731 by a more sumptuous baroque building with yet another organ in 1754. The choristers at the grammar school joined those of the Kreuzschule towards the end of the century in the opera chorus in the theatre 'auf dem Linckeschen Bade', and like the poorer members of the Kreuzschule, sang on the street to collect for alms. The function of the grammar school as a choir school was terminated in 1877. The secularized Dreikönigsschule and the church were both destroyed in 1945, although the latter has since been rebuilt.

We have seen how the municipal authorities acted in various ways to blur the distinction between Church and city functions. This tradition reaches far back in history. From early times, the tower keeper of the Kreuzkirche was required to ring the bell to sound the fire alarm. More specifically musical pursuits were ordered by the civic authorities in about 1420: three players of wind instruments to play at all the major feasts and festivals in the organ gallery of the Kreuzkirche. The municipal wind players *(Stadtpfeifer)* were increased to four in 1572. Their duties included playing in four parts from the church tower, reinforcing the Kreuzchor at the major festivals, on Sundays and on such occasions (weddings, funerals) as the elaborate nature of the music performed required. By the early seventeenth century the group had been extended to include crumhorns, recorders, side-blown flutes, dulcians, trumpets and cornetti. Proud of their quasi-monopolistic rights they were incensed at the way in which other bodies of wind players, both military and from the Court, tried to muscle in on the act at weddings, with consequences, as we shall see later, for the instrumentation of Schütz's *Christmas Story*. The links between Church and municipal authorities were strengthened in 1675 when the *Stadtmusicus*, the official director of music for the city, was required to bring together the Stadtpfeifer and the Kreuzchor for the celebrations of Christmas, Easter and the Ascension, and the role of the Stadtpfeifer was extended even further to include using the trainee musicians at church services in the Sophienkirche and the Frauenkirche whenever the senior pastor of the Dresden churches held the sermon in those churches. By the end of the eighteenth-century *Stadtmusicus* Daniel Weber had extended the players to include both wind and strings under the new title of *Stadtkapelle*. By the end of the eighteenth century this body of municipal musicians was not only performing at all the major churches, it had found a new role as the accompanying orchestra for the newly founded secular choral societies who, on the English model, performed oratorios and the like with large amateur resources. In 1872 this admirable institution was dissolved by the municipal authorities, bringing to life in its place the *Gewerbehaus-Orchester* (to use but one of its many names).

The early records of music at the Court are patchy and reach back to the beginning of the thirteenth century, the age of minstrelsy. Notable visitors to the Court include Walther von der Vogelweide (c1170–c1230), arguably the most significant of the 'German' *Minnesänger*. 'German' at that time, long before unification in the late nineteenth century, referred solely to the language spoken. Walther was in residence from 1210 until 1211, followed by Heinrich von Morungen. Margrave Heinrich 'the Illustrious' ruled over the territory for 60 years (1227–88), and established Dresden for some of the time as his seat. An extraordinarily talented and cultured ruler, he fostered art throughout the region of his sway and himself composed songs, six of which still survive in the Manesse manuscript in Heidelberg. His settings of the Kyrie and Gloria were sanctioned by Pope Innocent IV in 1254 for liturgical use.

Dresden was not the main seat of the Court during this period so there is a lack of documentary evidence of the kind of music performed in Dresden throughout the fourteenth century, and the fifteenth century saw the region embroiled in dynastic and religious strife. In 1464, however, Dresden became again the permanent seat of the Court, there being at one stage two households, that of Elector Ernst and of his brother Duke Albrecht (thus the 'Ernestine' and the 'Albertine' lines of the Wettin dynasty referred to in the historiography of Saxony: see Appendix 1). With greater political stability surrounding the city, both the Ernestine electoral and the Albertine ducal establishments were able to maintain musicians, probably primarily wind players and timpanists.

Dresden's Lutheran *Hofkantorei* 1548–1697

The decisive moment for the glorious history of music at the Saxon Court in Dresden came with the foundation of a post-Reformation *Hofkantorei* in 1548 under Duke Moritz, who had been elevated to the status of Elector in the previous year. The choir was bound by the statutes introduced in 1539, and these defined its liturgical responsibilities for nearly 200 years. Music flourished throughout the latter half of the sixteenth century, not only under Johann Walther but also under his successors Matthaeus le Maistre (1505–

77) and Antonio Scandello (1517–80), whose Passion settings and *historiae* were later to serve as the stimulus for settings by Schütz over four decades in the seventeenth century, and Rogier Michael (1552–1619). Although all of these go down in history as *Kleinmeister* or 'minor composers' they established the reputation of Dresden as a place where the music mattered. The spread of provenance of these four first *Hofkapellmeister* in Dresden is also significant (native Thuringia, Netherlands, Bergamo, Netherlands respectively) and sets the trend. Dresden was to act as a magnet to Europe's leading musicians, and the catalyst for many of its own native musicians.

Towards the end of his life Michael became too infirm and feeble to carry out his duties in the Court Chapel. The Elector made virtue of necessity and succeeded in bringing the most respected Lutheran composer of the time, Michael Praetorius (c1570–1621), to Dresden on what was conceived as a one-year release from contract in Wolfenbüttel. A variety of circumstances meant that Praetorius, whom no-one would care to dismiss as a *Kleinmeister*, managed to prolong his stay for a further eighteen months, and even when he returned to Wolfenbüttel, the seat of the dukes of Braunschweig (Brunswick), the Saxon Elector continued to pay him a salary. Praetorius's stay in Dresden became significant for a variety of reasons. The most immediate of these was that he was able, as acting Hofkapellmeister, to direct the music for the Electoral Diet in Naumburg in 1614, impressing the gathered rulers of the Holy Roman Empire with the excellence of Dresden's Hofkapelle.

While Praetorius was fulfilling his temporary contract, Elector Johann Georg I was on the lookout for the inevitable imminent successor to his ailing Hofkapellmeister. His first choice was Heinrich Schütz (1585–1672), a still relatively young composer at the time, who had recently returned from Venice where he had been studying with the great Giovanni Gabrieli at St Mark's, having been granted a scholarship from Moritz, the Landgrave of Hesse. Schütz assisted Praetorius at various important musical events with the Dresden Hofkapelle and so impressed the Elector that he set out to wrest the man of his choice from his contract with the less powerful Landgrave. After protracted haggling, Landgrave Moritz was finally forced to release Schütz, who was a Saxe-Thuringian by birth. The man later to be dubbed 'the Father of German Music' took up the post of Hofkapellmeister in Dresden in 1617. The short period of interaction with Praetorius was fruitful for both men. Schütz brought with him fresh impulses from Venice and the 'polychoral' style that was famous throughout Europe: sumptuous music, written to be performed by groups of musicians scattered round the various galleries of the cathedral. Through the young Schütz, Praetorius was influenced by the prevailing Venetian style. Through Praetorius, Schütz experienced how this Venetian music could be harnessed to the German Lutheran liturgy, as manifested in his first German opus, the *Psalms of David,* published shortly after in 1619.

With Praetorius and Schütz, the Elector was able to send out a powerful message as to the excellence of his musical establishment. Furthermore Schütz remained in office (though not necessarily all the time in Dresden) for forty years in a full-time capacity, with a further fifteen years from 1656–72 in an advisory role. The continuity of his long stay in office was to prove crucial in later years when Protestant church music, throughout a Germany that had been devastated by war, needed a fresh start.

Schütz's appointment coincided with the outbreak of the Thirty Years War (1618–48), waged between the predominantly Catholic Imperial armies loyal to the Holy Roman Emperor and the predominantly Protestant allied armies led by Gustavus Adolphus, the King of Sweden. The Saxon Elector tried to maintain a neutral or ambiguous posture, with the result that Saxony was made to suffer by both parties. The effect on Dresden was devastating.

On his appointment, Schütz had a *Kapelle* comprising nearly twenty trebles and lay clerks and at least the same number of instrumentalists. Virtually from the beginning, the Kapelle had been a mixture of native Saxon, Italian and Netherlands performers. In the 1620s they were augmented further by viol players from England so that, despite the war, Schütz could still call on nearly 40 members in 1632. By the end of the decade the number had been reduced virtually to single figures. No longer was he able to compose poly-choral works, elaborate *historiae* (oratorios) and brilliant motets for solo voices with varied instrumental accompaniments, as in the previous decade. Schütz's output, *de rigueur,* had been reduced in the mid-1630s to works for a handful of solo singers with no instrumental accompaniment other than a keyboard instrument, perhaps doubled by a bass viol or dulcian (bassoon).

Schütz marked the end of the war with a collection of motets, *Geistliche Chormusik* (1648). It is dedicated to the *Thomaner,* the choristers attached to St Thomas', Leipzig where in the next century J.S. Bach became *Kantor.* The town council here had kept its church music establishment in working order, in contrast with the situation in electoral Dresden. Of particular poignancy is motet No 4, *Verleih uns Frieden genädiglich*: Grant peace in our time, O Lord.

From and in Dresden, Schütz devoted the final twenty-five years of his life to the composition of works that mirror those written before the devastation of the 1630s: each new work has an earlier counterpart. So, for instance, the enduring *Christmas Story* (c1664) mirrors in more modern form the *Resurrection Story* of 1623, which itself had been a modernization of the setting made by Scandello in 1568 shortly after his appointment. One small detail of the *Christmas Story* highlights the complex relationship between Court, church

Figure 53. Christian Spetner's portrait of *Heinrich Schütz* aged 65. Courtesy of Manfred Lauffer.

and municipality in Dresden. The work was available on hire to any church with the necessary musical resources to perform it. Unlike in similar places, the ruler, at this time, did not exercise monopolistic rights over music written for performance by the Hofkapelle. It was at this time, however, that the Stadtpfeifer had complained to the Elector that his and other horn players were usurping their time-honoured right to play at weddings. In consequence the Elector banned the use of horns in all churches outside the Hofkirche. The result was that the horns used in the *Christmas Story* to characterize the exotic three Kings had to quickly disappear when performed elsewhere. Their parts were adapted for violins instead, and it is in this form that we generally still hear the work today.

The unaccompanied *Passions according to St John, Luke* and *Matthew,* which have likewise endured to the present day, are the only major works of Schütz's final years that do not have an earlier counterpart. A fourth Passion setting, a *Mark Passion,* has now been identified as the work of the Italian Marco Peranda (1625–75), the Hofkapellmeister for the last three years of his life. The long-standing conflict between the German and the Italian elements in the Hofkapelle was to have far-reaching consequences.

The pupils of Schütz from within the ranks of the Hofkapelle proved crucial in the revitalization of Lutheran music in the latter half of the seventeenth century. His most significant protégé was Christoph Bernhard (1627–92). Musical histories tend to honour him for his treatises on singing and on composition. However, it is as a composer that we should most revere him, especially for his motets for solo voices with instrumental accompaniment in the *Geistliche Harmonien* published in Hamburg in 1665. Particularly worthy of mention from that collection are the motets *Aus der Tiefe* ('Out of the deep') for soprano and two violins, and *Was betrübst du dich?* ('Why art thou so downcast?') for alto, violin and bass viol, both of which bear comparison with even the finest similar works by his great mentor. Schütz commissioned from Bernhard a motet to be sung at his funeral. Like many early manuscripts, it has failed to survive the various calamities that have befallen the city. It was ironic that the man who had risen to deputy Hofkapell-meister in 1655 and had brought some outstanding singers back to Dresden from a study visit to Italy, should have felt himself so overshadowed by the (better-paid) Italian element that he seized the first opportunity to take up an appointment elsewhere. On the death of Weckmann in 1674 he returned to Dresden as Vize-Kapellmeister and, in 1681, when in a cost-cutting exercise the new Elector, Johann Georg III, had dismissed all the highly paid Italians, he became finally Hofkapellmeister.

Another significant pupil of Schütz to move to Hamburg (1655) was the above-mentioned Matthias Weckmann (c1619–74). He is unusual among pupils of the more voice-and-text-orientated Schütz in having made his name as an organist. From his position as organist at the Jacobikirche he was able to influence Bernhard's appointment as Kantor of the same church. Recent scholarship has challenged the authenticity of some of the keyboard works hitherto attributed to him. His Annunciation dialogue (soprano and two recorders, tenor and two violins) *Gegrüßet seist du, Maria*, 'Hail Mary, full of grace', is absolutely in the Schütz mould, especially in the way in which the two violins accompanying the Angel Gabriel play in rapid short notes in strict canon throughout, representing vividly the twitching of the angel's wings. A further Weckmann dialogue *Tobia und Raguel* was published earlier in the same century as a work of the one-time Leipzig composer Johann Rosenmüller. Rosenmüller's solo motets, *Kernsprüche*, published in Leipzig shortly after the end of the Thirty Years War, likewise show a debt of gratitude to Dresden's undisputed doyen of Protestant music. Other notable and influential pupils from the Dresden stable include Christoph Kittel (active in the Hofkapelle 1640–80) and Constantin Christian Dedekind (1628–1715).

While Schütz was predisposed to a preference for sacred music, it would be totally wrong to infer that the Hofkapelle served only a liturgical function. Increasingly Court functions called upon the Hofkapelle to contribute to a full range of festivities, of which often the music was only a part and competed with fireworks and hunting. Consequently Schütz was required to compose the first German opera *Dafne* (performed at the residence in Torgau, 1627) and a further opera *Orpheus und Euridice*, written for the marriage of the heir to the electoral throne in 1638. Significantly, the Elector was able to finance this latter event, whereas the musical establishment had fallen apart for the day-to-day liturgical needs of the Hofkirche. Sadly, neither of these operas has survived. As we shall see, however, the conflicting interests of sacred and secular operatic music and of German and Italian musicians increasingly dominate the musical life of the Court, with opera and Italian performers the ultimate winners during the golden age of the Hofkapelle in Dresden.

One of the reasons for Christoph Bernhard's departure to Hamburg was the persistent preference given by the Elector to the Italian musicians. Ten years earlier, Schütz had recommended Bernhard for the vacant position of *Vizekapellmeister*, but the position was awarded to the male soprano Giovanni Bontempi (1624–1705). It was for Bontempi that we may assume Schütz wrote the part of the Angel in the *Christmas Story*, Angelini or Angelino being his original name, meaning 'little angel'. The Court records show that the Italians were better paid than their native colleagues, causing bitter resentment. It is significant that, following the death of Schütz, there was an unbroken succession of Italians directing the Hofkapelle: Marco Peranda (1672–75); Sebastiano Cherici (1675); Vincenzo Albrici (1675–80). Only financial hardship ended this, as the Elector dismissed the Italians and tempted back Bernhard, who held the post until his death in 1692. The preference for Italian composer-directors was doubly significant. It showed that the function of the Hofkapelle had changed drastically from the liturgical body envisaged by Luther and Walter to a political instrument: ostentatious opera performances by the Court musicians had become a means by which political and economic power could be made manifest.

A Catholic Ruler and a Protestant Town, 1697–1763

The radical change that took place in 1697, when Elector Friedrich August I, that is Augustus the Strong, who had acceded to the Electoral throne in 1694, converted for political reasons to Catholicism, was probably not quite as dramatic and abrupt as it may seem. The musical climate in favour of Italian musicians and Italianate music had long been apparent. This was so much so that, some thirty years earlier, Constantin Dedekind had founded a *kleine deutsche Kapelle* as an instrument of Lutheran church music performed only by Germans. Even with the conversion of the Elector to Catholicism, a Lutheran element was maintained, with its own chapel and a very modest budget to maintain minimal resources for unpretentious musical support to the liturgy. Forty years later even this came to an end, when the chapel was converted into living quarters and the services transferred to the Sophienkirche and the tender mercies of the unpredictable Wilhelm Friedemann Bach.

At all events, the change from a Lutheran Electoral establishment to that of a Catholic King of Poland and Elector of Saxony in 'personal union' (with an additional 'Royal Polish Chamber Music') coincided with Dresden's meteoric rise in prestige in all the arts, but especially music. Virtually all the major figures in music in the first half of the eighteenth century can be related in some way to the Court in Dresden, especially in respect of opera. Handel came in 1719 to poach the best singers for the enterprises in which he was involved in London. The King was so enraged at their defection that he temporarily disbanded the opera in 1720. It was in Dresden, in 1717, that the famous musical duel between Johann Sebastian Bach and the French virtuoso Louis Marchand had been arranged, only for the latter to beat an ignominious retreat before the event actually took place.

A catalogue of all the important figures in Dresden would outstrip the confines of this chapter, but a few names may be used to point to the many. Antonio Vivaldi, although not present in person, dedicated a set of violin sonatas to Johann Georg Pisendel (1687–1755), his former pupil and the Elector's Konzertmeister (leader of the orchestra), as did also Albinoni. Another virtuoso violinist at the Court was Pantaleon Hebenstreit (1667–1750). Hebenstreit's Christian name became the name by which an instrument he designed came to be known. The 'pantalon' was a sophisticated form of the rustic zither, its dynamic range influencing the advance of the pianoforte in the mid-eighteenth century. Early pianofortes were often named 'pantalon' after him. There is an amusing account of a musical encounter between the Leipzig Kantor Johann Kuhnau (clavichord), the Prague lutenist Count Losy and Hebenstreit on his own instrument. The Count, on hearing the pantalon for the first time, was beside himself, storming out of the room and protesting to Kuhnau that he had 'heard all the fine things that music has to offer, but never before . . . anything like this'.

There is a further link between Count Losy and Dresden in the person of Leopold Silvius Weiss (1686–1750), an almost exact contemporary of Johann Sebastian Bach, and the two knew each other. Weiss was the outstanding performer of his day and, by 1744, the highest paid member of the Hofkapelle. His recitals throughout Europe brought him to London in 1718. An unfortunate incident in 1722 nearly ended his prodigious career. He gave hospitality to a French violinist by name of Petit who was applying for a post in the Hofkapelle. When Petit failed to gain the post he assumed that Weiss had put in an unfavourable word behind his back, and took his revenge by attempting to bite off his host's thumb. Fortunately Weiss and his thumb survived the attack. All contemporary reports speak of the magic of his playing. His tribute to Count Losy, *Tombeau sur la Mort de M. Losy*, is arguably the finest, most poetic work in the lute repertoire, and certainly one of the most moving works written for any instrument in the course of the eighteenth century.

The revival of the lute and related instruments in more recent times has helped to bring Weiss to our attention. There were, however, many composers attached to the Dresden Court at some time who are now likewise undergoing revaluation following a period in relative obscurity. One other such is Antonio Lotti (c1667–1740), the *maestro di capella* at St Mark's in Venice who, in 1717, was commissioned to write an opera for the wedding of the Elector. Lotti's four major stage works over the next two years, written in Dresden, won such acclamation that he was allowed to keep the coach and horses placed at his disposal for his return journey. Thereafter Lotti composed no more operas and undertook no further trips outside Venice. His various settings of the *Crucifixus* for up to ten voices have survived in libraries scattered around Europe, a testament to the high esteem in which the composer was held in his time.

The very opposite is true of Lotti's pupil, the Bohemian composer Jan Dismas Zelenka (1679–1745). He first came to Dresden as a double bass player, but was allowed protracted leave of absence from 1715–19 to study under Fux in Vienna and Lotti in Venice. For many years he acted as Kapellmeister during the long illness suffered by the existing incumbent, Johann David Heinichen (1683–1729), who had been appointed in 1719. Heinichen's premature death from tuberculosis robbed the Elector not only of a very capable composer but of a theoretician whose treatise on *Der General-Bass in der Composition* (1728) was much admired throughout Europe. An incident during rehearsal of Heinichen's opera *Flavio Crispo* (1720) between the composer and the singer Senesino over an alleged inappropriate setting

Figure 54. Balthasar Denner, Johann Adolph Hasse, 1740. Courtesy of Manfred Lauffer.

of an Italian word led to such acrimony (Senesino tore up the part!) that reconciliation proved well-nigh impossible. The King finally supported the authority of his Kapellmeister by sacking all the Italian singers for their arrogance. When, in 1733, Heinichen's post was advertised, it went not to Zelenka, but to Hasse. Zelenka was made to content himself with the minor title of *Kirchen-compositeur*, completely up-staged by the opera composer. Worse still, the Elector forbade copies of Zelenka's sacred music to be made for circulation outside the Court. Consequently his highly individual and original compositions remained unknown for two centuries, and the divide between the music of a Catholic Court and its Protestant *Hinterland* was increasingly accentuated.

Johann Adolf Hasse (1699–1783), the preferred candidate in 1733, was the most feted opera composer of the mid-eighteenth century in Germany and Italy, in the period dominated in England by Handel and terminated by the advent of the young Mozart. Handel was a great admirer of his and borrowed almost 50 of his arias for various stage works produced in London in the 1730s. Hasse was also the favourite composer of Frederick the Great of neighbouring Prussia, and many of his Dresden operas were also produced in the Royal Opera in Berlin. Ironically it was Frederick the Great who brought about the end of Hasse's time in Dresden with the bombardment of the city in 1760, as a consequence of which much of Hasse's music was destroyed, especially the chamber works. Hasse is reported to have said that if the Prussian monarch had realized that the bombardment was to destroy so many of the composer's scores, he would have alerted him in advance, so that the music could be placed in a safer place. The same bombardment and subsequent defeat of Saxony in the Seven Years War (1756–63) also temporarily brought the sumptuous period of music in Dresden to an end, as economic necessity proved incompatible with the massive indulgence that the music at Court had represented. Hasse never came to London, although he asserted that he had received many invitations. This is in part made credible by the dedications of the opera *Demetrio* to the Earl of Middlesex and *Euristeo*, composed in Venice in 1732, 'to the English Nation'. Hasse's fame was as short-lived as it was prodigious. He died in Venice and only a handful of mourners attended his funeral.

One further Dresden personality in the years leading up to the outbreak of the Seven Years War merits attention: Princess Maria Antonia Walpurgis (1724–80), sister of the Bavarian Elector Maximillian III Joseph (1727–77), one of the finest viola da gamba players Charles Burney had ever heard. Maria Antonia married the heir apparent, Friedrich Christian, (by proxy) in 1747. Irritated at the great Metastasio's harsh criticisms of an opera libretto she had written, and impatient at waiting for Hasse to advise her on matters of composition, she set about doing the whole thing herself. In 1754 she delighted the Court with her own opera *Il Trionfo della Fedeltà*. Within months, word of the opera had reached Paris and, in May 1755, a lengthy review of the work appeared in the *Journal Etranger*, followed in January 1756 by the publication of one of the arias from the opera in full in the same journal. A second opera was to follow: in about 1760 her second opera *Talestri, Regina delle Amazzoni* was performed at her brother's Electoral Court in Bavaria, and published five years later by Breitkopf in Leipzig. It was one of the first scores to be printed using the revolutionary movable type fonts. The first Dresden performance appears to have been in August 1763, almost the last opera to be performed at the Court before the great break. Dr Charles Burney was in Munich in 1772 when the opera was being revived there, and in 1770 the overture to the opera was published in England in full, while a keyboard arrangement of the overture to her first opera was published in Leipzig in 1761. Copies of both of these editions, and indeed of both the full opera scores, are held by the British Library in London.

Unlike others in her position Maria Antonia was desperate for all Europe to know of her achievements. She corresponded on the subject with Empress Maria Theresa in Vienna, with Frederick the Great in Berlin, and with his sister Wilhelmine in Bayreuth. Wilhelmine was very similar to Maria Antonia and had also composed an opera of her own *(Argenore)* several years earlier. Maria Antonia's determination to publicize her works (and she did compose others) might be taken as 'protesting too much'. The suspicion still lingers that someone, possibly Hasse, possibly someone at the Court in Munich, may have helped her more than was made apparent. Alternatively she should be given full credit for two operas of which any Court composer in Europe at that time would have been proud.

The Decline of Court and Church and the Rise of New Institutions, 1763–1918

Music at the Court, especially the Italian Opera, went into decline in the early 1760s, and the link between the Electorate of Saxony and the Kingdom of Poland was also ruptured. The early death of Maria Antonia's husband, the heir apparent, in 1763 resulted in this highly talented lady living out her days as the Dowager Electress (in royal terms the Queen Mother) of Saxony and the most artistically gifted queen that Poland never had. Slowly the Italian Opera and the Hofkapelle were reinstated, not least by the efforts of Elector Friedrich August III, himself a highly competent musician. Now the members of the Court orchestra fulfilled all three functions as opera, church and chamber musicians, whereas in its heyday these musical activities had been more differentiated. More crucially, in Dresden as elsewhere, music was becoming a middle-class preoccupation, as private and municipal enterprises wrested music away from the strongholds of Church and Court.

The Congress of Vienna in 1815 created the Kingdom of Saxony. A municipal Deutsche Oper was soon called into being and competed with the Court institutions that had already been opened up to a paying non-aristocratic public. The middle classes, not surprisingly, showed a distinct preference for German works, and it is in this context that we see the rise of Carl-Maria von Weber (1786–1826). The composer's early death in London brought to a premature end the series of operas comprising *Der Freischütz, Euryanthe*

Figure 55. John Hayter's portrait of Carl-Maria von Weber completed in 1829, after the composer's death. Courtesy of Manfred Lauffer.

and *Oberon*. With his death, the future of German opera in Dresden seemed doomed, but the Italian Court opera was disbanded in 1832, and by the time the magnificent Royal Saxon Opera House, designed by Gottfried Semper, was opened in 1841, German-language opera was on offer to the general public in an institution that was no longer subject solely to the will of the monarch. For all that, however, the premature death of Weber was a bitter blow to the evolution of quality German 'light' opera in a post-Mozartian tradition. Weber brought new standards of orchestral playing (meeting initially with much hostility from the musicians, before gaining their respect and admiration). Weber also concerned himself with the acting, the sets and the costumes, seeing musical stage works as the amalgam of all these constituent parts. His greatest contribution was, perhaps, the physical reforms that he introduced to the orchestral pit in 1817. Hitherto the space had been very cramped and contact between the conductor, the orchestra and the singers almost non-existent. Weber sought to remedy this, but once again his reforming zeal met with disapproval, this time from the King, who indirectly ordered a return to the *status quo*. Weber countered with an open written appeal to the public. He justified all the new measures, introduced in the interests of improved visibility, balance and greater space for more players, pointing out that the musical demands made of the players by contemporary music were no longer to be equated with the simplistic scoring of much Italian *opera buffa*. A mere detail in all this is the fact that Weber conducted not from the keyboard, and not with a roll of music as had hitherto been the custom, but with a baton. Weber seems ultimately to have won the admiration of the King, for shortly after he was accorded the title of 'royal' conductor. He was the beneficiary of his own reforms for all too short a period, but the real beneficiary in subsequent years was his successor, Richard Wagner (1813–83), with his truly sophisticated orchestral scores. It is small wonder, therefore, that it was Wagner who spearheaded the campaign for the return of Weber's mortal remains from the Roman Catholic burial ground in Moorfields in London to the Catholic cemetery in the Dresden suburb of Friedrichstadt. The reinterment took place on 15 December 1844, in a family vault designed by none other than Gottfried Semper, the architect of the Dresden Opera House.

Wagner was born in Leipzig, educated at the Kreuzschule in Dresden, and returned to Dresden after appointments in Riga and Paris. Whilst Kapellmeister in the Opera House, he composed the oratorio *Das Liebesmahl der Aposteln*, that was first performed in the Frauenkirche with Wagner himself conducting. Before his political activities necessitated a hasty farewell from the royal capital in 1849, his early operas in Dresden, *Rienzi, Der fliegende Holländer, Tannhäuser, Lohengrin,* had established German beyond all doubt as a medium for serious opera. By the time Wagner returned to Dresden, in 1862, his operas had become firmly fixed in the repertoire of the Royal Opera.

During the early Wagner years in Dresden public concerts were also held by Robert Schumann (1810–56) and his wife Clara *née* Wieck (1819–96). Their protracted love affair and its tragic consequences for Robert are well enough known not to be dwelt upon here. Clara's half-sister, Marie Wieck, continued with these concerts in the 1850s. Dresden was now emerging as a middle-class music metropolis, attracting the foremost virtuosi and conductors of Europe – Spohr, Paganini, Berlioz and Mendelssohn, to name but a few,

Figure 56. Unknown painter, portrait of Richard Wagner during his last visit to Dresden 1880. Courtesy of Manfred Lauffer.

and in 1856 the Dresden Academy for the training of aspiring musicians was formally instituted.

Throughout the nineteenth century the number of municipal and private music institutions steadily increased, with a plethora of orchestras, choirs, and concert series quite outside the hold of the Elector. In 1870 a new concert hall, the *Gewerbehaussaal,* was built and in its wake a new orchestra was formed, the Dresden Philharmonic Orchestra, which formally adopted the shortened title of Dresdner Philharmonie in 1923. Semper's first opera house burnt down in 1869 and was replaced by a second Semper-Oper nine years later. In the meanwhile the Königliche Kapelle, as the former Hofkapelle was now known, held its concerts in the municipal *Gewerbehaussaal* until

Figure 57. Richard Strauss (photograph by Dr. Gertrud Ulmer). Courtesy of
Manfred Lauffer.

able to return to the opera house. Among the outstanding musical directors
of this period was Ernst von Schuch, who presided over the rise of the opera
for over thirty years until his death in 1914. During those years such notable
figures as Brahms, Tchaikovsky, Dvořák and Rachmaninov (who lived in
Dresden from 1906–9) stepped on the podium as conductors of the *Phil-
harmonische populäre Künstlerkonzerte* given by the Philharmonic Orchestra.
These have continued to the present day under the title of *ausserordentliche*

Figure 58. Richard Strauss, seated centre, with, on his right, Alfred Reucker, the General Manager of the Semper Opera and, on his left, Fritz Busch, the Director of Music (Alois Mora and Leonhard Fanto behind). Courtesy of Manfred Lauffer.

(extraordinary or special) *Konzerte*. However, the leading figure in the first half of this century has to be Richard Strauss (1864–1949), who, with a string of premieres in Dresden, beginning with *Feuersnot* in 1901, to be followed by *Salome* in 1905, *Elektra* (1909) and *Rosenkavalier* (1911), not only cemented his own position in the world of opera but confirmed Dresden as a city at the leading edge of musical developments in Europe.

The Weimar Republic, Nazism and the Destruction of the City in 1945

Between the World Wars this tradition was maintained as Fritz Busch put on further Strauss premieres, notably *Intermezzo* in 1924 and *Die ägyptische Helena* in 1928, conducted not by Busch but by the composer himself. Busch was hounded out of office by the Nazis, but Clemens Krauss continued the Strauss link with the premiere of *Arabella* in 1933. Karl Böhm conducted the first performance of *Die schweigsame Frau* in 1935, but it was discontinued by the Nazi authorities after only four performances when they discovered that its librettist Stefan Zweig was a Jew. Strauss had not only consciously carried on collaborations with Jewish librettists, he had a Jewish daughter-in-law and therefore Jewish grandchildren. That compromised him in his dealings with the Nazi authorities, a fact not always acknowledged by commentators in subsequent years. Other significant premieres by Hindemith *(Cadillac)* in 1925, Busoni *(Doktor Faust)* and Kurt Weill *(Der Protagonist)* in 1926, also took place in the inter-war years in Dresden.

The GDR Years, 1945–89

The horrendous events in Dresden at the end of the Second World War in 1945 are too well known to be reiterated here and are indeed the motivating factor behind the present publication. Despite the scene of unbelievable destruction, the Dresden Philharmonic resumed giving public concerts in June 1945. The orchestra's first artistic manager under the new post-war GDR regime was Heinz Bongartz who remained in office until 1963 and was succeeded by H. Förster (1964–7) and more tellingly by Kurt Masur (1967–72).

There were similar developments with the resuscitated Staatsoper and Staatskapelle, as the erstwhile Hofkapelle, subsequently the Königliche Kapelle, had been known since the dissolution of the monarchy in 1918. Among the list of resident conductors in the post-war years the most notable was Rudolf Kempe (1950–3). The rebuilding programme meant that in 1969 the Dresden Philharmonic could move into the new Palace of Culture, and this then also became the orchestral home of the Staatskapelle. Both orchestras undertook extensive tours abroad. At the height of the Cold War, with prejudice against the GDR at its worst in the Federal Republic, the first tour of West Germany by the Staatskapelle under Lovro von Matacic in 1956 met with effusive critical acclaim in Munich and in Hamburg. It is undeniably true that the touring activities of both orchestras served the political aim of using cultural institutions to impress the outside world and encourage it to make deductions about the political and economic standing of the country from whence they came. But it must be pointed out that this had been historically the function of the Staatskapelle for most of the 400 years of its existence, and that it was not as a purely altruistic gesture that powerful Western governments were likewise exporting their cultural wares to Eastern Europe during the Cold War years.

The revival of music in Dresden in the aftermath of the destruction of 1945 was also fostered by the musical activities in and emanating from the *Kreuzkirche*. Notable, here, was the role played by Rudolf Mauersberger (1889–1971), whose period in office as Kreuzkantor from 1930 extended from the final years of the Weimar Republic, through the difficult years from

Figure 59. Rudolf Mauersberger conducting choir boys in the Zwinger, pre-war. Courtesy of Manfred Lauffer

Hitler's *Machtergreifung* (seizure of power) in 1933 and the ensuing war, to the founding and consolidation, for better or for worse, of the German Democratic Republic (GDR) after the war. In 1955 Mauersberger instituted the famous *Heinrich-Schütz-Tage*. His death in 1971 precluded his participation in the international tercentenary celebrations of the death of Heinrich Schütz, a composer whose world-wide rediscovery in the post-war years owed much to the early recordings made by Mauersberger and the Kreuzchor of such major works as *Die Musikalischen Exequien*. Despite his reputation as a Schütz interpreter, Mauersberger was also a champion of contemporary church music, and the name of the Kreuzchor became associated with performances of such leading German composers as Distler and Pepping. Under him, however, the Romantic repertoire was somewhat neglected, though this is not a charge that can be held against his recent successors Martin Flämig and Gothart Stier.

Mauersberger's long association with the Kreuzchor lived on in the performances still held, though no longer annually, of the *Dresdner Requiem*. This was composed in 1948 as a substantial (polychoral) sequel to the motet to the opening words of the Lamentations of Jeremiah, *Wie liegt die Stadt so wüst, die voll Volks war?* (How doth the city sit solitary, that was full of people?) that the Kreuzkantor had written for Good Friday 1945 in the immediate aftermath of the calamity, when among the dead were ten of his boy choristers and three of the clergy attached to the Kreuzkirche.

The Kreuzchor, like Dresden's two leading orchestras, also became involved in major tours abroad. Often singers used these tours as a means to defect, with the result that frequent and lengthy travel bans were then imposed on the choir, the authorities in a sense cutting off their nose to spite their face, for in so doing they were inhibiting the powerful politico-cultural message they were so at pains to propagate. Among *alumni* who have achieved international status in post-war years are Karl Richter, with his somewhat eccentric interpretations of Bach, the Wagnerian bass Theo Adam, and the tenor (more recently conductor) Peter Schreier, whose extensive list of recordings began as the boy alto soloist in Mauersberger's early recording of Bach's *John Passion*.

Mauersberger's elegiac motet and the *Dresdner Requiem* and are by no means the only works written with the events of 1945 in mind. In 1996, shortly before his death, the Dresden composer Rainer Kunad wrote his oratorio *Die Pforte der Freude* (The Gates of Joy) and this was performed in the Kreuzkirche on February 13. Benjamin Britten's *War Requiem* was first performed for the consecration of the new Coventry Cathedral in 1962. Britten specifically wrote the work for performance by a Russian soprano (Galina Visnevskaya), an English tenor (Peter Pears) and the German baritone Dietrich Fischer-Dieskau. Coventry and Dresden, having shared similar fates in the war, had long been twinned. It was therefore appropriate that the first performance outside Britain should be held in Dresden in 1965 to mark the twentieth anniversary of the destruction of the city. The performance took place in the Martin-Luther-Kirche with the Dresdner Philharmonie under Kurt Sanderling. Britten, a committed pacifist and Quaker, wrote in the programme: '*I was delighted to hear that my Requiem is soon to be performed in Dresden, and I am moved that you should have chosen to perform it on the day that marks the anniversary of those dreadful events.*' In subsequent performances of the *War Requiem* in Dresden in 1974 Fischer-Dieskau felt it appropriate for 'his' role to be taken by Theo Adam, who ran perilously near to damning Britten's masterpiece with faint praise in describing it as 'a grandiose, sincere work, and a modern composition that sounds good'!

There is a similar – and more intriguing – tale to tell in relation to the Russian composer Dmitri Shostakovich (1906–75). In 1960 he was in Dresden in connection with the writing of a film score and, while he was there, dedicated the score of his Eighth String Quartet 'to the victims of fascism and war'. This is at least the official version of that dedication. There is, however, a more sinister sub-text. Shostakovich had at this time been forced to join the Communist Party. Depressed at the evolution of things in the USSR he contemplated suicide, incorporating in the Quartet various quotations from other of his works as a sort of summing-up of his achievements. The dedication was intended primarily as a means of ensuring publication of the composition. Ultimately he was dissuaded from taking his own life, but whether or not this unofficial account of the work's background is true, the 'Dresden' dedication remains.

The names of Britten and Shostakovich remind us of a musical tradition that has marked the musical life of the city over the past century-and-a-half: Dresden as a leading venue in the performance of contemporary music, a tradition that survived undiminished during the years of the GDR. Even in 1947, the *Staatsoper* was able to premiere the West German composer Boris Blacher's opera *Die Flut*. This was followed by premieres of new operas by the Swiss Robert Oboussier and by Fidelio Friedrich Finke (1891–1968), a Czech-born composer who moved to Dresden after the war, and by two other major Dresden composers, Rainer Kunad (1936–96) and Udo Zimmermann, yet another *Kruzianer*, born in Dresden in 1943. Zimmermann is currently the director of the *Dresdner Zentrum für zeitgenössische Musik* (Dresden Centre for Contemporary Music), which, since 1986, has held an annual festival of contemporary music, known as *Dresdner Tage der zeitgenössische Musik*.

Music in Dresden since Reunification

The mainstream orchestral, chamber and choral repertoire has never ceased to be well represented in the musical life of Dresden, and continues to flourish with a host of ensembles, orchestras, choirs and enterprises too lengthy to list in detail. Modern music, as we have seen, continues to be well catered for, and the area of Early Music, meaning the performance of music before 1800 using historic instruments and deploying historic performance practices, has likewise made its mark on the life of the city with a *Gesellschaft zur Pflege alter Musik* (Society for the Promotion of Early Music) attached to the State Conservatory and specialist ensembles such as the *Dresdner Barock-orchester* and *Das Ensemble Alte Musik Dresden*, both of which have taken part in performances with the Kreuzchor.

Understandably one encounters a certain coyness when enquiring into the constraints that obtained during the forty years of the GDR. Indubitably there were problems and indubitably there were conflicts of political and artistic interest. The shift from a centrally directed economy to a market-driven economy is, likewise, not bereft of problems as other non-artistic criteria begin to set the agenda in questions of subsidy and financial viability. The musical history of Dresden, however, has been marked by upheaval, disaster, adaptation and triumphant resurgence. One can only hope and assume that this will long continue to be the case, and that a rebuilt Frauen-kirche will resume its place in that process.

Dresden's Literary and Theatrical Traditions

Judith Purver

Blühe, *deutsches Florenz*, mit deinen Schätzen der Kunstwelt!
Stille gesichert sei *Dresden Olympia* uns.

Blossom, Germany's Florence, rich storehouse of art's choicest treasures!
Preservèd in peace be thou ever, Dresden Olympia, for us.

Johann Gottfried Herder (1744–1803)

The picture of Dresden presented in this book would be incomplete without looking at the part played by literature and the theatre in the cultural and social life of the Saxon capital over the past four centuries. Although less well known than its contribution to the European heritage in other areas, such as architecture, music, or painting, the arts based on the written and spoken word are equally important for a full appreciation of the city's cultural significance. This is particularly so because of the interaction between the different arts, and between them and other intellectual and social developments at major junctures of Dresden's cultural and political history.

The origins of German literature are rooted in pre-Christian culture. The earliest German poetry – like Old English poetry, to which it is closely akin – was not rhymed but alliterative, and celebrated the deeds of warrior heroes in the context of a pagan Germanic religion. It was almost wholly destroyed in the Christian era, but an example of it is preserved in the eighth-century *Hildebrandslied* (Lay of Hildebrand) and its influence is apparent in the early thirteenth-century *Nibelungenlied*, on which Wagner drew for his *Ring* cycle.

The development of the German literary tradition is closely connected with that of the standard language. Here, the role of Saxony was crucial. The power of the Wettin state, the influence of the Lutheran Bible and the Reformation, and the work of writers and scholars of the later eighteenth century established East Middle German (Upper Saxon) as the basis for modern High German. Of major importance in this process was Johann Christoph Adelung (1732–1806), Librarian in the Dresden Royal Library, who published a five-volume dictionary of standard German in 1774–86 and a German grammar in 1781.

In the Middle Ages Dresden did not play a prominent role in literary production, although the great flowering of medieval poetry around 1200 owed much to the patronage of Landgrave Hermann of Thuringia at the Wartburg castle above Eisenach, where Luther, under the protection of the Elector of Saxony, was later to translate the New Testament. The city does, however, figure in literary and theatrical history from the late sixteenth century onwards. Overshadowed as it was by Leipzig – which boasted Germany's leading university and became, with Frankfurt, a major centre of the German book trade – Dresden was often little more than a literary backwater. The periods at which the city entered the mainstream of literary and theatrical development, however, were epoch-making not only for Dresden and Saxony, but for Germany and Europe as a whole.

In 1586 Lord Leicester's *Englische Komödianten* (English Comedians), the generic name given to the troupes of strolling players who travelled throughout Germany in the late sixteenth and seventeenth centuries, gave guest performances at the Dresden court on the recommendation of the Elector of Brandenburg. This was both the first visit of English Comedians to any German venue and the first recorded theatrical performance in the city. The repertoire of the *Englische Komödianten* included works by most of the Elizabethan and Jacobean dramatists, performed in prose adaptations in the original language, and from about 1604 onwards in German. In the earlier years most of the audience would have been unable to understand the dialogue, so the actors aimed at strong visual effects, ranging from eloquent gestures and rich costumes to realistic scenes of bloodshed. In Dresden and several other cities they obtained court protection and, after 1592, some of them stayed permanently in Germany, recruiting native actors into their ranks. Even after German was adopted as the language of performance, however, the repertoire remained predominantly English and the name 'Englische Komödianten' was used until the middle of the seventeenth century.

During that century, Saxony attained a leading position in Germany both culturally and economically, but was less significant for German literature of the period than for intellectual history, for music, and for the theatre. There is, in fact, no equivalent in seventeenth-century Germany of the great age of classical literature in France under Louis XIII and Louis XIV: the ravages of the Thirty Years War and the absence of a unified cultural and political centre prevented this. Nevertheless, 1626 saw the German premiere of *Hamlet* in Dresden; in the following year the great baroque poet Martin

Opitz (1597–1639) translated Rinuccini's *Daphne* for performance in the city to music by Heinrich Schütz; and in 1685 Johannes Velten (1640–92 or 1693) and his company of actors entered the service of Elector Johann Georg II, soon afterwards introducing the plays of Molière and Corneille to the repertoire.

Together with the neighbouring states of Thuringia and Silesia, Saxony also played a major role in Protestant hymn writing of the period. Martin Rinckart (1586–1649), best known as the author of *Nun danket alle Gott* (Now Thank We All Our God), was a pastor in the Saxon town of Eilenburg, while Gottfried Arnold (1666–1714), whose hymns were especially popular among the pietistic community, spent some time as a private tutor in Dresden.

It was not until the eighteenth century, however, that the city's cultural florescence really began. While the literature of the 'Augustan Age', in marked contrast to the splendours of its architecture, consisted largely of court poetry of inferior quality, Dresden became the catalyst for a development that was to prove one of the most significant in the whole of German and European cultural history. It was here that the art historian Johann Joachim Winckelmann (1717–68), who became the most important antiquary of the eighteenth century and is regarded by many as the founder of the discipline of classical archaeology, joined the circle of the Saxon court and studied examples of classical sculpture in the collections established by Augustus II, publishing in 1755 his polemical essay *Gedanken über die Nachahmung der griechischen Werke in der Malerei und Bildhauerkunst* (Thoughts on the Imitation of Greek Painting and Sculpture), which became the manifesto of German Classicism. His conception of the antique as noble, elevated, serene, and simple (*eine edle Einfalt und eine stille Größe*) exercised a decisive influence on Lessing (1729–81), Goethe (1749–1832), Schiller (1759–1805), and other writers and was of seminal importance in the development of European Classicism.

Both Goethe and Schiller paid a number of visits to Dresden, which was geographically quite close to the Classical centre of Weimar. In 1768, while a student in Leipzig, Goethe had admired the collection of paintings in the Johanneum on the Neumarkt and viewed from the dome of the Frauenkirche the devastation wrought by Prussian bombardment of the city during the Seven Years War. In April 1813, at the beginning of the Wars of Liberation against Napoleon, he watched the entry of the Russian Tsar and the King of Prussia into the city from a window of the painter Gerhard von Kügelgen's house in the Hauptstraße (now home to the Museum of Early Romanticism). Like many other illustrious contemporaries, Goethe and Schiller were also guests in the house of Christian Gottfried Körner, who composed the first musical setting of Schiller's *Ode to Joy* and at whose summer residence in Loschwitz Schiller worked on his tragedy *Don Carlos*, the basis for Verdi's

Figure 60. Johann Friedrich Schiller (1759–1805) and the Loschwitz Summer
House, where he worked on Don Carlos (see p. 167). Courtesy of the
Kupferstichkabinett, Sächsische Landesbibliothek, Deutsche Fotothek.

opera of that title. When Goethe died in 1832, a memorial performance at the Dresden court theatre of his Classical drama *Iphigenie* marked the end of an era.

That era, extending approximately from the middle of the eighteenth to the end of the first third of the nineteenth century and often known – somewhat misleadingly – as the 'Age of Goethe', had seen an unprecedented upsurge of creative activity in all areas of German cultural, artistic, and intellectual life. It was to have a profound and lasting influence not only on Germany but on Europe as a whole. To gain some idea of this, one only has to think of the Weimar Republic, which owed its name to the immense authority exerted by German Classicism; of the Grimms' collection of fairy tales, which arose from the Romantic concern with a common *national* heritage, yet is now, after the decline in knowledge of the Bible and classical mythology, the only cultural heritage that *Europeans* still hold in common; of the powerfully symbolic paintings created by Caspar David Friedrich in his Dresden studio; and of the Romantic music of Weber, Schumann and others which still has a major place in the concert and operatic repertoire throughout the world. All this would be unthinkable without the role played by Dresden in its genesis.

It was, in fact, not only Classicism to which the Saxon capital acted as midwife; it may fairly claim a decisive role in the birth of Romanticism as well. In contrast to the situation in France, where the two movements are clearly distinct from one another and widely separated in time, the position in Germany is more complex. The legacy of the Thirty Years War meant that Classicism came late to Germany, and Romanticism followed it so closely that it is not always easy to separate the two. From a European perspective, Goethe and Schiller may appear to be Romantics; viewed from a German perspective, however, they are the epitome of literary Classicism and regarded themselves as such. Whether Classicists, Romantics, or classifiable under neither heading, however, nearly all the leading figures of that uniquely fertile period of German culture spent time in Dresden, drank deep of its artistic and architectural splendours, and drew inspiration from them for their own work.

Just as Dresden's collections of sculpture had been an essential factor in the development of Classicism, so the paintings of the Dresden gallery played a similar role for Romanticism. One painting above all, Raphael's Sistine Madonna, became the Romantics' cult picture. In the summer of 1796 two young men from Berlin, Ludwig Tieck (1773–1853) and Wilhelm Heinrich Wackenroder (1773–98), viewed it together, and at the end of that year published *Herzensergießungen eines kunstliebenden Klosterbruders* (Outpourings of the Heart of an Art-loving Monk), with a portrait of 'Der

Göttliche Raphael' (The Divine Raphael) as frontispiece. This was followed in 1798, after Wackenroder's death, by Tieck's Romantic novel of the artist's life *Franz Sternbalds Wanderungen* (Franz Sternbald's Travels) and in 1799 by a jointly authored collection of essays, *Phantasien über die Kunst* (Fantasies on Art). These writings, in particular the *Herzensergießungen* (the bulk of which is by Wackenroder) and Tieck's novel, are seminal texts for early German Romanticism. In them, Italian Renaissance painters – especially Michelangelo, Leonardo da Vinci, and above all Raphael – are extolled alongside the German Dürer as vessels of quasi-divine revelation, and Tieck's novel contains important reflections on the role of landscape in painting. These works influenced Romantic painters, particularly Philipp Otto Runge, Ludwig Richter, and the Nazarenes. The latter in turn inspired the Aberdonian William Dyce, who painted the frescoes in the Parliament buildings in London.

August 1798 saw another important encounter between early Romantic writers and the paintings of the Dresden gallery. In the following year two members of the group, August Wilhelm Schlegel (1767–1845) and his wife Caroline (1763–1809), published in the periodical *Athenaeum*, edited by August Wilhelm and his brother Friedrich, a dialogue, *Die Gemählde* (The Paintings), which discusses many of the pictures and culminates in a eulogy of the Sistine Madonna and a number of poems inspired by the paintings. It also includes a description of Dresden that gives a good indication of how the Romantics viewed the city and its surroundings:

> Hier, dächte ich, ließen wir uns nieder: wir können keinen bequemeren und anmuthigeren Sitz finden. Vor uns der ruhige Fluß; jenseits erhebt sich hinter dem grünen Ufer die Ebne in leisen Wellen, dort unten spiegelt sich die Stadt mit der Kuppel der Frauenkirche im Wasser, oberhalb ziehn sich Rebenhügel dicht an der Krümmung hin, mit Landhäusern besäet und oben mit Nadelholz bedeckt.

> Here, I should think, we might sit down [the German verb also translates as 'settle' or 'settle down']; we cannot find any more comfortable and pleasant spot. In front of us the peaceful river; on the other side, beyond its green bank, the plain rises in gentle waves; below lies the city with the dome of the Frauenkirche reflected in the water; above, hugging the bend of the river, stretch vineyards dotted with villas, their higher slopes covered with conifers.

A similar, if more ornate description may be found in E.T.A. Hoffmann's fantastic tale *Der goldne Topf* (The Golden Pot), written in Dresden in 1813:

> Dicht vor ihm (Anselmus) plätscherten und rauschten die goldgelben Wellen des schönen Elbstroms, hinter demselben streckte das herrliche Dresden kühn und stolz seine lichten Türme empor in den duftigen Himmelsgrund, der sich hinabsenkte

auf die blumigen Wiesen und frisch grünenden Wälder, und aus tiefer Dämmerung gaben die zackichten Gebirge Kunde vom fernen Böhmerlande.

Directly in front of Anselmus the golden yellow waves of the beautiful River Elbe rippled and murmured, while beyond it the magnificent city of Dresden stretched its gleaming spires boldly and proudly into the translucent expanse of the sky which hung over the flowery meadows and fresh green forests, and the jagged peaks half-hidden by twilight announced the far land of Bohemia. [Translation by Ritchie Robertson.]

Hoffmann (1776–1822) – who is the author of the story on which the *Nutcracker* ballet is based and the central figure in Offenbach's opera *The Tales of Hoffmann* – wrote these words after witnessing horrific scenes of carnage and suffering in and around Dresden in the opening months of the Wars of Liberation. His story evokes the mythical kingdom of Atlantis to which, after many trials, the poet Anselmus is finally granted entry. The tale is set, however, in recognizable locations in Dresden: Atlantis is not some far-off country, but the 'magnificent city' of Dresden – reality transfigured in the light of the creative imagination. Aspects of the work recall Mozart's *Magic Flute*, which Hoffmann had conducted in Dresden immediately before writing it.

Hoffmann left the city in December 1813, never to return. Tieck, however, did visit Dresden again and, in 1819, settled there with his family. The readings of plays, poetry, and other works that he gave at his house on the Altmarkt gained him a European reputation, and the great 'Schlegel-Tieck' translation of Shakespeare's plays, begun by August Wilhelm Schlegel and completed in Dresden under Tieck's direction by Count Wolf Baudissin (1789–1878) and Tieck's daughter Dorothea (1799–1841), represents, together with Luther's Bible, probably the finest example of the translator's art in German literature. Tieck's love of Shakespeare and the theatre was expressed not only in this enterprise and in his play-readings – *A Midsummer Night's Dream* was a particular favourite – but also in his critical and editorial work, his reviews in the *Abend-Zeitung* (Evening Newspaper), and his practical concern with theatrical production. From 1825 to 1841 he was dramaturge of the Dresden court theatre, staging a number of Shakespeare's plays and works by Spanish Golden Age dramatists as well as the Dresden premiere of Goethe's *Faust* and dramas by Heinrich von Kleist (1777–1811), who was later to be recognized as one of Germany's major writers.

In 1808 Kleist, together with the conservative political philosopher and aesthetician Adam Müller (1779–1829), had founded in Dresden the monthly periodical *Phöbus – Ein Journal für die Kunst* (Phoebus – a Journal for Art)

Figure 61. Carl Christian Vogel von Vogelstein, David d'Angers modelling a bust of Ludwig Tieck. At Tieck's left is his daughter Dorothea, the Shakespeare translator. Courtesy of the *Museum der Bildenden Künste Leipzig*.

in which a number of Kleist's works and a series of lectures on drama held by Müller in Dresden in 1806 first appeared. The cover illustration by the Romantic painter Ferdinand Hartmann shows the sun-god Phoebus Apollo (who is also the god of poetry, music, healing, and prophecy), surrounded by figures of classical mythology and signs of the zodiac, driving the chariot of Oceanus, drawn by four sun-horses, through the sky above Dresden; a number of the city's landmarks, including the Hofkirche and the dome of the Frauenkirche with lantern, Cross, and Orb, are clearly visible. *Phöbus* folded after twelve issues but remains the most ambitious journal ever published in Dresden.

In due course Kleist's dramas, together with those of Shakespeare, Goethe, Schiller, and other classics, gained a secure place in Dresden's theatrical repertoire. Like audiences everywhere, however, the Dresden public expected primarily to be entertained. The history of the performing arts in the Saxon capital from its beginnings to the present day bears witness to this; it also reveals fluctuations in public taste and in the social composition of audiences.

23 Ferdinand Hartmann:
Phoebus über Dresden

Figure 62. *Phoebus over Dresden*, Ferdinand Hartmann, Woodcut, 1808.
Courtesy of the Sächsische Landesbibliothek, Deutsche Fotothek.

As we have seen, the English Comedians laid great stress on visual aspects of performance. This was necessary at first in order to overcome the language barrier; it was also characteristic of productions in Elizabethan England, where theatre-going, at least in London, was a form of mass entertainment. At that time, however, Dresden possessed no equivalent of the Globe Theatre. When not engaged at the court, the actors were permitted to perform in the suburbs only; the opera house on the Taschenberg, completed in 1667 under Johann Georg II, was intended solely for musical performances such as opera and ballet. An exception was made for Velten's troupe, but Caroline Neuber (1697–1760), probably the most important reformer in the history of the German theatre, never gained social recognition in Dresden, although she performed there a number of times and in 1737 acted before Augustus II. She died, alone and impoverished, in the suburb of Laubegast, where in 1776 a simple memorial was erected to her.

For most of its history the Dresden theatre was a court theatre. Up to the middle of the eighteenth century there were five main theatre buildings: the Taschenberg opera house; the half-timbered French theatre of 1696 and Pöppelmann's opera house of 1719, both dating from the reign of Augustus the Strong; the Mingotti theatre, a small private theatre made of wood which was built inside the Zwinger in 1746 but was destroyed by fire two years later; and the Kleines Hoftheater (Small Court Theatre), a half-timbered construction on the Theaterplatz between the Zwinger and the Elbe, built in 1755 as a private theatre by the Italian Pietro Moretti and acquired by the court in 1765. In 1776 a summer theatre was opened at the Linckesches Bad, a popular open-air restaurant and garden where the actors of the court theatre performed several times a week during the summer months – outdoors in daylight and fine weather, otherwise in a small half-timbered building. The repertoire included the tragedies of Shakespeare and dramas by Lessing and Schiller, but also plays by popular dramatists such as Iffland and Kotzebue.

From the middle of the 1770s, theatrical performances for a paying public were staged in the Small Court Theatre on a regular basis. Plays by Molière and Goldoni, as well as by German dramatists such as Gellert and Lessing, were put on there. Tickets for French plays, however, cost several times as much as those for German plays, reflecting the court preference for things French. During the Wars of Liberation the court theatre was dissolved and placed under state control, but after the King returned to Dresden in 1815 it reverted to its former status.

This was a mixed blessing. On the one hand, the royal theatres were financed by the Elector; on the other hand, the posts of theatre director and theatre secretary were court appointments, and this led to friction. Karl Gottlieb Theodor Winkler (1775–1856), better known under his pseudonym Theodor Hell, was for many years both theatre secretary and co-editor (with Friedrich Kind (1768–1843), the *Freischütz* librettist), of the *Abend-Zeitung*, also known as the *Vespertina*, which achieved one of the highest circulation figures in Germany. Most of the contributions to the *Vespertina* were banal in the extreme; the same was true of the pseudo-Romantic works read aloud by dilettante writers at gatherings of the 'Liederkreis' (Poetry Circle), the literary society under whose auspices the newspaper had been founded in

1817. Hell was also responsible, with Tieck, for determining the repertoire of the royal theatres, offering the audience a diet of lowbrow dramas in preference to the more demanding fare selected by Tieck. Hell was, however, a better judge of public taste than Tieck: in 1826 a production of Calderón, a dramatist favoured by Tieck, was booed off the stage.

Amateur scribbling was much in vogue among both men and women of the educated classes in 1820s Germany: the 'literary teas' characteristic of such circles were memorably satirized by Heine. Alongside groups of this kind there still existed literary salons reminiscent of an earlier era: the most notable of these in Dresden was presided over by Elisa von der Recke (1756–1831), the companion of the author C.A. Tiedge (1752–1841), who had published hymns, poems, and a four-volume travel diary. In her house on the Kohlmarkt (afterwards Körnerstraße) in Dresden's Neustadt she entertained writers, artists, and intellectuals, and was said to be one of the most intelligent and cultured women of her time.

The royal house of Saxony also had its share of literary talent. Amalie, Princess of Saxony (1794–1870), who wrote under the pseudonym Amalie Heiter (Amalia Merry), was a prolific and highly successful dramatist whose plays were performed not only in Dresden and in the little court theatre at Pillnitz but at commercial theatres throughout the German-speaking lands. Her collected works were published in six volumes between 1836 and 1842, and an English translation of six of her plays appeared in London in 1848. Her brother, Prince Johann (1801–73), whose equestrian statue stands in the Theaterplatz, produced under the pseudonym of Philalethes an acclaimed translation of Dante's *Divine Comedy*, founding the *Accademia Dantesca* in 1832 to assist him in this task. Both Tieck and the Shakespeare translator Baudissin were members of this group, which met in the Taschenberg Palais: thus through them, and through the German Romantic concern with translation, a link was established between Dresden and the two giants of European letters – the medieval Italian poet and the Renaissance English playwright. If Tieck's interest in Spanish drama is also taken into account, it can be seen that cultural interchange between Dresden and other European countries was not confined to the visual and musical arts but involved literature and the theatre as well. In 1830 Dresden was, in fact, the only place in Germany that still had an Italian theatre.

The year 1841 marked a watershed in the city's theatrical history: in that year Tieck relinquished his position as dramaturge and the new court theatre, designed by Gottfried Semper and doubling as an opera-house, opened. Semper saw the building as a correlative of theatrical performance, an idea that fascinated Wagner, with his Romantic-inspired conception of the *Gesamt-kunstwerk* fusing music, drama, and visual presentation. The building, in its turn, amply justified its creator's vision: both drama and opera flourished there in the years that followed its inauguration.

Many of those engaged at the theatre were of outstanding ability. This is especially true of Eduard Devrient (1801–77), who was appointed as actor-director in 1844, and his talented, if vain, younger brother Emil (1803–72), the darling of the Dresden public, whose skills both in acting and singing met with an enthusiastic reception throughout Germany and even in London. He retired in 1868, his last part being the lead in Goethe's *Torquato Tasso*. Of equal merit were Franziska Berg (1813–93), who played Ophelia in the first production of the Schlegel-Tieck version of *Hamlet*, and Marie Mayer-Bürck (1820–1910), who was said to possess all Emil Devrient's advantages without any of his weaknesses. Devrient and Mayer-Bürck were particularly impressive in dramas by Schiller. Another actress of note was Caroline Bauer, whose memoirs, published posthumously in 1871, provide an entertaining, if unreliable account of theatrical, literary, and social life in Dresden during her employment there from 1835 to 1844.

In the first half of the nineteenth century women began to make their mark in Dresden, as elsewhere in Germany, not only in the theatre and the salon but also in literature. The 'Liederkreis' had a number of female members, among them Helmine von Chézy (1783–1856), the much-maligned librettist of Weber's *Euryanthe,* and contemporary accounts list many other women writers. Although women were less prominent in the literature of Germany than in that of Britain or France at this time – there is no German equivalent of Jane Austen, the Brontës, George Eliot, or George Sand – they were sufficiently visible to provoke derogatory comments on the part of men. This, together with the emphasis placed on feminine 'modesty' in the society of the time, discouraged many of them from advertising their authorship publicly: the names of Dorothea Tieck, Caroline Schlegel, and Princess Amalie are absent from the works to which they put their hand. This remained a common practice among women writers throughout the century.

A notable exception to this rule is the aristocratic novelist and travel-writer Countess Ida Hahn-Hahn (1805–80). When she settled in Dresden, in 1845, she was the most famous and widely read writer in Germany. She became the centre of a socially and intellectually exclusive circle, and although she lived openly with her lover, Baron Bystram, she was even granted recognition by the court. Her novels reflect her own negative experience of marriage and plead the claims of love above those of the existing moral and social order. After the publication of a parody of her best known novel in 1847, however, her popularity declined. She was further affected by Bystram's death and by the revolutions of 1848–9. In 1850 she converted to Catholicism and retired to a convent, achieving renewed success as a writer in the service of the Church. An interesting comment on her conversion as a response to post-1848 disillusionment appears in an essay by Karl Gutzkow (1811–78), a writer of liberal tendencies who, in 1847, was appointed as dramaturge at the court theatre in Dresden. A personal friend of Emil Devrient and a highly successful playwright, Gutzkow devoted particular attention to reviving the fortunes of the classics on the Dresden stage as well as putting on modern dramas. However, he soon quarrelled with the actors and in 1848 offended the Saxon court by a speech that he made to a public gathering in Berlin, where revolution broke out in March of that year. When unrest spread to Dresden on 3 May 1849, the court theatre was closed and the contracts of all employees except Emil and Eduard Devrient were terminated. Gutzkow's contract was one of the few not to be renewed after the revolution was put down on 9 May. He was, however, allowed to direct the performances in celebration of the centenary of Goethe's birth in August that year. These included his comedy *Der Königsleutnant* (*The King's Lieutenant*) which had been specially written for the centenary, and the world premiere of two acts of Goethe's *Faust*, Part II.

The Goethe centenary of 1849 rings down the curtain on one of the most fascinating epochs of Dresden's intellectual life and of its cultural history as a whole. In considering the role of the theatre and literature in the city during this period, it is important to remember that these institutions, and particularly the theatre, functioned as a substitute for participation in public life, which was denied to Germans not merely in Saxony but in other states as well. They are therefore of more than intrinsic interest and have, directly or indirectly, a political as well as an aesthetic and social dimension.

In Dresden, both amateur and professional theatre played a particularly large role at this time, and there was greater interest in literature among the educated population than elsewhere in Germany – a significant fact in view of the cultural importance of literature throughout the German-speaking lands during this period. This reflects the lack of political interest among the inhabitants of a city that had known too much of the sufferings of war during the previous century. After the 1830 revolution in Paris, however, politics for a time displaced literature and the theatre as the chief object of interest among the educated population even in Dresden.

At about the same time, there was a fundamental change in the trend of German literature itself. The period of Romanticism and Classical idealism – called by Heine the *Kunstperiode* (artistic period) – came to an end with the death of Goethe and several Romantic authors. Romanticism fell into disrepute, while realism and subjects of contemporary interest came to the fore. Liberal authors such as Heine and Gutzkow demanded greater political, religious, social, and sexual freedom, and although they never formed a coherent group became known collectively as 'Junges Deutschland' (Young Germany), the name under which their works were banned by a decree of the Bundestag (Federal Diet) in 1835.

It was Leipzig that became the centre of liberalism in politics and literature during the period leading up to the revolutions of 1848–9, whereas Dresden largely remained the haunt of second-rate pseudo-Romantics and imitators of Classicism. The city was, however, by no means isolated from modernizing influences: one of the most important events of the time was the opening in 1839 of the Leipzig–Dresden railway, the first inter-city railway in Germany. Its significance for the country as a whole was comparable to that which the Liverpool and Manchester Railway (opened in 1830) had for Britain: it paved the way for the spread of industrialization and urbanization and irrevocably changed people's sense of space and time. This change was reflected in literature and, although its impact in that sphere was much stronger in Leipzig than in Dresden, the Saxon capital was touched by it.

Notwithstanding its relative backwardness in literary terms, Dresden witnessed important scientific and technological developments at this time. One figure in particular links writing, painting, philosophy, medicine, and psychology, as well as the heritage of the Romantics and of the Classical Goethe: the 'universal genius' Carl Gustav Carus (1789–1869), after whom the Faculty of Medicine at the Dresden University of Technology is named. Besides writing a pioneering textbook on gynaecology – he was for many years Professor of Obstetrics at the Dresden Academy of Medicine and Surgery and was also the King's personal physician – Carus is responsible for the first documented use of the term 'the unconscious' ('das Unbewußte'). This occurs in his work *Psyche* (1846), which is based on lectures given in Dresden in 1829–30. Both Freud and Jung, and especially the latter, are indebted to Carus, though the Freudian conception of the unconscious owes more to Romantic literature, notably E.T.A. Hoffmann, than to Romantic psychology.

Hoffmann himself, however, had been decisively influenced by the work of the Dresden physician and *Naturphilosoph* (philosopher of nature) Gottfried Heinrich von Schubert (1780–1860), whose *Ansichten von der Nachtseite der Naturwissenschaft* (Views on the Night-Side of Natural Science), originally a series of lectures given at the Palais Carlowitz in 1808, was published in the city in the same year and dedicated to Gerhard von Kügelgen. Schubert writes of a primordial Golden Age in which human beings were in harmony with nature and which is reflected in ancient myth. This state, though lost to us at present, will be regained on a higher level at the end of time and is accessible to the individual in death and through borderline psychic phenomena such as clairvoyance, telepathy, dreams, and somnambulism. These ideas, which represent a partly secularized form of Christian doctrine – Paradise lost and regained – were of great importance for later Romantic writers and for Wagner. In another of his works, *Die Symbolik des Traumes* (The Symbolism of Dreams), which was published in Dresden in 1814, Schubert develops a systematic rhetoric of dreams which to some extent anticipates Freud.

In the same year the philosopher Arthur Schopenhauer (1788–1860) settled in Dresden, where he wrote his main work, *Die Welt als Wille und Vorstellung* (The World as Will and Idea), one of the most significant books ever to be produced there. It was published in Leipzig in 1819 and exerted a considerable influence on Wagner, Nietzsche, and the novelist Thomas Mann.

It was politics rather than psychology, the life of the times rather than that of the mind, however, which chiefly concerned the young writers associated with Julius Mosen (1803–67), who practised law in Dresden from 1834 until 1844. Apart from four poems – one of which, *Der Nußbaum* (The Walnut Tree), was set to music by Schumann – Mosen's work is virtually unknown today, but in his time he was the main representative of modern literature in Dresden. His circle included Hoffmann von Fallersleben (1797–1874), who wrote the German national anthem, and the left-wing radicals Ernst Theodor Echtermeyer (1805–44) and Arnold Ruge (1802–80), co-editors from 1838 to 1841 of the journal *Hallische Jahrbücher für deutsche Wissenschaft und Kunst* (Halle Yearbooks for German Science and Art), which numbered Friedrich Engels among its contributors. When it was banned in Prussia in 1841, the editors moved its headquarters to Dresden and it continued to appear anonymously under the title *Deutsche Jahrbücher für Wissenschaft und Kunst* until 1843, when it was banned in Saxony and subsequently in all other German states. Soon afterwards Ruge, who for a time had been the most important political journalist in Germany, left Dresden; in 1844 he co-edited a journal with Karl Marx in Paris. He left behind him in the Saxon capital a literary museum that he had helped to found in the Café français on the Promenade, a revival of the reading room run by the bookseller Arnold from 1825 to 1834, which took 160 German and foreign periodicals and was unrivalled by any institution elsewhere in Germany or even in Paris, Florence, or London.

A further important meeting place for artists and intellectuals in Dresden was the salon founded in 1845 by the composer Ferdinand Hiller (1811–85). Among its habitués were Robert Schumann, Berthold Auerbach (1812–82), the author of the *Schwarzwälder Dorfgeschichten* (Village Stories of the Black Forest), and Eduard Devrient, while the soirées held by Major Friedrich Anton Serre and his wife Friederike attracted not only Dresden's leading personalities but also foreign visitors such as Hans Christian Andersen and non-Europeans including Prince Aquasi Boacchi, an African studying mining in Freiberg, and the Javanese painter Raden Saleh. After 1840, well-to-do Jewish families also gained prominence in Dresden, and the houses of the bankers Kaskel and Oppenheim were open to guests of the most diverse viewpoints and interests.

Two notable writers who settled in Dresden in the 1840s were Otto Ludwig (1813–65), a representative of the literary movement known as Poetic Realism, and the playwright and social novelist Gustav Freytag (1816–95), whose praise of commerce and the middle classes made him the characteristic literary figure of his generation. Germany's greatest nineteenth-century novelist, Theodor Fontane (1819–98), also spent some months in Dresden from 1842 to 1843, working as a pharmacist and writing in his spare time. He drew inspiration for his writing from the outstanding Shakespeare productions that he saw at the Dresden theatres during this period.

Another Shakespeare devotee who came to the city in the same decade was the Romantic writer Joseph von Eichendorff (1788–1857), perhaps the most truly popular of all German poets, but best known in Britain as the author of the texts of Schumann's *Liederkreis* (Song Cycle) (op. 39) and of the last of Richard Strauss's *Vier Letzte Lieder* (Four Last Songs), *Im Abendrot* (In the Sunset). Eichendorff, a native of Silesia, had first visited Dresden at the age of eleven, and had recorded in his diary his youthful impressions of the collections in the Grünes Gewölbe and the picture gallery. In 1805 and 1806 he had passed through the city as a student, attentive to the beauties both of the landscape and of the Saxon women. In April 1813 he was briefly there again, this time as a volunteer on the way to join the regiment in which he had enlisted. Finally, in April or May 1848, now a retired Prussian civil servant, he sought refuge in Dresden from the revolutionary upheavals in Berlin, only to become caught up in similar events in the Saxon capital a year later. Although he was an aristocrat and had close family ties with the military, he had greeted the revolutions of 1848 and 1849 with a measure of hope. Their bloody suppression wrung from him a sharply satirical fairy-tale, written in Dresden, which ends with the withdrawal of the Lady Liberty to her dream castle, *das aber seitdem niemand wieder aufgefunden hat* (which no-one has ever been able to find since).

One of the most striking passages in Eichendorff's Dresden letters describes how, from the windows of his doctor's house on the Neumarkt, he witnessed the procession of several thousand people to the memorial service held in the Frauenkirche for Robert Blum, the revolutionary leader executed near Vienna in November 1848. As a Catholic and an opponent of liberal politics, Eichendorff was doubly excluded from this event; that he watched it with interest, however, suggests some degree of sympathy with Blum, a position not incompatible with a number of the poems that he wrote around this time. There is certainly no trace in his writings of relief at the brutal restoration of civil order in Dresden.

In 1846 it was estimated that up to a hundred writers lived in the Saxon capital, a number of them of some reputation. From about 1843 onwards the press had become radicalized and many new journals had come into being in the brief 'Dresden Spring' preceding the revolution. The theatre audience, too, was far less dominated by aristocrats than it had been. After the suppression of the revolution, however, Dresden's cultural scene lost its sparkle. Literary and theatrical life nevertheless continued and in some respects even flourished.

Overt theatre censorship in Dresden after 1848 seems to have been relatively liberal in practice; references to religion and the Church were, however, forbidden, and there was clearly a good deal of covert control as well as self-censorship. When the court theatre re-opened on 1 June 1849, controversial plays were avoided in favour of comedies and other politically 'safe' forms of entertainment. Similar fare was already on offer at the theatre at the 'Linckesches Bad', which had been refurbished and had become a miniature court theatre staging light society dramas performed by leading actors and attended by the court nobility and the *haute bourgeoisie*. The work of Gustav Räder, an actor and writer of comic and popular plays, was particularly in vogue both there and at the court theatre itself.

In 1844 a second summer theatre, with performances from May to October, had opened in Reisewitz's Garden. Here, too, a popular restaurant with an attractive garden was linked with the theatre. Everything was on a larger scale, however, especially the new theatre building with seating for 600. As the theatre at Lincke's restaurant progressively lost its popular character, so the importance of the Reisewitz theatre increased. It could bear comparison not only with Lincke's theatre but also with the court theatre in respect of the quality of its repertoire, which consisted chiefly of farces, comedies, musical plays, and dialect plays. Some of the dramas were by well-known writers, such as the Austrian playwrights Nestroy, Raimund, Bäuerle, and Bauernfeld. The standard of both the productions and the acting was high, and premieres were sometimes staged there. In 1854 a third summer theatre was established in the Großer Garten. Performances were given there until 1881; three years later the theatre was demolished.

Gottfried Semper's court theatre was destroyed by fire in 1869; in the same year a temporary theatre was erected in the grounds of the Zwinger. In 1876 the famous company of the Meiningen Court Theatre opened their first Dresden season there with a production of Shakespeare's *Julius Caesar.* Thereafter they acted in the Residenztheater in the Zirkusstraße, which had been built as a private theatre in 1872. The inspiration behind their style of acting may be traced back to Edmund Kean's 'Shakespeare Revivals', although it went beyond this, aiming at the presentation of drama as a *Gesamtkunst-werk*. The historical accuracy of the set and costumes pointed forward to Naturalism, and in December 1887 the Meiningen company performed one of the most controversial Naturalist plays, Ibsen's *Ghosts* (1881), in Dresden. The performance was banned the next day, but between 1889 and 1894 four further dramas by Ibsen – *Pillars of Society, A Doll's House, An Enemy of the People,* and *Rosmersholm* – were staged in the city, signalling the advent of naturalism there. The Norwegian Ibsen (1828–1906) spent the most influential period of his life in Germany, living from 1868 to 1875 in Dresden; his first address was An der Frauenkirche 6. From 1869 to 1871 the Russian writer Dostoevski (1821–81), too, lived in the city, where he wrote his novel *The Possessed* (1871).

Naturalism, a form of detailed realism that developed in Europe in the late nineteenth century, came to Germany around the mid-1880s, reaching a climax in the early 1890s. Its most important German representative is Gerhart Hauptmann (1862–1946), whose first play, *Vor Sonnenaufgang* (Before Sunrise), treating of the degenerative effects of alcoholism, was premiered in Berlin in 1889. As a young man, Hauptmann briefly studied at the Dresden Academy of Arts in 1884; as an old man close to death, he was destined – as he felt – to share the sufferings of his people when he witnessed the destruction of the city in 1945. His culturally most significant connection with Dresden, however, came about through his dramas, which were frequently performed there.

In 1894, Count Nikolaus Seebach (1854–1930) became director of the court theatre. At this time Dresden was, with Stuttgart, one of the few German cities where modern drama was performed, but it also continued to put on the classics – Schiller was especially popular – and works by post-Classical dramatists such as Kleist, the Austrian Franz Grillparzer (1791–1872), Friedrich Hebbel (1813–63), and Otto Ludwig. During Seebach's period of office Dresden became Germany's leading court theatre in respect of the literary quality of the dramas staged there.

In 1913 a new theatre building was opened on the Ostra-Allee opposite the Zwinger, replacing the Albert-Theater on the Bautzner Platz, which had been inaugurated in 1873 as the first theatre in Dresden built by ordinary citizens. The Albert-Theater had been leased by the court theatre since its completion and in 1895 had passed into royal ownership; in 1913 it became a private theatre. When the First World War broke out, the King ordered that the court theatre should remain open in order to maintain morale, but foreign plays were dropped from the repertoire; in earlier years, dramas by

Figure 63. Dresden Schauspielhaus, originally built in 1912–13, destroyed in 1945 and rebuilt in 1948 and 1990–94. Courtesy of Manfred Lauffer.

George Bernard Shaw and Oscar Wilde had been performed in Dresden. At first, people stayed away from the theatre and its income fell sharply. Many of the actors and members of the orchestra were called up and a number were killed in action. As time went on, however, theatre-going increased again, and towards the end of the war there was a full house at almost every performance. Seebach was the only court theatre director in Germany to remain in office after 1918.

The most important artistic and cultural movement in Germany in the years before, during, and after the First World War was Expressionism, which, like Romanticism, embraced both literature and – most strikingly – the visual arts. The influence of this movement is still apparent in Germany and there is continued interest in it in Britain as well. A major event in Manchester's recent cultural life was the city's International Festival of Expressionism in 1992. This included an exhibition of postcards by members of the *Brücke* (Bridge) group of painters, founded in Dresden in 1905, together with an exhibition and a conference on literary Expressionism.

Before the First World War, the cultural and especially the literary climate of Dresden was not particularly favourable to new ideas. It was characterized largely by conservative writers and artists and a public that included a high proportion of pensioners, civil servants, and army officers. By 1911 all the *Brücke* painters had left the city owing to lack of recognition, and in the same year the poet Friedrich Kurt Benndorf (1871–1945) wrote in his diary: '*So geht mirs ja auch mit Dresden: Kleinbürger, Hofleute, Militärs, Musiker, aber die Dichtkunst Stiefkind und unbekannt*' ('That's how I feel about Dresden, too: petty bourgeois, courtiers, military personnel, musicians, but literature is a poor relation and unknown'). The city had as yet no university, and between 1910, when literary Expressionism first made its appearance in Germany, and the outbreak of war in 1914, it had no periodical devoted to modern literature either. Even so, the influence of contemporary verbal as well as visual art became increasingly apparent in Dresden in the pre-war years, and during and immediately after the war the city became one of the most important centres of late Expressionism.

In January 1914 a major exhibition of Expressionist paintings was held in Dresden and from 1916 onwards the movement began to develop a strong presence in the city. In that year the Dresden-based physician and writer Heinrich Stadelmann, a collaborator on the Expressionist periodical *Die Aktion*, published a treatise, *Die neue Kunst* (The New Art) in which he attempted to consider Expressionism both in connection with the literary currents of the day and in a wider historical context. In the autumn of 1916 Franz Benndorf, the brother of Friedrich Kurt Benndorf, made a first attempt to bring together artists and intellectuals living in and around Dresden, including the writers Alfred Günther (1885–1969), Iwar von Lücken (1874–1935), and Walter Hasenclever (1890–1940). In 1917 the painter and writer Oskar Kokoschka (1886–1980) came to Dresden, later becoming an honorary member of the group of painters known as *Sezession. Gruppe 1919* and from 1920 to 1928 a professor at the Dresden Academy. There was also a woman writer, Bess Brenck Kalischer, who was older than the others and published her first volume of work, *Dichtung* (Poetry), in Dresden in 1917. Several Expressionist publishing houses were founded in the city, and in October 1917 the 'Expressionistische Arbeitsgemeinschaft Dresden' (Dresden Expressionist Study Group) was formed. In January 1918, it launched the journal *Menschen* (Human Beings), of which Hasenclever was for a time a co-editor. The 1919 numbers of this journal were particularly substantial and made an impact far beyond Dresden. In May 1918 a second Expressionist journal, *Neue Blätter für Kunst und Dichtung* (New Journal for Art and Literature), was launched. Another new journal, *Die Neue Schaubühne* (The New Stage) was devoted primarily to Expressionist theatre, and there was also a short-lived journal entitled *Der silberne Spiegel* (The Silver Mirror). *Der Zwinger*, whose early numbers in 1917 still had the subtitle *Blätter der*

Dresdner Hoftheater (Journal of the Dresden Court Theatre), published an increasing number of Expressionist works.

Around the time of the First World War, as in the first half of the nineteenth century, the verbal arts became a substitute for participation in the public sphere and at times a vehicle of critical comment on current events. This is particularly so in the case of drama. In 1916 the Dresden court theatre had appointed its first and only dramaturge of Jewish origin, Karl Wolff, who staged plays by Strindberg and Euripides as well as by German writers. Between 1916 and 1918 the Dresden theatres also mounted pioneering productions of several Expressionist plays, the first being Hasenclever's *Der Sohn* (The Son), which was premiered in Dresden on 8 October 1916. This was followed on 3 June 1917 by the performance of three plays by Kokoschka, directed by the author, at the Albert-Theater. The first of these, *Mörder Hoffnung der Frauen* (Murderer, the Hope of Women), written in 1907 and published in 1910, is regarded as the earliest German Expressionist play; the others were *Hiob* (Job) and *Der brennende Dornbusch* (The Burning Bush). The most sensational theatrical performance, however, was the premiere at the court theatre on 12 February 1918 of *Seeschlacht* (Naval Battle) by Reinhard Goering (1887–1936). The military command attempted to have the performance banned, but Seebach, who had good relations with the court, managed to gain permission for a single performance before an invited audience. The action of the play takes place in the gun-turret of a battleship at the battle of Jutland (31 May 1916), and in order to render this as authentically as possible Seebach had brought in a naval expert as a collaborator. The representation of the battle was so realistic that it caused panic among the audience and occasioned a theatrical scandal. The reviewers of the *Dresdner Neueste Nachrichten* (Dresden News) and the *Dresdner Anzeiger* (Dresden Advertiser) disagreed as to the play's import; as a result, details of the performance became known to a much wider public than the theatre audience alone.

The Dresden Expressionists were not a homogeneous group: they held differing opinions, which resulted from divergent political and artistic attitudes as well as from age differences. The main unifying factors between them were their opposition to the war, their desire to help end it by fostering human solidarity across national boundaries, and their rejection of the Wilhelmine Empire. The first generation of Expressionists had volunteered enthusiastically in August 1914, but their experience of battle had shocked and disillusioned them and they had attacked the war in their writings. The later Expressionists had gone straight from school and university to the front as conscripts, so that for them the experience of warfare had been even more decisive.

When revolution came to Dresden on 8 November 1918, resulting in the fall of the monarchy and the establishment of a provisional workers' and soldiers' soviet, the Expressionists, almost without exception, embraced the revolutionary and republican cause. They formed a propaganda committee and the poet Iwar von Lücken was appointed Saxon Minister of Culture, with the theatre, opera, and orchestra under his Ministry's control. From 1918 to 1921 Berthold Viertel was director of the state theatre, and on 9 October 1919 he staged the premiere of Friedrich Wolf's expressionist drama *Das bist du* (That's You). The set by the painter Conrad Felixmüller – who, like Kokoschka, was a member of the *Sezession. Gruppe 1919* – translated Wolf's conception of anti-Naturalist theatre into visual terms. Numerous other Expressionist plays were performed in Dresden in the post-war years, although a production in 1924 of Ernst Toller's *Hinkemann*, about the plight of a returning soldier emasculated during the war, caused an unprecedented scandal and the play was banned after a single performance. After this, modern dramas of social criticism could be performed only at the Aktuelle Bühne (Topical Theatre), an experimental theatre in the city.

Eventually the old conflicts between the different Expressionist tendencies erupted in Dresden, and the writers either retreated into inwardness or took up a political cause, which changed the nature of their writing. The group broke up without having been able to influence the direction of Germany's social and political development, the periodicals ceased publication, and most of the writers left Dresden. For most of them, the end of Expressionism meant the end of their literary careers, and by 1933 their works had been so thoroughly forgotten that, unlike those of better known Expressionists, they were not banned by the Nazis. Even so, they played a significant and honourable role in the cultural history of the Saxon capital.

The town of Hellerau near Dresden, founded in 1910 on the model of the English 'garden city', also merits comment in connection with the period around the First World War. It had its own flourishing cultural life centred on the Institute of Eurhythmics, which was conceived and directed by the Swiss Emile Jaques-Dalcroze in collaboration with his fellow-countryman, the theatre designer and theoretician Adolphe Appia. The Institute provided for the citizens of Hellerau and students of many nationalities a unique programme of training through experimental work in music, movement, lighting, stage design, and performance, which has been said to mark the birth of the modern theatre. Appia's far-reaching lighting and scenic reforms, in particular, provided much of the basis for modern theatrical practice.

The Institute's Festival Theatre, partly planned by Appia, did away with the proscenium arch and raised stage, substituting for them, for the first time since the Renaissance, a completely open performance area. This consisted of a large, high rectangular hall enclosing performers and audience with no barrier between them. It held 600 people and was illuminated by thousands of lights, installed behind translucent linen and operated centrally so that the walls and ceiling radiated light, which was used as a visual correlative to the music. In 1912 and 1913, the Institute held public exhibitions of its work that were attended by most of the leading theatre artists of the time, including Shaw, Stanislavsky, and Max Reinhardt. It was of major importance for ballet and opera as well as for drama, and many of its pupils – Marie Rambert being one of the most celebrated – became innovators in the performing arts. On 5 October 1913 a gala premiere of Paul Claudel's lyrical drama of 1912, *L'Annonce faite à Marie* (The Tidings Brought to Mary), took place there in the presence of many famous writers, including Hauptmann, Kokoschka, and Rilke.

On the outbreak of war in 1914, the Institute was closed and the building taken over by the German government. From 1937 onwards it was used by the SS and after the bombing of Dresden the linen cloths that covered its walls and ceiling were torn down to make bandages. From the end of the Second World War until 1992 it was occupied by Russian troops. It is now being carefully restored and was formally re-dedicated in 1998. It is important for theatrical history, and, together with the town as a whole, which has remained largely intact, it represents an early and highly successful expression of the holistic concept of existence.

One of the many writers who visited Hellerau or made it their home was the Scottish poet, novelist, and critic Edwin Muir (1887–1959), who spent some years there in the early 1920s and was friendly with Iwar von Lücken. In his autobiography, Muir describes both Hellerau and Dresden, where he also lived for a time, with wistful affection. In Hellerau his wife, Willa, taught at the school set up by the educational reformer A.S. Neill in the Institute's building.

Hellerau's influence on Dresden was limited, however. In the late 1920s the Dresden state theatre concentrated chiefly on unimaginative productions of the classics. Brecht's *Dreigroschenoper* (Threepenny Opera) of 1928 – a reworking of John Gay's satirical *Beggar's Opera* of 1728 – had a successful run in 1929 at the Albert-Theater, with the character actor Erich Ponto (1884–1957) in the role of Peachum, but was not included in the repertoire of the State Theatre.

During the Nazi period, theatre employees of Jewish origin and those considered to be politically liberal were dismissed and the repertoire acquired a national, *völkisch* flavour. The Albert-Theater was taken over by the city authorities in 1936 and renamed *Theater des Volkes* (People's Theatre). Even so, productions of the classics continued to be staged at the state theatre and attendance remained high, not least in the war years. Fourteen productions were planned for the 1944–5 season, five of which were premieres; performances ceased, however, after a production of Goethe's *Iphigenie* on 31 August 1944, three days after the 195th anniversary of the author's birth. Of all Goethe's plays, this is the purest expression of his ideal of *Humanität:* it proclaims the triumph of truthfulness, courage, and humane ideals over barbarism and the urge for vengeance. In 1827, Goethe had written on a flyleaf of a copy of this play lines that end with the words: *Alle menschliche Gebrechen/Sühnet reine Menschlichkeit* (For all our human frailties/Pure humanity atones). A less appropriate sentiment for a period of 'total war' – to which the theatre building as well as the city in which it stood were to succumb less than six months later – can scarcely be imagined. As a motto for Dresden's rebirth, however, it could hardly be more apt.

The spirit of this rebirth manifested itself as early as 10 July 1945, when the curtain rose in what is now the *Kleines Haus* (Small Theatre) in the Neustadt on a production of *Nathan der Weise* (Nathan the Wise) by Lessing, who was himself a native of Saxony. In this play, written in 1779, the parable of the three rings of equal value, representing the three great monotheistic religions of Judaism, Christianity, and Islam, points a lesson about the need for tolerance of religious and cultural diversity that is no less relevant now than at the time of the play's composition, or in 1945, when Germany lay in ruins after six years of conflict and intolerance on a hitherto undreamed of scale. As in the nineteenth century, or in the aftermath of the First World War, the theatre once again functioned as a substitute for a defective or non-existent public sphere.

Unlike the other Dresden theatres, which were completely destroyed in 1945, the theatre on the Ostra-Allee, though it had suffered severe damage, was still standing. Rebuilding work began soon after the war, and on 22 September 1948 the building was re-opened as a home for opera and ballet as well as drama with a performance of Beethoven's *Fidelio*. Besides the classics, the post-war theatrical repertoire emphasized plays that had not been performed during the Nazi era as well as contemporary dramas. However, performance of *Des Teufels General* (The Devil's General) by Carl Zuckmayer (1896–1977), a powerful presentation of high-level political and military life in Berlin during the Second World War, was not permitted. Erich Ponto resigned his post as theatre director in protest at this decision. Martin Hellberg, who succeeded him for a year, sought to combine Shakespeare productions with performances of modern dramas of international provenance. Eventually, several plays concerned with the recent German past were staged, and during the GDR period both the Russian classics and modern Soviet dramas were performed with increasing frequency. Thanks to the work of the actor-producer Hannes Fischer, Dresden also became an important centre for productions of Brecht during the 1960s.

After the construction of the Berlin Wall in 1961, a number of Dresden's best actors were sent to Berlin to replace those who had left for the West. Nevertheless, the GDR premiere in Dresden of *Der Besuch der alten Dame* (The Visit) by the Swiss writer Friedrich Dürrenmatt (1921–90), with Antonia Dietrich in the main role, was a sensation. The mid-1960s saw the arrival of the director and producer Hans Dieter Mäde, who adhered closely to the official party line. Besides noteworthy productions of the classics, he included a number of contemporary plays in the repertoire, but none made a major impact. He was succeeded by Hannes Fischer, who failed to repeat his earlier achievements. However, three plays by Peter Hacks (1928–) were successfully premiered in Dresden and won critical acclaim outside the city as well.

At the beginning of the 1980s, Horst Schönemann and Gerhard Wolfram took over as theatre directors. After the re-opening of the Opera House in 1985, opera and ballet were transferred from the building in the Ostra-Allee, sole use of which reverted to the state theatre. In the dying years of the GDR, young people in particular flocked to see the controversial productions staged there. Innovative presentations both of modern plays and of classics such as Kleist's *Penthesilea* (1809), with its politically and psychologically disturbing treatment of the themes of state power and the battle of the sexes, and Hebbel's 'German tragedy', *Die Nibelungen* (1862), which deals with guilt and failure in face of the demands of history, played a decisive role in Dresden's rise to a leading position among GDR theatres. Touring productions by the Dresden company met with an enthusiastic response in West Germany and Vienna, and the state theatre staged plays that had been banned elsewhere in the GDR. One of the most important contemporary plays produced there was *Die Ritter der Tafelrunde* (The Knights of the Round Table) by Christoph Hein (1944–), which was premiered in 1989 and despite the author's disclaimer was taken as a parable on the political situation in the GDR. *Die Übergangsgesellschaft* (Society in Transition) by Volker Braun (1939–), a native of Dresden, was also well received.

When, in the spring of 1991, the Dresden state theatre was awarded the German Culture Prize for 1990 in recognition of its artistic and political work, Christoph Hein declared in his laudatory address that it had helped put an end to a regime that had lost all dignity and meaning. In other words, the theatre had not only acted as a substitute for the public sphere; it had also, for the first time in the history of Dresden, of Germany, and of Europe, played its part in bringing about a lasting social transformation. There could be no more convincing endorsement of its cultural function or of its *raison d'être* than that. Not only had the Dresden state theatre become what Germany's writers had so long desired, a truly national theatre; Hein's use in his play of the European heritage of the Arthurian legends, or the 'Matter of Britain', as they are also known, accords with the international spirit manifested by Dresden's literary and theatrical traditions since their earliest days.

There is, however, one writer born and bred in Dresden whose international popularity exceeds that of all the rest. *Emil and the Detectives* (1928) has achieved greater renown than any other German children's book this century, but the Dresden origins of its author, Erich Kästner (1899–1974), are less well known. Kästner spent much of the Second World War in Dresden; although his books were publicly burned by the Nazis and he was forbidden to publish, his attachment to his native city and country made him unwilling to live in exile. In his autobiography, *Als ich ein kleiner Junge war* (When I was a Little Boy), published in 1957, Kästner paints a vivid picture of the city both as it was in his childhood and as it was later to become. This description may be cited as a fitting conclusion both to the present chapter and to the main body of this book:

Dresden war eine wunderbare Stadt, voller Kunst und Geschichte [. . .]. Die Vergangenheit und die Gegenwart lebten miteinander im Einklang. Eigentlich müßte es heißen: im Zweiklang. Und mit der Landschaft zusammen, mit der Elbe, den Brücken, den Hügelhängen, den Wäldern und mit den Gebirgen am Horizont, ergab sich sogar ein Dreiklang. Geschichte, Kunst und Natur schwebten über Stadt und Tal, vom Meißner Dom bis zum Großsedlitzer Schloßpark, wie ein von seiner eignen Harmonie bezauberter Akkord. [. . .]

Ja, Dresden war eine wunderbare Stadt. Ihr könnt es mir glauben. Und ihr müßt es mir glauben! Keiner von euch, und wenn sein Vater noch so reich wäre, kann mit der Eisenbahn hinfahren, um nachzusehen, ob ich rechthabe. Denn die Stadt Dresden gibt es nicht mehr. Sie ist, bis auf einige Reste, vom Erdboden verschwunden. Der Zweite Weltkrieg hat sie, in einer einzigen Nacht und mit einer einzigen Handbewegung, weggewischt. Jahrhunderte hatten ihre unvergleichliche Schönheit geschaffen. Ein paar Stunden genügten, um sie vom Erdboden fortzuhexen. Das geschah am 13. Februar 1945. Achthundert Flugzeuge warfen Spreng- und Brandbomben. Und was übrigblieb, war eine Wüste. Mit ein paar riesigen Trümmern, die aussahen wie gekenterte Ozeandämpfer. [. . .]

Noch heute streiten sich die Regierungen der Großmächte, wer Dresden ermordet hat. Noch heute streitet man sich, ob unter dem Garnichts fünfzigtausend, hunderttausend oder zweihunderttausend Tote liegen. Und niemand will es gewesen sein. Jeder sagt, die anderen seien dran schuld. Ach, was soll der Streit? Damit macht ihr Dresden nicht wieder lebendig!

Dresden was a beautiful city, filled with art and history [. . .] The past and the present lived in unison with one another, or rather gave forth a two-part melody. And together with the landscape, the Elbe, the bridges, the hillsides, the forests,

Figure 64. The Kästner Memorial in front of the Café Kästner in the Albert Platz. Courtesy of Manfred Lauffer.

and the mountains on the horizon, they even formed a triad. History, art and nature cast their enchantment over the city and the valley, from Meissen Cathedral to the park of Grosssedlitz castle, like a chord enraptured by its own harmony. [...]

Yes, believe me, Dresden was a beautiful city. You have to believe me, for not one of you, even if your father were ever so rich, can go there by train to see if I am right. The city of Dresden is no more. Apart from a few remains it has disappeared from the face of the earth. In a single night and with a single blow, the Second World War wiped it away. It had taken centuries to create Dresden's incomparable beauty and yet so few hours were sufficient to banish it from the earth. It happened on 13 February 1945 when eight hundred aeroplanes dropped explosive and incendiary bombs and all that remained was a wasteland with a few enormous ruins, looking like capsized ocean liners. [...]

The governments of the major powers still argue about who murdered Dresden and about whether there are fifty thousand, one hundred thousand or two hundred thousand lying dead beneath the nothingness. No-one admits responsibility, every-one says the others are to blame, but what's the point of all the arguing? No amount of arguing will ever bring Dresden to life again!

Kästner was both right and wrong in this assessment. Arguing never rebuilt a community, a city, or a single edifice; as this book seeks to demonstrate, however, determination, co-operation, and conciliation have already resurrected an impressive part of Dresden's fabric and are continuing to do so. In the course of this process the city – which can never become an exact replica of its former self but must be recreated for the new millennium – has erected a touching memorial to Kästner. In doing so it has recognized its debt to one of its best loved sons who is much more than a 'mere' children's author and can still prove one of its most effective ambassadors and advocates.

New Beginnings: An Epilogue

Alan Russell

Conclusions, in a book such as this, would be wholly inappropriate because Dresden's story is far from over.

As the earlier chapters recall, Dresden began as a simple trading outpost with no particular claims to cultural distinction. In the sixteenth century it developed into a small Renaissance city known for architecture as well as for exchange. The great period of musical pre-eminence that followed might have been matched in other fields of endeavour had the Thirty Years War not intervened. Yet due to a chance combination of mineral deposits, a ruler with an iron will and a population talented in many crafts, it rose again in the eighteenth century, like a butterfly from its chrysalis, to become one of Europe's greatest baroque cities. The Seven Years War dealt it cruel blows. However, it reinvented itself a third time and, before nineteenth century industrial expansion took it back to its trading roots, it became one of the key centres of the Romantic Movement. A century later, having been stripped of its royal status, it was degraded by the Nazis, shattered by the Allies and – in a fourth but not a final metamorphosis – was dressed by its communist masters in unwonted and unwanted plebeian garb.

It is now emerging from yet another chrysalis to become one of the great twenty-first century centres of industry and culture in Saxony, in Germany and in the Euro-Region that extends into Polish Silesia and Bohemia. A city whose *Kruzianer* (choir boys) could sing in 1945 in the still-smoking ruins of their city, whose conservationists worked in the early post-war period with little pay or food and in a climate of near total political alienation, and that, in the face of crippling financial restraints, succeeded in quickly re-establishing its five great artistic enterprises – the Staatskapelle, the Semper-Opera, the Philharmonic, the Kreuzchor and the Schauspielhaus, or playhouse – is no mean place. As Lord Menuhin recalls in the closing pages of this volume, its human heart and its musical and artistic soul have never died.

Unhappily, the dense fabric of the city centre cannot be restored. However, enough remains to enable today's planners to ensure some degree of visual continuity. The Zwinger and the Opera House, the Catholic Cathedral and the Residence or Royal Castle, all fully restored, are by any standards world-class buildings. With thousands of the old stones being carefully reused, the Frauenkirche rises daily towards the pinnacle of George Bähr's soaring dome, on which the British-made Orb and Cross will have been placed, before Dresden celebrates its eighth centenary in 2006. Surprisingly beautiful townscapes are re-emerging along the Elbe, on the Brühl Terrace and in the Neustadt, and once the Frauenkirche has been completed, significant archaeological reconstruction will begin in the area of the Neumarkt too.

The art collections are splendidly intact again and, within months of the millennium, the *Grünes Gewölbe* will have been restored to its rightful place in the Residence. In 1996, when the stunning new crypt of the Frauenkirche was inaugurated as both church and concert hall, the Comedy Theatre, founded in 1667, reappeared. It has quickly become a regular feature, with the Playhouse, of Dresden's theatrical life. Together with the city's Theatre of the Young Generation, it prompts the mind to wander back across the centuries to the English Comedians who gave the first theatrical performances in the Saxon capital.

The many and varied cultural events that take place in Dresden every year remind us, moreover, that, however fractured the cityscape may still be, there is real continuity of artistic spirit and endeavour. Each and every year there are tens of exhibitions covering everything from fashion to film making and from architecture to art, over a dozen operas and ballets in addition to the three hundred or so regular performances in the Semper, ten or twelve new theatrical performances including several of Shakespeare's plays, music galore – both classical and jazz – and forty to fifty festivals of all kinds that give structure to the seasons and the year.

On 13/14 February, Dresden mourns in the Kreuzkirche and in its market squares, before – on the Monday before Lent – celebrating present and future life in fancy dress. As the weather improves, the Spring Fair and the Spring Market take place beside the Elbe and in the Altmarkt, against the backdrop of some of Europe's most long-established riverboats. In May, Dresden's music festivals – Dixieland and Classical – occur. Through the summer months they are followed by celebrations with a more outdoor and/or regional flavour: the Elbehangfest on the meadows stretching from the Carola Bridge to Pillnitz, the joint Saxon-Bohemian Festival of Music, the Wine Festival, the Vogelwiese or Festival of Shooting, the Dresden Town Festival, and festivities in celebration of Dresden's – and Saxony's – Polish links. October sees the Festival of Contemporary Music, November the traditional Striezelfest and December – just before Christmas – the Stollenfest.

Such a summary as this can be no more than indicative but it underlines the fact that, for all the suffering and death, for all the migration westwards, and for all the post-war immigration from the south and east, the Dresdeners remain a loyal and cohesive community, whilst Dresden itself re-emerges, step-by-step, as one of Europe's significant cultural centres.

That Dresden will again pass through difficult times cannot be doubted. Despite the creation of tens of thousands of new jobs (for example in the Siemens-owned microchip factory, in the new Volkswagen plant, in 'high tech' industries and in tourism) unemployment remains stubbornly high. However imaginative plans for the rebuilding of the centre in general are, argument still rages over the architectural, planning and sociological concepts that should underpin them. But there can be little doubt that a city that has lived through so many changes and such real catastrophe in the past will be able to find its way through. Its route, its solutions and its achievements will be worth watching and will certainly provide lessons for us all: as Lord Menuhin says, 'Dresden may yet serve as a beacon for the whole of Europe'.

Dresden: City of Music and Culture

Yehudi Menuhin

Dresden is, for me, the most cultured, cultivated, musical city in the world. This is not a statement lightly made; it is not empty rhetoric. In Dresden, in a remarkable way, succeeding cultures fed and fertilized each other. The cultures that composed the Czech, German and Polish peoples were largely cohabitant in Dresden – and the kings and princes of Dresden were more concerned with a balancing act than a conquering act. Their pleasure and pride, it seems to me, derived more from the pursuit of refinement and beauty than from military glory.

Whether ecclesiastical, of diverse creeds, secular, aristocratic, or middle class, Dresden always revolved around its core purpose – the satisfaction of our highest creative and aesthetic aspirations in artistic musical expression. I was again reminded of this when in 1989, at a concert in the restored Semper Opera House, the city celebrated sixty years since my debut with the then great Generalmusikdirektor Fritz Busch in 1929.

During the period of six decades when I have known the glorious city of Dresden at the height of its beauty, have grieved deeply with its people over its destruction in 1945, have played with the fine Russian conductor Kyrill Kondraschin in the GDR period and have finally lived to see the City restoring itself to its noble stature, I repeatedly encountered wonderful people, cultivated, civilized, loyal, loving and still full of faith. For me it has been a lesson in humanity and humility. It is impossible to know whether the people saved their culture or whether the culture saved the people. It is no doubt a reciprocal process – and one of which I am particularly aware and grateful each time I find myself in Dresden.

Dresden is at the very heart of Europe, where the Slav, the Teuton and the Latin have always rubbed shoulders and, when not at war, produced the highest art – all-encompassing and both artistically and intellectually compatible. It is in these regions where the same will that is now rebuilding the Frauenkirche will proudly proclaim our united Europe – united in its respect for the richest diversity and intermingling of cultures – where the autonomy of each and the representation of all cultures and heritages will create a Europe that will no longer murder its own people but will provide humanity with an example and a model for a most colourful non-uniform collective society, evolving towards a world where the obligations and responsibilities that go with rights lead us towards the highest ideals as well as towards the care of the downtrodden and the suffering, where there is mutual service and reciprocal relationships and where a creative life – a singing and dancing life in our arts and sciences as in our daily occupation – can be assured to everyone.

In this way, Dresden may yet serve as a beacon for the whole of Europe, providing indeed, for our agonizing and ignorant humanity, that shining light, produced through the interaction of cultures, which should be Europe's way of making human progress.

The House of
Wettin in Dresden

Herzog/Kurfürst/König	*Dates of reign*	*Duke/Elector/King*
Herzog Albrecht der Beherzte	1443–1500	Duke Albrecht the Bold
Herzog Georg der Bärtige	1500–1539	Duke George the Bearded
Herzog Heinrich der Fromme	1539–1541	Duke Henry the Pious
Herzog und Kurfürst Moritz	1541–1553	Duke & Elector Maurice
Kurfürst August I	1553–1586	Elector Augustus
Kurfürst Christian I	1586–1591	Elector Christian I
Kurfürst Christian II	1591–1611	Elector Christian II
Kurfürst Johann Georg I	1611–1656	Elector John George I
Kurfürst Johann Georg II	1656–1680	Elector John George II
Kurfürst Johann Georg III	1680–1691	Elector John George III
Kurfürst Johann George IV	1691–1694	Elector John George IV
Kurfürst von Sachsen und König von Polen Kurfürst Friedrich August I (August der Starke) als König von Polen August II	1694–1733	Elector of Saxony and King of Poland Elector Frederick Augustus I (Augustus the Strong), as King of Poland Augustus II
Kurfürst Friedrich August II, als König von Polen August III	1733–1763	Elector Frederick August II, as King of Poland Augustus III
Kurfürst Friedrich Christian	1763	Elector Frederick Christian
Kurfürst Friedrich August III, von 1806 König Friedrich August I (Friedrich August der Gerechte)	1763–1827	Elector Friedrich Augustus III from 1806 King Frederick August I* (Frederick Augustus the Just)

König Anton (Anton der der Gütige)	1827–1836	King Anton (Anton the Good)
König Friedrich August II	1836–1854	King Frederick Augustus II
König Johann	1854–1873	King John
König Albert	1873–1902	King Albert
König Georg	1902–1904	King George
König Friedrich August III	1904–1918	King Frederick Augustus III

*The title Elector ended with the formal dissolution of the Holy Roman Empire in 1806.

Appendix 2

Worldwide Support for the Frauenkirche

Background

More than half of the overall cost of rebuilding the Frauenkirche is coming from non-official sources – that is from individuals, charitable bodies and companies. Appropriately for such an international collaborative effort, contributions are flowing in from all parts of Germany and from many parts of the world.

In Dresden, the Society for the Promotion of the Rebuilding of the Frauenkirche, which now has nearly 5,500 members, takes the lead in fund-raising. Its work is complemented by a student support group and by a number of regional associations, based in Bad Kreuznach, Bad Salzuflen, Celle, Köln/ Düsseldorf, Freckenhorst/Warendorf, Gedern, Hamburg, Lippstadt/Soest, Munich, Oldenburg, Osnabrück, and Remagen.

Outside Germany there are three well-established support groups – wholly independent but comparable: Britain's Dresden Trust, the Frauenkirche Association in Paris and the Friends of Dresden in the United States.

Gifts, large and small, have been received from around half a million people and the total number of all committed members/contributors both inside and outside Germany is now approaching 15,000.

The Dresden Trust

The Dresden Trust was established as a Charitable Trust on 16 August 1993; it launched its Frauenkirche Appeal six months later in February 1994. Its registered objectives are:

- the advancement of religion by the restoration of the Church of our Lady in Dresden; and
- the commemoration of the victims of aerial bombardment in the two World Wars.

As well as HRH the Duke of Kent as its Royal Patron, the Trust has, as Patrons the past and present Bishops of Coventry; Richard Balfe, Baroness Chalker, Hugh Dykes, Giles Radice, and Lord Walker from the worlds of politics and business; Professor Gerald Bernbaum and Lord Dahrendorf from the academic world; Lord Watson of the British German Association and, until his recent death, Lord Menuhin from the world of music. Its Trustees reflect a similarly broad spectrum of British life:

Mr John Beale, Chairman, Historical Collections Plc
Sir Nigel Broomfield, KCMG, Ambassador to the GDR 1989–90 and to the FRG 1993–97
Mr Timothy Everard, CMG, Ambassador to the GDR 1984–88
Group Captain Peter Johnson, DSO, OBE, DFC, AFC, Bomber Command (Retd); Civil Air Attaché, British Embassy, Bonn 1950–56[†]
Mr David Marsh, Director and Head of Research, UK and Europe, Robert Fleming & Co Ltd
Mr Peter Nardini, Architect and Senior Lecturer, South Bank University, London
Canon Emeritus Paul Oestreicher, International Consultant, Coventry Cathedral
Dr Judith Purver, Senior Lecturer in German, University of Manchester
Dr Alan Russell (Chairman), Senior Official (Retd), Commission of the EC
Mrs Tonie Smith, JP, Member of the Meissen Commission
Professor Wolfgang van Emden, Emeritus Professor of French, University of Reading

From the beginning, the Trust has set itself four main objectives: the manufacture of the Orb and Cross for the Frauenkirche; playing a leading role in the financing of the Lantern; the creation of a British Window surrounded by sixty individually gifted stones; and – as and if requested – the provision of art work for the Crypt. It hopes, in addition, to be able to finance or to achieve sponsorship for a number of scholarships for the study of architecture, the arts and communications technologies in Dresden/Saxony and in the United Kingdom, prior to bringing its activities to a close in 2006 or soon thereafter. The first of these is being launched in Oxford, with the aid of Reuters Foundation, in the academic year 2000/2001.

In the early days, the Trust's fund-raising was directed primarily at British professional bodies and associations concerned with the peace and reconciliation, art and architecture, and international politics and British/German trade. Since then, it has broadened its activities to include concerts (in London, Cambridge, Coventry, Oxford, Norwich and York), exhibitions in twenty cities (Bath, Birmingham, Bournemouth, Cambridge, Cardiff, Chichester, Coventry,

Exeter, Glasgow, Liverpool, London, Manchester, Newcastle, Norwich, Oundle, Oxford, Poole, Portsmouth, Sheffield, York), dinners and receptions in St James' Palace (hosted by HRH the Duke of Kent for Saxon Minister-President Kurt Biedenkopf), and in the Palace of Westminster and the display of the completed Orb and Cross in Windsor Castle and in several British cathedrals. It has also had support from over sixty British companies, notably from the Goldsmiths' Company, British Gas and British Petroleum, from RMC and Rovers, and from Rolls Royce Aero- Engines and Historical Collections.

The Trust is essentially an expression of the wish of people in the United Kingdom, from many different backgrounds, to offer the hand of friendship and reconciliation to Dresden. Its underlying aims are the rebuilding and creation of spiritual and human links, the fostering of friendship and forgiveness and the recognition of the Frauenkirche as a monument to the victims of aerial bombardment not only in Dresden but all over Europe and indeed the world.

Chairman and information: PO Box 23, Arundel, West Sussex BN18 9AA, UK. Tel. + 44 1903 884070. Fax + 44 1243 786930. Email nardinp@sbu.ac.uk

The Frauenkirche Association in France

The Association Frauenkirche Paris was set up as a charitable organization (Association Loi 1901) in late 1993 by two French citizens, Jean-Francois Benoit (President) and Charles Delamare together with an English-born resident of Paris, Malcolm Livesey. René Monory, the former President of the French Senate, graciously accepted the post of Honorary President. The management team also includes natives of Dresden (Gisela Paul and Brigitte Schubert-Oustry) and one of Cologne (Catrin Unkel).

To date the Association's activities have primarily taken the form of exhibitions and concerts. In 1994 and 1995 it presented a small exhibition of historical photographs of the Frauenkirche and of old Dresden, which was expanded in 1996 into a larger exhibition at the Institute of German History. Somewhat different material, on the work of reconstruction, was shown at the Goethe Institute in mid-1997.

Several concerts have been organized, within the context of the Parisian National Trust, beginning with a chamber concert in the Marais district, where the President is very active in conservation and heritage work. Subsequently concerts involving well-known German, French and other artists have been organized in the prestigious Palais Beauharnais, the residence of the German Ambassador.

In addition to ticket sales, funds are raised through a membership campaign, through individual contributions and through Franco-German trading companies.

All these activities, like the reconstruction work itself, are creating opportunities for the French public to become more familiar with German baroque architecture and with German culture in general.

Vice President: Brigitte Schubert-Oustry, Eglise Allemande, 25 rue Blanche F75009, Paris, France. Tel: 0033 187439929 Fax: 0033 142948070.

Friends of Dresden

Friends of Dresden was founded in 1994 by Professor Günter Blobel, of Rockefeller University, Frank Wobst, Chairman of the Huntington Bank, Dr Carl Wolf of New York Hospital and Dr Peter Stern of the Burke Rehabilitation Hospital in Rye, New York. Together, they envisioned an organization that would raise US public awareness together with much needed funds for efforts to rebuild Dresden's architectural wonders. As reconstruction for the Frauenkirche was well under way, the board voted to support the rebuilding of this famous church.

Its honorary directors are Henry H. Arnhold, George N. Fugelsang, Richard C. Holbrooke, Hermut Jahn, Philip Johnson, Henry A. Kissinger, Ronald S. Lauder and David Rockefeller. Its board of directors consists of: Günter Blobel, president; Frank Wobst, treasurer; Carl F.W. Wolf, Secretary; Peter Stern, Vice President; Winfried H. Spaeh, chairman of the executive committee; and Kim Boylan, Betsy Hills Bush, Richard Lormer, Iris Love, Laura Maioglio, Steven C. Rockefeller Jr, John P. Schmitz and Frederick Seitz. Ms Anne-Thelma Radice is the executive director. It is inspired by the belief, voiced by Henry Kissinger, that 'the rebuilding of Dresden's Frauenkirche demonstrates an international commitment to overcome the cruelties of war and to build bridges among nations'.

Friends of Dresden has set a goal of $10 million as the American contribution to this end. Its campaign focuses on individual gifts, on the adoption of individual stones (400 to date, to be concentrated in the Chancel) and on the financing of the exterior portion of the church behind the high altar (which – for campaign purposes – Friends of Dresden calls 'the American Wing'). In addition to major individual cash donations, funds are being raised by the sale of gold certificates ($2,000, resulting in the adoption of a stone), and silver ($1,200), and bronze ($400) certificates. Fund-raising events have included dinners (for example, for Saxon Minister-President Kurt Biedenkopf and Dresden's Lord Mayor Herbert Wagner), exhibitions, receptions, lectures and outreach activities in schools, universities, German associations and so on. All these activities are vitally supported by Dresdner Kleinwort Benson North America, by Myer Brown and Platt and by Huntingdon Bank Shares.

1675 Broadway, Suite 1900, New York, NY 10019-5820, Tel. +1 (212) 506 2310. Fax +1 (212) 506 2312.

Bibliography

Dresden and the Dresden Trust

Annan, Noel (1995), *Changing Enemies,* London: HarperCollins
Clare, Frank (1998), *The Cloven Pine,* London: Hutchinson
Davies, Norman (1996), *Europe: A History,* Oxford: Oxford University Press
FitzHerbert, Katrin (1997), *True to Both My Selves,* London: Virago
Johnson, Peter (1992), *The Withered Garland: Reflections of a Bomber,* London: New European Press
Panayi, Panikos (ed.) (1996), *Germans in Britain since 1500,* London: Hambledon Press
Vonnegut, Kurt (1970), *Slaughterhouse 5,* London: Jonathan Cape

Dresden 1206–1918

Bachlev, H. and Schlechte, M. (1990), *Sächsisches Barock,* Leipzig: Prisma Verlag
Gretschel, M. (1995), *Die Dresdner Frauenkirche,* Hamburg: Ellert und Richter Verlag
Löffler, F. (1992), *Das Alte Dresden,* Leipzig: Seemann Verlag
Tenbrock, R.-H. (1968), *Geschichte Deutschland*s, Munich: Hueber

Dresden 1919–45

Bergander, G. (1977), *Dresden im Luftkrieg,* Cologne: Böhlau
Graml, H. et al (1970), *The German Resistance to Hitler,* London: Batsford
Hastings, Max (1979), *Bomber Command,* London : M. Joseph
Jäger, W. and Brebbia, C.A. (eds) (2000), *The Revival of Dresden, Southampton and Boston,* WIT Press
Irving, David (1963), *The Destruction of Dresden,* London: Kimber
Manvell, R. (1971), *The Conspirators: 20th July 1944,* New York: Pan/Ballentine
McKee, Alexander (1982), *Dresden 1945: The Devil's Tinderbox,* London: Souvenir

Dresden and East Germany 1945–90

Hahn, H-J (1998), *Education & Society in Germany,* Oxford: Berg
Maier, C. (1987), *Dissolution, the Crisis of Communism and the End of East Germany,* Princeton: Princeton University Press

McCauley, Martin (1983), *The German Democratic Republic since 1945*, Basingstoke: Macmillan
Marsh, David (1994), *Germany & Europe: The Crisis of Identity*, Reading: Mandarin
Radice, Giles (1995), *The New Germans*, London: Michael Joseph

Dresden: its Destruction and Rebuilding 1945–85

Official City Council sources

1950: *Planungsgrundlagen für den Neuaufbau der Stadt Dresden*
1967: *Generalbebauungsplan und Generalverkehrsplan der Stadt Dresden*
1979: 'Zur Entwicklung des Wohnungsbaues in der Stadt Dresden seit der Gründung der DDR', *Jahrbuch zur Geschichte Dresdens*
1984: *Rekonstruktionsgebiet Neumarkt in Dresden*, Rat der Stadt Dresden

Other material

Brauer, H. (1953), 'Kritische Bemerkungen zur Neugestaltung Dresdens' *Deutsche Architektur*, 1, pp 13–19
Funk, G. (1954), 'Wettbewerb für die städtebauliche und architektonische Gestaltung der Ost-West Magistrale in Dresden', *Deutsche Architektur*,7, pp 240–247
Hempel, E. (1953), 'Wiederaufbau von Dresden', *Europa*, Salzburg, pp 19–25
Hempel, O. (1955), 'Vorschlag für die Rekonstruktion des historischen Viertels um die Frauenkirche in Dresden', *Deutsche Architektur*, 8, pp 107–171
Jäger, W. and Brebbia, C.A. (eds) (2000), *The Revival of Dresden*, Southampton and Boston, WIT Press
Michalk, H. (1982), 'Zur baulichen Entwicklung der Stadt Dresden nach ihrer Zerstörung', *Sächsische Heimatblätter*, pp 49–59
Michalk, H. (1983), 'Dresden: der Wiederaufbau des historischen Stadtkerns', *Stadt und Gemeinde, Dresden*, pp 28–33
Möbius, D. and Hartmann, G. (1985), 'Die städtebauliche und architektonische Gestaltung des Dresdner Altmarkts – ein bleibendes Beispiel der architektonischen Entwicklung in der DDR', *Dresdner Hefte, Beiträge zur Kulturgeschichte* 3, pp 48–60
Rauda, W. (1952 & 1953), 'Bauliches Gestalten im alten und neuen Dresden', *Wissenschaftliche Zeitschrift der Technischen Hochschule Dresden*, pp 965–976
Rauda, W. (1956), 'Raum und Formprobleme im alten und neuen Dresden', *Jahrbuch zur Pflege der Kunst*, I, pp 44–84
Schneider, H. (1956), *Das neue Dresden: Natur und Heimat*, Leipzig: VEB
Schuster, G. (1989), 'Der Aufbau Dresdens schreitet voran!', *Deutsche Architektur*, 3, pp 121–126
Thümmler, G. (1959), 'Die Stadt Dresden, ein grosser Bauplatz', *Sächsische Heimatblätter*, pp 49–84
Wermund, H. (1947), *Wiederaufbau der Stadt Dresden*, Dresden: Stadtverordnete zu Dresden

The Renaissance of Dresden after 1985

Official City Council sources

1990: *Stadtgestaltskonzept Dresden 2006, Technische Universität Dresden*
1991: *Denkschrift zum künftigen Städtebau und Stadtverkehr in Dresden*
1991: *Planungsleitbild Innenstadt-Entwurf Landeshauptstadt Dresden*
1992 *Rahmenkonzept Stadtentwicklung, Zwischenbericht zur Flächennutzungsplanung Dresdens*
1994: *Planungsleitbild Innenstadt-Entwurf Landeshauptstadt Dresden*
1995: *Dresden 2000, Projekte und Visionen*

Other material

Féderation Suisse des Architects Indépendents, (1993), 'Zum Beispiel Dresden', *Archithese* 3
Just, G., Oelsner, N. et al (1995), 'Der Dresdner Neumarkt', *Dresdner Hefte, Beiträge zur Kultureschichte* 44, 4/95 pp 1–120
Michalk, H. (1986), 'Zur Entwicklung des innerstädtischen Bauens im Stadtzentrum von Dresden', *Studium zu Städtebau und Architektur*, pp 57–63, Berlin
Peters, P (ed), *Dresden 1992: Erfahrungen – Perspektiven*, Cologne: Müller Verlag
For further information: – the architectural section of the Library of the Technical University Dresden, the *Sächsische Zeitung* and other Dresden papers

Dresden's Architectural Traditions and its Surviving Heritage

Biedenkopf, Kurt, et al (1992), *Dresden, die Kunststadt,* Munich and Berlin: C. J. Bucher
Delau, Reinhard, translated Marjorie Willey, (1995), *Taschenberg Palais Dresden,* Halle: mdv
Gesellschaft zur Förderung des Wiederaufbaus der Frauenkirche (1995, 1996, 1997, 1998), *Die Dresdner Frauenkirche: Jahrbuch zu ihrer Geschichte und zu ihrem archäologischen Wiederaufbau,* Weimar: Hermann Böhlaus Nachfolger
Giebel, Wieland (ed) (1992), *Dresden Insight Guide,* Dresden: Apa Publications
Güttler, Ludwig et al (1992), 'Die Dresdner Frauenkirche – Geschichte – Zerstörung – Rekonstruktion', *Dresdner Hefte, Beiträge zur Kulturgeschichte,* 32, 4/92, pp 3–101
Hélas, Volker (1996), 'Die Geschichte der Friedrichstadt', *Dresdner Hefte, Beiträge zur Kulturgeschichte* 47, 3/96, pp 14–21
Hempel, Eberhard (1965), *Baroque Art and Architecture in Central Europe,* London: Penguin
Hoffman, Gabriele (1988), *Constantia von Cosel,* Bergisch-Gladbach: Bastei-Lübbe-Taschenbuch

Kunze, Peter (1996), 'Das Friedrichstädter Krankenhaus', *Dresdner Hefte, Beiträge zur Kultureschichte* 47, 3/96, pp 22–29

Lerm, Matthias (1993), *Abschied vom alten Dresden – Verluste historischer Bausubstanz nach 1945*, Leipzig: Forum Verlag

Löffler, Fritz (1994), *Das alte Dresden,* Leipzig: E.A. Seemann Verlag

Lühr, Hans-Peter (ed) (1997), 'Gartenstadt Hellerau – der Alltag einer Utopie', *Dresdner Hefte, Beiträge zur Kulturgeschichte,* 51, 3/97, pp 3–108

May, Walter (1992), 'Die höfische Architektur am Hof Christian 1', *Dresdner Hefte, Beiträge zur Kulturgeschichte,* 29, 1/92, pp 63–71

May, Walter (1994), 'Italienische Impressionen in der Dresdner Architektur', *Dresdner Hefte, Beiträge zur Kulturgeschichte,* 40, 4/94, pp 6–14

Menzhauzen, Joachim (1994), 'Dresdens italischer Himmel', *Dresdner Hefte, Beiträge zur Kulturgeschichte,* 52, 4/97, pp 2–94

Milde, Kurt et al (1992), *Matthäus Pöppelmann 1662–1736,* Dresden: Verlag der Kunst

Schumann, Paul (1992), *Dresden,* Leipzig: E.A. Seemann

von Kracke, Friedrich (1972), *Das Königliche Dresden,* Boppard am Rhein, Harald Boldt Verlag

von Nostitz, Helene (1941), *Feierliches Dresden: die Stadt Augusts des Starken,* Berlin: Hans von Hugo

The Art Collections of Dresden

Arnold, K. (1993), *Porzellan im Dresdner Zwinger,* Dresden: Galerie Verlag

Arnold, W. et al (1993), *The Green Vault of Dresden,* Leipzig: Edition Verlag

Biedenkopf, K. and Paul, Jürgen (1992), *Dresden – die Kunststadt,* Dresden, Munich and Berlin: C. J. Bucher

Gleeson, Janet (1998), *Arcanum: the Extraordinary True Story of the Invention of European Porcelain,* London: Bantam Press

Haase, G. (1995), *Kunstgewerbemuseum Dresden Schloss Pillnitz,* Dresden: Galerie Verlag

Kollmann, E. (1975), *Meissner Porzellan,* Brunswick

Marx, H. (1993), *Picture Gallery, 'Old Masters',* Leipzig: E.A. Seeman Verlag

Marx, H. (1994), *The Dresden Masterpieces,* Leipzig: E.A. Seeman Verlag

Neidhardt, L. (1994), *The Rape of Europa: The Fate of Europe's Treasures in the Third Reich and the Second World War,* London: Macmillan

Sponsel, J. (1925–32), *The Green Vault,* Leipzig

Dresden: A Music Metropolis

Blume, F. (ed) (1949), *Musik in Geschichte und Gegenwart,* Kassel: Bärenreiter

Blaschke, K. et al (1991), *Schola Crucis, Schola Lucis,* Gütersloh: Bertelsmann

Fürstenau, M. (1861), *Zur Geschichte der Musik und des Theaters am Hofe zu Dresden*, Frankfurt: Peters Verlag. Reprinted Leipzig 1971

Hartwig, D. (1970), *Die Dresdner Philharmonie: eine Chronik des Orchesters von 1870–1970*, Leipzig: VEB

Laux, K. (1964), (trans: L. Jaeck), *The Dresden Staatskapelle*, Leipzig: VEB

Long, A. Yorke (1954), *Music at Court: Four Eighteenth Century Studies,* London: Weidenfeld

McCulloch, D. (1990), *Aristocratic Composers in the 18th Century*, Guildford, University of Surrey: doctoral thesis

Moser, H. (trans. and ed. D. McCulloch) (1967), *Heinrich Schütz: a Short Account of his Life and Works*, London: Faber

Sadie, S. (ed) (1984), *The New Grove Dictionary of Music and Musicians*, London: Macmillan

Schmidt, E. (1961), *Der Gottesdienst am kurfürstlichen Hofe zu Dresden*, Göttingen: Vandenhoek und Ruprecht Verlag

Wilson, E. (1994), *Shostakovich Remembered*, London: Faber

Dresden's Literary and Theatrical Traditions

Andrews, K. (1989), 'Nazarenes and Pre-Raphaelites', *Bulletin of the John Rylands University Library of Manchester*, 71, pp 31–46

Anon. (1846), *Dresden und die Dresdener oder Spiegelreflexe aus Dresdens Gegenwart: Frescogemälde und Federzeichnungen in niederländischer Manier*, Leipzig: Otto Wigand

Beacham, R. (1994), *Adolphe Appia: Artist and Visionary of the Modern Theatre*, Chur, Switzerland: Harwood

Garland, Henry and Mary (1986), *The Oxford Companion to German Literature*, Oxford: Oxford University Press

Gaskill, H. (1979), 'Edwin Muir's friend in Hellerau: Iwar von Lücken', *German Life and Letters*, 32, pp 135–47

Hoffmann, E.T.A. (1990), *Fantasiestücke in Callots Manier*, Frankfurt: Insel

Hoffman, E.T.A. (1992), *The Golden Pot and Other Tales*, trans. R. Robertson, Oxford: Oxford University Press

Kästner, E. (1966), *Als ich ein kleiner Junge war*, London: Harrap

Kötzschke, R. and Kretzschmar, H. (1965), *Sächsische Geschichte: Werden und Wandlungen eines deutschen Stammes und seiner Heimat im Rahmen der deutschen Geschichte*, Frankfurt am Main: Weidlich

Kratzsch, K. (1990), *Dresden und seine Geschichte*, Leipzig: Sachsenbuch

Kummer, F. (1938), *Dresden und seine Theaterwelt*, Dresden: Heimatwerk Sachsen von Baensch

Ludewig, P. (ed) (1988), *Schrei in die Welt: Expressionismus in Dresden*, Berlin: Der Morgen

Paulin, R. (1985), *Ludwig Tieck: A Literary Biography*, Oxford: Oxford University Press

Purver, J. (1996), 'Steps beyond the private sphere: women writers of the Vormärz and the challenge to exclusion', H. Koopman and M. Lauster (eds) *Vormärzliteratur in europäischer Perspektive I: Öffentlichkeit und nationale Identität*, Bielefeld: Aisthesis, pp 247–63

Raabe, P. (ed) (1965), *The Era of Expressionism*, London: Calder and Boyars

Scherzlieb, E. (G.W. von Lüdemann) (1830), *Dresden wie es ist*, Zwickau: Schumann

Schlegel, A.W. (1996), *Die Gemählde: Gespräch*, Amsterdam: Verlag der Kunst

Stopp, E. (1989), 'Carl Gustav Carus' emblematic thinking', *Bulletin of the John Rylands University Library of Manchester*, 71, pp 21–30

Walker Chambers, W. and Wilkie, J. (1978), *A Short History of the German Language*, London: Methuen

Wilton, A. and Bignamini, I. (eds) (1996), *Grand Tour: the Lure of Italy in the Eighteenth Century*, London: Tate Gallery

Zumpe, D. (1992), 'Auf der Bühne und hinter den Kulissen: Die Rolle des Theaters, in *Dresden: die Kunststadt*, Munich and Berlin: C.J. Bucher, pp 141–148

Index